America First Updated Edition

BY

RACHEL LEBOWITZ

AN UPDATED AND EXPANDED EDITION OF
AMERICA FIRST
BY LAWTON B. EVANS

Copyright © 2019 A Charlotte Mason Plenary, LLC

All rights reserved. No part of this publication may be reproduced, stored in a retrieval system, or transmitted in any other means such as electronic, mechanical, photocopying, recording or otherwise, without the prior permission of the publisher. Doing so is in violation of the copyright © held by A Charlotte Mason Plenary, LLC.

This edition published 2019 by A Charlotte Mason Plenary, LLC.
www.cmplenary.com
Author: Rachel Lebowitz
Author: Lawton Evans
Format: Paperback
ISBN-13: 978-1-7324321-3-0
ISBN-10: 1-73243-213-9

STORIES OF OUR OWN HISTORY

AMERICA FIRST
UPDATED EDITION

TABLE OF CONTENTS

INTRODUCTION BY THE ORIGINAL AUTHOR v
PREFACE TO THE UPDATED EDITION vi
1. LEIF, THE LUCKY 1
2. HOW THE SPANIARDS CONQUERED MEXICO 3
3. THE CONQUEST OF PERU 9
4. THE FOUNTAIN OF YOUTH 13
5. DESOTO DISCOVERS THE MISSISSIPPI 17
6. SIR WALTER RALEIGH 21
7. THE LOST COLONY OF ROANOKE 25
8. SOME ADVENTURES OF JOHN SMITH 29
9. MORE ADVENTURES OF JOHN SMITH 33
10. PERSECUTIONS OF THE PILGRIMS AND PURITANS 37
11. THE ADVENTURES OF MILES STANDISH 41
12. BUILDING A CANOE 45
13. THE FLIGHT OF ROGER WILLIAMS 47
14. OLD SILVER LEG 51
15. WILLIAM PENN AND THE QUAKERS 55
16. THE CHARTER OAK 59
17. BLOODY MARSH 63
18. THE SAVING OF HADLEY 67
19. SIR WILLIAM PHIPS AND THE TREASURE SHIP 71

20. A Young Surveyor	77
21. The Adventures of Young Washington	81
22. How Detroit was Saved	85
23. The Story of Acadia	89
24. Blackbeard, the Pirate	93
25. The Adventures of Daniel Boone	95
26. Sunday in the Colonies	99
27. The Salem Witch Trials	103
28. Traveling by Stage Coach	107
29. King George and the Colonies	111
30. Patrick Henry and the Parson's Cause	115
31. Paul Revere's Ride	119
32. The Green Mountain Boys	125
33. The Father of His Country	129
34. Nathan Hale	133
35. The Bravery of Elizabeth Zane	137
36. Capturing the Hessians	141
37. How Lafayette Came to America	145
38. The Patriotism of Lydia Darrah	149
39. Captain Molly Pitcher	153
40. Marion, The Swamp Fox	157
41. Outwitting a Tory	161
42. Supporting the Colors	165
43. Nancy Hart, The War Woman of Georgia	169
44. Mad Anthony Captures Stony Point	173
45. The Execution of Major Andre	179

46. How General Schuyler was Saved	181
47. How the Northwest was Won	185
48. Benjamin Franklin	189
49. Nolichucky Jack	195
50. Eli Whitney Invents the Cotton-Gin	199
51. Thomas Jefferson	203
52. The Burning of Philadelphia	207
53. The Expedition of Lewis and Clark	211
54. Pike Explores the Arkansas Valley	217
55. How the Pumpkins the Family	221
56. Old Ironsides	225
57. Tecumseh	231
58. The Star-Spangled Banner	235
59. Traveling by Canal	239
60. Lafayette's Return to America	243
61. Osceola, The Seminole Chief	247
62. An Early Journey by Railroad	251
63. Old Hickory	253
64. Daniel Webster	257
65. Henry Clay	261
66. John C. Calhoun	265
67. The Heroes of the Alamo	269
68. Sam Houston Wins Freedom for Texas	273
69. The Invention of the Electric Telegraph	277
70. The Discovery of Gold in California	281

71. Crossing the Continent 285
72. The Pony Express 289
73. The Boy Who Saved a Village 293
74. The Rescue of Jerry McHenry 297
75. Abraham Lincoln 301
76. Robert E. Lee 305
77. Stonewall Jackson 309
78. Stealing a Locomotive 313
79. Sam Davis 319
80. An Escape from Prison 323
81. Running the Blockade 327
82. Through the Heart of the South 331
83. The Surrender of General Lee 335
84. Laying the Atlantic Cable 339
85. The Story of the Telephone 345
86. Thomas A. Edison, The Great Inventor 349
87. Clara Barton and the Red Cross 353
88. Hobson and the Merrimac 357
89. Dewey at Manila Bay 359
90. Conquering the Yellow Fever 363
91. The Sinking of the Lusitania 367
92. The Last Race of Private Treptow 371
93. Frank Luke, Jr., Aviator 375

Introduction by Lawton B. Evans

When children advance beyond the nursery age, no story is so wonderful as a true story. Fiction to them is never as appealing as fact. I have often been faced with the inquiry: whether or not a story is a true one. The look of gratification, when told that "it actually happened," was most satisfying to me as a story-teller.

The nearer a story is to the life and traditions of the child, the more eagerly it is attended. True stories about our own people, about our neighbors and friends, and about our own country at large, are more interesting than true stories of remote places and people. We naturally are interested in our own affairs, and the nearer they are to us the greater the interest we feel.

That history is just a long, thrilling story of the trials and triumphs of pioneers and patriots is well known to those who have had to do with the teaching of history to youthful minds. That the dry recital of political and governmental history does not interest children is also well known. History should be made vital, vibrant, and personal if we expect children to be stirred by its study.

To gratify the love of children for the dramatic and picturesque, to satisfy them with stories that are true, and to make them familiar with the great characters in the history of their own country, is the purpose of this volume.

It is hoped that through appeal to youthful love of adventure, this collection of stories, covering the entire range of American history, will stimulate the ambition and strengthen the patriotism of those young citizens whose education has been the constant concern of the author for many years.

Lawton B. Evans

Building a Canoe

Preface to the Updated Edition

– To Parents –

AMERICA FIRST by Lawton Evans has always been my favorite book for elementary American History. The author has such a wonderful narrative style that always keeps students engaged. Both my children have thoroughly enjoyed this book.

However, as a parent, I was dismayed at some of the language used in the book, as well as some of the subjects chosen. The author, Lawton Bryan Evans (1862-1934), published this book in 1920. Unfortunately, the book contains language and attitudes from that time period that are racially insensitive. In addition to the racial language, Evans sometimes chose subject matter that I consider inappropriate for young children, including tales that are too violent as well as stories that not only glorify Confederate soldiers during the Civil War, but also suggest that slaves were well-treated.

I have tried to remedy this so that parents can enjoy reading this book to their children without having to edit as they read it aloud. Or, in the case of children reading this book independently, so that parents are not having to explain why certain disrespectful words and attitudes were common when the book was published.

Therefore, I have made the following changes to the 1920 edition of America First:

I have edited or removed any disrespectful and offensive language and subject matter that appeared in the original publication. Derogatory terms have been replaced with "person" or "citizen," or, when referring to enslaved peoples prior to or during the Civil War, any derogatory terms have been replaced with the word "slave." The term "white men" has been changed to "explorers," "English colonists," "colonists," or simply, "citizens" or "people," depending on the context.

Other updates to the book include restoring dignity to the descriptions of enslaved peoples. An example of this includes changing the title of one chapter from "The Rescue of Jerry" to "The Rescue of Jerry McHenry." McHenry was an escaped slave who found freedom in the north. Evans continually refers to him by his first name, whereas he refers to other persons by their last names. "Jerry" has been replaced with "McHenry" throughout the chapter so that Mr. McHenry receives the same respect as any other person mentioned in the book.

Likewise, changes have been made to the chapter titled "Through the Heart of the South." In this chapter, Evans uses "dialect" speech whenever a freed slave speaks. Her dialogue lines have been updated to modern English.

The book originally contained 100 chapters; it now contains 93 chapters. The following chapters were removed:

> Hannah Dustin
> Israel Putnam Captures the Wolf
> How the Indians Treated Major Putnam
> An Indian Trick that Failed
> Christmas on the Plantation
> Colter's Race for Life
> The Exploits of Sergeant York

Dates have been updated from "a few years ago" or "a hundred years ago" to the actual date or time period, so as to not confuse the reader.

I have also included new illustrations. Almost every chapter now has an illustration.

All in all, I hope you and your children enjoy the revised and updated edition of AMERICA FIRST.

For a complete listing of books and study guides, or for more information regarding the Charlotte Mason method of education, please see The Plenary website at CMPLENARY.COM.

Rachel Lebowitz
July 2019

Vikings explore North America

STORIES OF OUR OWN HISTORY

CHAPTER 1
LEIF, THE LUCKY

Leif was a bold Norseman, and was called "Lucky" because he came safely through so many dangers. He was the bravest seaman of his race, and the sailors believed that whatever boat carried him would come safely into port, no matter how fierce the storm.

When voyagers from the far seas brought word to Iceland that fair lands covered with forests lay to the west, for they had seen them, Leif the Lucky called for thirty-five strong and true men. "Let us sail to this country, and get wood for our ships, and perhaps gold and silver to sell to the kings of Europe," he said. The men came forward and the ship set sail in the summer.

They went by way of Greenland, where they stopped for more news of the strange lands, and then sailed southwest for many days. The first place they saw was a land of ice and mountains. This was probably Newfoundland. Then they reached a level country covered with trees. This was probably Nova Scotia. Still sailing onward, the little ships with their brave crews came to a beautiful country abounding in trees, grass, and flowers. Here they landed, and carried all their baggage ashore with them. The place was so beautiful, they resolved to spend the winter there, and at once set about building houses. This was probably somewhere in Rhode Island.

When the Norsemen had built their houses, Leif said to his men, "Let us explore the land; some of us will stay to guard the houses, and the rest will find out what there is to see." So they set forth into the interior.

Soon they came upon an abundance of grapevines hanging from trees and covered with luscious fruit. Leif was delighted, and at once named the country Vinland, or the Land of Vines. So they gathered grapes, and cut wood for their ships, and built more houses, and settled down to spend the winter in this delightful spot. The cold came on, but the Norsemen did not mind it, for they had plenty of food and great fires; besides which, they were accustomed to cold weather.

In the spring they loaded their ships with timber, and sailed for home. Here they narrated their marvelous story of the new land. Leif offered his ship to his brother, Thorwald, and told him he might go and spend a winter in Vinland. So Thorwald fitted himself out and started for the new country, but he was not as lucky as his brother. He found the homes that had been built by those who had been before him; but the Native people attacked his party one night, and killed Thorwald with a poisoned arrow. He was buried on the shore, and his men set sail for home as soon as the weather allowed them to leave.

About eight hundred years after this, a skeleton clothed in armor was found buried in the earth at the head of Narragansett Bay. No one knew who it was; but we have every reason to believe that it was the remains of the brave old Norse warrior, Thorwald, or, maybe, of one of his followers. At any rate, the Skeleton in Armor has been the subject of much romance and poetry, and the traditions of the Norsemen have been handed down to us as sagas in the writing of the seafaring Icelanders.

Chapter 2

How the Spaniards Conquered Mexico

The one thing the early Spaniards wanted above all else was gold. For it they were willing to abandon their homes and families in the Old World, undergo all kinds of hardships and suffering, treat the native people of the Americas with great cruelty, and often imperil their own lives. Thus we see what men will do when possessed of a greed for wealth!

In Cuba there lived a Spanish gentleman named Hernando Cortez. He was the son of wealthy parents, and he had studied law. But when nineteen years of age, he had run away from home to find adventures in America. He possessed wonderful courage and great command over men; but by nature he was very cruel. He loved gold, as all the others did in those days, but he loved power and adventure as much as he did wealth.

Hernando Cortez

Cortez heard stories about the wonderful wealth of the King of Mexico. It was said that gold was so common among them that the very people ate and drank from golden vessels. The King was said to live in a palace so covered with gold that it shone like the sun, while he and all his attendants were believed to wear gold embroidered clothes every day. These fabulous stories were told by the natives, and the Spaniards were wild with excitement.

Cortez was placed at the head of an expedition designed to conquer Mexico, and with him were the bravest of the Spanish captains and the wildest adventurers in the New World, Nothing suited Cortez better than this expedition, and with hope he and his men set forth.

The ruler of Mexico was the proud Montezuma. He lived in a palace, and fared sumptuously upon the dainties of his land. Was it not said of him that he ate fresh fish, brought every day from the coast by runners who came in relays over two hundred miles? Around him was every kind of comfort and luxury, and Mexico, the capital city, showed many evidences of a high civilization.

When Cortez landed at Vera Cruz, runners carried swift word of the stranger to Montezuma, as he sat on his throne in Mexico City. The King turned pale as he heard of the men, riding strange animals, killing their enemies with the aid of weapons that gave out smoke and made noises like many thunders. He cried in dismay, "They are the children of the sun, who, according to the traditions of my country, have come to take away my throne. Alas! woe is me, and woe is Mexico!" And the brave monarch shed tears of distress.

The runners were sent back to Cortez, bearing presents of gold, jewels, and rich cloth, and begging him to begone with his men and leave the country in peace. When Cortez saw the gifts, his eyes blazed with greed, and he said, "Go tell your Montezuma we will visit him in his palace, even if we have to force our way. Tell him also that we have a disease of the heart; it will take much gold to cure us!"

The King heard this message with dismay, for he did not understand why men should want gold. They could not eat or wear it, and he feared their coming to his beautiful capital.

Cortez burned his ships, so that his men could not think of retreat, and then set out on his march to Mexico City. The terrified natives fled before him at the sight of his horses, and at the sound of his cannon and guns. The roads over the mountains were smooth, with here and there a stone house built nearby for the convenience of traders.

At last Cortez and his adventurers came to a point where they could look down over the city of Mexico. Great white stone buildings, were seen on an island in the middle of a lake, connected with the mainland by means of bridges. The temples and palaces were reflected in the clear water, and the whole scene was peaceful and beautiful. "The Land of Gold! The City of Plenty!" exclaimed Cortez, and he rested awhile before preparing for his triumphal entry.

Montezuma sat in his palace with his attendants around him. "The strangers are in the mountains," announced his chief warrior. "Shall I drive them away, or let them enter?" Montezuma thought awhile, and replied, "It will be of no avail to try and drive them away. Let them enter the city."

Cortez, on a fine horse and covered with all the trappings of war, attended by his captains and men, rode into the city. Montezuma was carried to meet him in a chair beneath a canopy of feathers. His mantle was decorated with gold and precious stones, and his bearers brought with them great quantities of food and rich gifts for the strangers. Alas for poor Montezuma! If he thought that was the way to get rid of the cruel and greedy Spaniard, he was much mistaken!

Cortez was given the freedom of the city. He went everywhere, observing the means of defense and the provisions of warfare. He visited the temples and saw the priests offering up sacrifices. He resolved to force these people to adopt the Christian religion. He was very arrogant, and made the Mexicans give him everything he demanded.

So matters went on for several weeks, until the Mexicans showed plainly that they wanted the Spaniards to leave. But the

Cortez and the Aztec King Montezuma

Spaniards wanted more and more gold, and Cortez became anxious, for the natives were growing tired and unfriendly. He felt that he was walking over a volcano that might blow up at any minute. A Mexican slew one of his soldiers. This proved to Montezuma's subjects that the Spaniards could be killed. Cortez demanded that the murderer be turned over to him for punishment, and, when this was done, the Spaniards burned him alive in the public square. The Mexicans became more sullen and dangerous.

Cortez had only two hundred men with him, and around him were thousands of Mexicans. He and his men, already loaded with plunder and in fear of their lives, resolved to escape with what they had. It would mean for them certain destruction if the Mexicans once began hostilities. Montezuma, whom Cortez had quite terrified, advised him to go, so as to escape the wrath of the Mexican people. Just about this time, Alvarado, one of the Spanish captains, witnessing the sacrifice of human lives at a Mexican religious festival, grew so indignant that he ordered his men to fire their cannon into the group, thereby killing some of the priests.

This brought matters to a crisis. The Spaniards must now indeed leave, and leave quickly. So they planned to go by night. But as they departed over the bridge that connected the city with the mainland, the Mexicans discovered them, and began a merciless attack upon them. They swarmed forth by the thousands, cutting away portions of the bridge, hurling stones and arrows, and rushing upon the Spaniards with their spears. Cortez lost many men before he could withdraw. The greedy Spanish soldiers would not follow his advice to drop their packs of gold as they fled. They clung to their plunder to the very last, and, in consequence, many were killed who might have escaped. In Spanish histories this is known as "the sorrowful night."

It took a whole year for Cortez to get enough men from Cuba and Spain to march again upon Mexico. In the meantime Montezuma had been slain by his own people, and Guatemazin reigned in his stead. This time the siege lasted three months, and thousands of the Mexicans were slain before the proud city gave way, and the conquest of Mexico was complete. Cortez had at last broken the heart of the ancient race, and from that time on Mexico was in possession of the Spanish conquerors.

Chapter 3

The Conquest of Peru

Francisco Pizarro was a Spaniard of low birth, and never in all his life did he learn to read and write. His parents were very poor.

When Pizarro became old enough to work, he took up the occupation of a swineherd, feeding and tending pigs. He became very rough and lawless, but like all other Spaniards of the day, was eager for conquest in America. So he ran away and shipped in a vessel bound for the West Indies. Here he met Vasco Nunez de Balboa, and was one of the party that went with this explorer when he beheld the waters of the Pacific Ocean. He heard a great deal about a land to the south, abounding in gold and silver.

Of course Pizarro wanted to conquer this land, just as Cortez had conquered Mexico. With a small party of men and some horses, he started out in one ship to explore the west coast of South America, where the Peruvians lived. As he went down the coast he saw signs of villages here and there, and some large towns with houses and streets. The people he noticed wore clothing, and appeared to have plenty of gold ornaments.

At one place a party of fifty of his men landed with their horses and began a march into the interior. The Peruvians came against them by the thousands, but the Spaniards fired off their guns and dismounted their

Francisco Pizzaro

horses. The strange noise of armor, and the appearance of an animal that could separate itself into two parts, for the natives thought the horse and rider were one, so terrified them that they fled in dismay.

Seeing the vast numbers of people in this new land, and also its limitless riches of gold and silver, Pizarro decided to return to Spain for larger forces and more supplies, and then to return for the complete conquest of Peru. So he made his way back to Spain and reported to his King what he had seen. The Spanish monarch told Pizarro that he might be governor of all the land he subdued, and in addition he might keep half the gold he found. But the King did not give him any money with which to buy ships and supplies.

Pizarro was not daunted, however, by this. After a few months he found enough men and borrowed enough money to start afresh. He landed again on the Peruvian coast, and remained a year in one place, awaiting reinforcements and supplies. He then started on his march inland, to meet Atahualpa, who was the King of the country. Atahualpa sent friendly messages, beautiful presents of gold, silver, and precious stones, together with plentiful provisions for the Spaniards.

Incan King Atahualpa

Pizarro marched over the narrow mountain passes with a few hundred men, while Atahualpa could easily have gathered fifty thousand soldiers to overwhelm him. But Pizarro's men were fierce as wolves, while the Peruvians were as timid as sheep. There was no opposition to the onward march of the Spaniards. At last they came to a large village, which had been abandoned by the inhabitants and left for the use of the Spaniards. In this village Pizarro quartered his men, and made himself comfortable.

He was now with about two hundred men in the heart of Peru, a thickly settled country of thousands, who could destroy him at any time they saw fit.

Pizarro fortified his town as best he could, and then sent his own brother, with forty men, to Atahualpa's camp to ask him to pay the Spaniards a visit. "Tell the Inca that he must come, or else I shall make him. I will take a few horses and my men, and lay waste all his country."

The terrified King then made haste to visit the Spanish camp.

Pizarro waited all day for Atahualpa to appear. Late in the afternoon he learned that the King and his men were on the outskirts of the village. So word was sent him that supper was prepared and that it would be kept waiting until he arrived. In the meantime, Pizarro made ready for an attack, inasmuch as he feared the treachery of the Spaniards.

Atahualpa appeared, borne on a litter, plated with silver and gold, and adorned with feathers. With him were five thousand soldiers, carrying clubs, slings, and bags of stones. The cortege halted in the great square, and Pizarro came forward to greet his guest. After an exchange of courtesies, a Spanish priest began to expound the Christian religion. The King listened, but acted as if he were not interested.

Then Atahualpa glanced around at his soldiers, speaking to them in their own language. The Spaniards thought this was a signal for war, drew their swords, and rushed upon Atahualpa's men. They met with but slight resistance. Hundreds of the Incan soldiers fell in the pursuit.

Those who bore the King's litter dropped it, leaving the poor monarch on the ground. He was easily taken prisoner, all of his army having fled with loud cries over the mountains.

Atahualpa saw what the Spaniards wanted, and offered to buy his life and liberty by giving up many wagon-loads of gold and silver. Pizarro agreed to this and the wagons began to come in, bringing riches in such abundance that it would have been impossible to carry all away. There were vessels, cups, bowls, earrings, ornaments of all kinds everything of pure gold or silver.

"Take this and leave my country. Also baptize me as a Christian, if you will, for I would serve your God if you will give me back to my people," said Atahualpa.

The eyes of Pizarro burned at the sight of so much wealth. If this were a part of it, why not have it all? His men gathered around the great pile and began to wonder at their own riches.

Pizarro, for no reason whatsoever, began to accuse his captive of treachery, claiming he had an army ready to overwhelm the Spaniards, and hence deserved death for his conduct. He then put the King in chains, and had him tried for treason and for being a heathen.

Poor Atahualpa was sentenced to be burned at the stake. In spite of his willingness to give up all his gold and silver, and to become a Christian, he was cruelly put to death. Thus did Pizarro carry out the practices of the early Spaniards in America, and complete the Conquest of Peru.

Chapter 4

The Fountain of Youth

Ponce de Leon was a brave Spanish soldier who came over with Columbus on his second voyage. He was so fine a soldier that he was made governor of a part of Hispaniola. One day he stood on a high hill, and saw the fair shores of Puerto Rico. "I will conquer that island," said he, and forthwith sailed across the waters, annexing it as one of his possessions and establishing himself as governor.

Like all the early Spaniards, he was cruel to the native people and greedy for gold. He made the natives work hard, and slew them for the slightest offenses. In consequence, De Leon was hated, as were all the Spanish oppressors of that period.

De Leon was getting old; his hair was white, his strength was waning, and he longed for the vigor and fire of youth. One time he complained to a native of his coming age. The native replied: "Across the seas only a few days sail from here, there is a beautiful land full of flowers and fruit and game. It is the most beautiful place in the world, far more lovely than this island. Somewhere yonder there is a fountain of magic water, in which, if one bathes, his hair will become black and his limbs will become strong. He then can carry his sword without fatigue, and conquer his enemies with his strong arm. He will again be a young man!"

De Leon listened gladly to the story of this native who was merely trying to get him and his men to leave Puerto Rico. He resolved to find the beautiful country, so that he might bathe in the

Fountain of Youth. He called his men to him at once and told them about the wonderful water. In a few days he set sail on his quest, full of foolish hope and pride.

It was in the early spring; the breeze was soft and the air was mild. In a short while the ship came to land, and De Leon named it Florida. He anchored his ship, and his men rowed him to shore. The spot where they landed was near the mouth of the St. John River, not far from where St. Augustine now stands. They were the first European men to set foot on the soil of the mainland of North America since the days of the Northmen five hundred years before.

Now began the vain search for the Fountain of Youth. Deep into the forests the soldiers plunged, wondering at the gorgeous flowers, the abundant fruit, and the plentiful game. The native people scurried away at the approach of the strange men's faces. De Leon and his men were bent on other things than flowers; they were hunting for their lost youth! In every stream, brook, river, and creek they bathed. Up and down the coast they wandered, trying the waters everywhere. They had never bathed as much before in all their lives, but it was all in vain!

No matter where or how often he bathed, Ponce de Leon's hair remained white, his skin was dried and his limbs were bent with age and fatigue. In vain he tried a hundred places, and at last exclaimed, "There is no such fountain here; we must return to Puerto Rico."

Accordingly, he set sail for the island from whence he had departed, just as old, just as white haired, and just as foolish in his belief as when he had started out on his fruitless mission. If De Leon did not find his Fountain of Youth, he at least did discover a beautiful country, and give a name to one of the future states of our Union.

For nearly a year afterwards, De Leon and his men wandered up and down the coast of Florida,

Perhaps they were still seeking the Fountain of Youth. One day, they were attacked and De Leon was wounded by an arrow. His followers put him on board ship and sailed away to Cuba. Here De Leon died of his wounds, with all his hopes unfulfilled

The Search for the Fountain of Youth

Chapter 5

De Soto Discovers the Mississippi

Hernando de Soto had been with Pizarro in Peru, and had seen there the temples all plated with gold. He was eager for conquests and wealth of his own, and called for volunteers to follow him into the unexplored lands which lay northward. Hundreds of warriors flocked to his standard, thirsting for gold and adventure. It was always so with the Spaniards of those days!

In May, 1539, De Soto, with six or seven hundred followers, landed at Tampa, in Florida. He carried blood-hounds to hunt the native people and chains to fetter them. A drove of hogs was brought along for fresh meat. The men were provided with horses, fire-arms, cannon, and steel armor. It was a cruel band, bent on war and on finding gold.

They had not gone far before out of the forests there stepped a man named Juan Ortiz who had been captive among the natives for ten years. He knew the native language well, and joined the adventurers as guide and interpreter.

The band marched northward, everywhere robbing the villages of food, and terrifying the people. A year passed, and there was no gold. Fear alone made the natives meet them with peace, but this was repaid by the Spaniards with many brutal deeds. At last they came to the banks of the "Savannah River, where they were met by a beautiful native Princess. As they neared the village, she came out to meet them and welcome them, hoping thus to make friends with them. She was borne on a litter by four of her subjects. She alighted before De Soto, and made signs of peace and friendship. Taking a double string of pearls, which she wore, she hung it around the neck of De Soto and bade him follow her into the village.

Here the party rested for awhile, entertained by the Princess and her people. But De Soto ill repaid her kindness. On leaving, he and his men robbed the village of all the valuables they could find, and took the Princess captive. They made her follow them into the wilderness. But De Soto gained little by this cruelty, for, after a few days marching, the Princess escaped, taking with her a large box of pearls, which De Soto had prized very highly.

They now marched westward and then southward, until they came to the town of Mavila, where Mobile, Alabama, now stands. The native Chief met De Soto with a great show of friendship, and begged him and a few of his soldiers to enter the palisade which protected the village. No sooner had they done so than the Chief shouted a word of insult and ran into one of the houses. In a moment a cloud of arrows swept from the houses, and many of the Spaniards fell dead. Only De Soto and a few of them escaped. Enraged by this treatment, the Spaniards assaulted the town, and a terrible battle followed, lasting nine hours. In the end the Spaniards won, but they lost many men, and nearly all of their property was destroyed. The town was burned and hosts of natives killed, but De Soto could ill afford to lose anything more, for his men were few and the natives were many.

A year and more had now passed, and the adventurers were tired of their journey. They had found no gold, but had experienced only hardship and battle and danger. They clamored to go home, but De Soto would not hear of it. He made them again take up their journey northward and westward.

It was now a strange-looking army. The uniforms with which they had started had worn out, and were replaced by skins, and mats made of rushes and bark. Their hair and beards had grown until they looked like wild men. All the hogs had long since been eaten, or had died on the march. The natives, forced to go along and carry the baggage, often escaped at night, taking with them or destroying before they left whatever they could. The remaining horses were gaunt and haggard. There was no longer any medicine, and but little ammunition for the guns. These men were sick at heart and sorely discouraged.

Onward they trudged, day by day, avoiding the natives as much as they could. Two years passed, and again it was May. One morning they marched out of the thick undergrowth, and stood on the banks of a great river. It was the Mississippi, the Father of Waters. It was a noble and imposing sight, as the vast volume of water rolled majestically before them on its way to the Gulf of Mexico.

Little, however, did De Soto care for the majesty or beauty of this river. In his heart still burned the desire for gold. He cried to his men: "Let us hasten and build boats that we may cross." It was a hard task for his enfeebled followers, but they undertook the labor, that

De Soto's First View of the Mississippi River

they and their few horses might get to the other side. Once over, they began the fruitless search, but always with the same result.

For another year they wandered over the country, west of the Mississippi. Sometimes they had to fight the natives, always losing a few men and shortening their ammunition supply. Sometimes they were kindly treated, and rested in the villages. At one place the natives thought De Soto was a god, and brought to him the sick to be healed and the blind to be cured. They were sorely disappointed at the result.

De Soto was now weary, emaciated and ill. He had at last lost his dreams, and the time had come for him to die. He had caught a fever from camping in a swampy place, and he knew his final hours were at hand. Calling his men around him, he begged their forgiveness for the perils and suffering he had made them endure, and appointed one among them to be his successor. The next day he died, and was buried near the camp.

His followers, however, feared the natives would attack them, should they discover that De Soto was dead, or find his body. For all along he had pretended that he was immortal and could neither die nor be slain. Therefore, at night, his body was taken up, wrapped in cloths filled with sand and stones, and carried to the middle of the river, where it was dropped into the keeping of the mighty current he had discovered.

What was left of the band of adventurers fashioned a few boats of rough material, and embarked on the river to make their way out of the wilderness. For many days and weeks they sailed and toiled, until at last a ragged remnant reached a settlement in Mexico, where they told the sad story of their wanderings and misfortunes.

Chapter 6

Sir Walter Raleigh

Walter Raleigh was a gallant young man of England, very bold and fond of adventure. He was an officer in Queen Elizabeth's army. One day, in London, he had an opportunity of attracting the attention of the Queen, herself. She was out for a walk in the royal park, attended by her courtiers, when the party came to a muddy place in the path over which the Queen must go. As she hesitated for a moment, there stepped from the bystanders a young man who threw his cloak down over the mud so that she might pass without soiling her shoes. When she had crossed, she called the young man to her side and offered to pay for the velvet cloak.

"The only pay I desire, your Majesty, is permission to keep the cloak; for since your Majesty's foot has pressed on it, it has become valuable indeed," was the reply of the young officer.

The Queen was pleased at the answer, and asked his name. "Walter Raleigh, most gracious lady," said he. The Queen passed on, but the next day she sent for him and made him one of the guards in the royal household.

Raleigh soon grew into favor with the Queen. Court life was

Sir Walter Raleigh

very cheerful in the reign of Elizabeth I. Raleigh was among the most brilliant and successful of all the courtiers. He had many suits of satin and velvet, he wore a hat with a band of pearls, and his shoe buckles cost several thousand dollars. He also had a suit of silver armor, studded with diamonds. He paid for all these things himself, for he was not only a fine soldier and sailor, but was also one of the best businessmen of his time.

Among the cherished plans of Raleigh was one to found a colony in the New World. The Queen said he might plant a colony in America anywhere he could find a place, but that he must do so at his own expense. The Queen was as thrifty as Raleigh was adventurous.

So he fitted out two ships, and collected a lot of poor people who were willing to go anywhere, and he sent them across the ocean to plant a colony in the New World. After four months' sailing, they came to Roanoke Island, off the coast of North Carolina. Taking a look at the land, they sailed back home, and reported that the country was very beautiful, but that they would rather be in England. Raleigh named the land Virginia, in honor of the Virgin Queen; he was not quite sure where it was.

The next year another company was sent out by Raleigh. They landed on Roanoke Island and started a colony, but in a short while they grew tired and a passing ship took them also back to England. Thus the second effort was a failure.

These colonists, however, brought back to Raleigh many products of the country, among other things some tobacco, which they told Raleigh the natives burned in their pipes, drawing the smoke through their mouths. Raleigh liked the idea of smoking, and soon began to use tobacco like the natives. As he sat in his room one day with his pipe, blowing the smoke into the air, his servant came in with a pot of ale. He was amazed to see smoke coming out of Raleigh's mouth. "The master is on fire," he cried in alarm, and threw the ale into Raleigh's face, very much to the latter's amusement and chagrin.

One day while smoking before the Queen, Raleigh laid her a wager he could weigh the smoke coming from his pipe. The Queen accepted the bet. Raleigh thereupon weighed a small quantity of tobacco, smoked it all, and then carefully weighed the ashes. The difference between the weight of the tobacco and the weight of the ashes, he said, must be the weight of the smoke. The Queen laughingly paid the wager.

Raleigh tried to found a third colony in America, but it came to grief and was lost; he therefore gave up all his plans of colonization. He had spent large sums of money, and besides he had married one of the Queen's maids-of-honor, which so displeased Elizabeth that Raleigh lost his favored place at Court. He managed to get up an exploring party to go to South America in search of gold. Soon after his return to England, the Queen died, and James I became King.

King James did not like Raleigh, and listened to his enemies, who were envious of his popularity. Charges were preferred against him, and he was thrown into prison. On the day of his trial, he pleaded his own cause with great eloquence. He spoke all day long, from early morning until dark, but he was condemned to death.

For some reason he was not executed for fifteen years, but was kept confined in prison, where he spent his time writing a history of the world.

He met death like a brave man, asking to be executed in the morning hours, for he had a fever at the time, and he knew that if he waited until evening the chill would come and he would shake;

thus his enemies might think he trembled for fear. His request was granted. As he mounted the block, he touched the headsman's axe, saying, "It is a sharp medicine, but it will cure all ills."

He then laid his aged head upon the block, and, when the axe fell, the old courtier's troubles were over.

Chapter 7

The Lost Colony of Roanoke

When Sir Walter Raleigh had tried a third time to plant a colony on Roanoke Island, he sent across the ocean farmers, mechanics and carpenters, with their wives, thinking that families would be more content to stay than single men. The expedition was in charge of Captain John White.

The colonists landed on the island, built houses and forts, planted gardens, and cultivated the fields. Raleigh had advised them to make friends with the natives. So, when one of the Chiefs came in, Captain White greeted him, and gave him some jewelry, a handkerchief, and a knife as presents. He then asked the native to kneel down while he conferred on him the title of Lord of Roanoke.

All went well with the little colony. The houses were ready for the coming winter, the crops were growing, and the natives were friendly. There was great rejoicing when it was announced that Mrs. Dare, the daughter of the Governor, had a little baby girl, the first child of English parents to be born in America.

Governor White thought he might safely sail back to England in order to get some supplies for the winter; he planned to return to his colony in a few weeks. So he went to England, leaving his happy people on Roanoke Island. But, when he reached England, he found that country in a state of great excitement over the threatened Spanish invasion.

It seems that a bold Englishman, Sir Francis Drake, had sailed into the harbor of Cadiz, in Spain, and had burned or captured all the ships there. This had made the Spaniards angry, especially as he had said, "I have singed the beard of the Spanish King."

The King of Spain fitted out a great fleet intended to destroy the English navy; he would land an army on English soil and plunder England herself! The fleet consisted of about one hundred and thirty ships, with 30,000 soldiers and sailors. It would not be considered wonderful in these days, but it was considered a great fleet then, and was called the "Invincible Armada."

This expedition created consternation in England, and everybody was hurried on board ships to fight the Spaniards. Hardly had the Armada sailed out of the harbor before a severe storm scattered the English ships; so that, later on, Drake and the other English sea captains fought the enemy singly. Fortunately, the English ships were light and were able to sail all around the big,, heavy Spanish ships, doing them much damage and not suffering much themselves. The Armada circled the British Isles, meeting storm after storm, and pursued and harried by the English. At last the great fleet was broken up in a terrible gale, many of the ships were lost, and the great Armada came to naught.

It took a long time for all this to happen, and, in the meanwhile, Governor White could not get back to his colony at Roanoke. One ship was fitted out and ready to sail, but the Government seized it and sent it off to fight the Spaniards. Another ship was made ready, and actually sailed, but the Captain turned pirate, and went after Spanish vessels in the West Indies. It was nearly three years before Governor White found himself on board his own ship, on his way to the colonists and to his little granddaughter.

We can imagine the feelings of the old Captain as he sailed over the seas, wondering what had become of his friends and family, and how they had fared all this time. They had looked for him to return to them in a few months, and here it was nearly three years!

Land was sighted one day just after dark, and a light glimmered on shore. "That must be the home of one of the colonists," exclaimed the Governor. Hastily, a boat was lowered and he was rowed to shore. On landing, his men with him looked about, called aloud, blew trumpets and fired off their guns, but there was not a sight or a sound of any of the colonists. 'On a tree nearby was carved the word 'Croatan.'

All night they searched, and next day. At last they came to a few huts, broken down and long unused; there were also some torn bits of clothing scattered about. No signs could be found of any colonists having been near in a great while. On a tree near by was carved the word, 'croatan.'

Governor White, when he saw this, thought he knew what had become of the colonists, because he had told them that if, for any cause, it was necessary for them to move away, they should carve on a tree or doorpost the name of the place to which they were going. Croatan was the name of a tribe of natives, and the Governor at once thought his colonists had

On a tree nearby was carved the word 'croatan.'

gone to the island where those natives lived.

He tried to reach this island, but storms arose and blew him off his path. Besides which, his crew demanded that he return home. So he set sail for England, leaving the lost colony to its fate. From that day to this no one has ever known what became of the lost colony of Roanoke, or of the little baby girl whose eyes first saw the light on the soil of America.

Chapter 8

Some Adventures of John Smith

Our hero of Jamestown, Virginia, was such a remarkable character that it is well for us to learn something of his adventures before he came to the New World.

As a boy, he was strong, active, and full of daring. When he was fourteen years of age, he ran away from home to join in the wars of Holland. For four years he served as a soldier; then, getting tired of obeying orders, he left his company and built for himself a hut in the woods. Here he did all his own work, cooked, and studied military tactics. He was determined to be a great soldier.

He now set out for the East. As he passed through France, he lost his money and had a hard time to keep himself from starving. Finally he reached a port, after walking many miles and begging food along the road, and he boarded a vessel bound for Italy.

After they had been out at sea for a few days, a storm arose, and the ship looked as though she were about to go down. The sailors were so frightened they began praying. One of them said, "We have. a lad here, not of our religion. He has brought on the storm. Overboard with him!" Thereupon, they seized John Smith, and cast him into the sea. But Smith was the best swimmer of his day, and the water was like land to him. So he swam for many hours, and finally landed on a strange shore.

We next hear of him in Austria, where he joined the army and again set out on his way to fight the Turks. Smith won a great name for himself in the following way: A Turkish officer, to amuse the ladies in his camp, sent a challenge to the Austrian army for single combat with any man they might send against him.

"I will accept the challenge," said Smith, and rode out in front of both armies. He dared the Turkish officer to come forth. They fought on horseback, and, as they rushed together, Smith directed his lance so that the point of it went through the eye of his opponent. The Turkish officer fell dead, and Smith cut off his head, carrying it away on his spear. This so enraged the Turkish soldiers that another officer rode out to avenge his comrade's death. But he shared a like fate, and Smith carried his head away on the end of his spear. Then with a great show of daring he rode up to the Turkish lines, and challenged another to come out and give him battle.

Nothing daunted, a third Turk, big and fierce, came forth on a fresh horse. Smith was tired out by this time, having killed two men, but he spurred his horse into the combat. As the two came together, Smith fell to the ground, and his companions thought he was dead.

The Turkish officer leaped from his horse to complete the victory, but Smith was up in a hurry and, sword in hand, awaited his enemy. Fiercely they fought for an hour, at the end of which time Smith's sword went through the body of the big Turk, and his head also was carried off the field.

By now the Turks had had enough fighting, and the ladies declared they were sufficiently amused for the day.

In one of the battles which occurred, Smith fell into the hands of the Turks and was made a slave, according to the custom of those days. He wore a ring around his neck, and worked about the house for his Turkish mistress. She was so much pleased with him that she sent him as a present to her brother, who lived in a distant town.

One day Smith dressed himself up as a Turk, and ran away, out of captivity. No one suspected him, for he spoke the Turkish language, and acted in every way as though he were a Turk.

Soon he came to the border of Russia, and from there went peaceably through Germany, France and Spain, finally making his way back to England, where he told everybody about the wonderful adventures which had befallen him.

AMERICA FIRST: UPDATED EDITION

Chapter 9

More Adventures of John Smith

When John Smith arrived in England, he found a ship with colonists on board ready to sail for the New World. He was asked to join the party and try his fortune in the strange land across the ocean. Of course, he agreed, and the ship soon set sail. Now, the King had arranged for the new colony to be governed by twelve counselors, whose names were put in a sealed envelope, not to be opened until the vessel reached America. There was much quarrelling on board as to which among the adventurers was the greatest; you may be sure that Smith did a deal of boasting, and would allow that no one was greater than he. His vain talk so alarmed some of those present and so enraged others that they put him in irons and kept him thus until they reached land.

They founded Jamestown, in Virginia but the colonists were not suited to the rude work of the wilderness. They were gentlemen who wanted gold, and they did not care to cut down trees, build houses, and plant gardens. Smith warned them they had better plant their gardens in the spring; if they wanted gold, they could seek it afterwards. But they would not listen to him, and went about the woods, digging around trees and seeking in the gullies for the precious metal. This made the natives laugh, for they knew that the winter would find the settlers without food. And so it came to pass. A terrible starving time fell upon them, and many of them died.

The natives would not sell corn to the colonists, and so Smith set out to make them. He and a few men went up the James River in a boat, until they came to a native village. Here they made signs that

Smith would exchange hatchets and beads for corn. The natives shook their heads, "No." The trinkets Smith offered did not tempt them, but they said they would give a small piece of bread for Smith's gun and sword.

Smith knew the natives were afraid of his gun, so he fired it off several times. This frightened the natives so much that they ran yelling into the woods, which gave Smith and his men the opportunity to seize a quantity of corn.

Later on, Captain Smith decided to explore the country, and, with a few men and two native guides he sailed up the Chickahominy River in search of adventure. After he had sailed for some distance, with a native guide he went ashore, leaving the rest of the party to boil the pot for supper. He had not gone very far before he heard cries and sounds of strife from the direction of the canoe. The natives had attacked the party and had killed every one of them. This left Smith and his guide alone in a wilderness, surrounded by hostile natives.

Smith now tied the native fast to his own arm, so that he could not escape and both began to run. An arrow whizzed out from the bushes, striking Smith in the thigh. Signs of natives were all around. Their forms moved in the undergrowth, and their arrows flew through the air. Smith seized his guide and held him in front as a shield to protect himself from the arrows. In this way the brave soldier tried to walk backwards towards his canoe, but, not seeing where he was walking, he backed into a quicksand up to his waist.

The natives, realizing the plight of Smith and the native guide, ran yelling from the woods, and made them both captive. They were pulled from the mud, washed clean, and their clothes were dried before a fire. Smith knew that this was all in preparation for a great time when he would be tortured to death.

Soon the natives came to their Chief, Opechancanough, who looked at the captive with an angry face. Smith thought his hour had arrived, but he resolved to put it off as long as he could. So he took out his pocket compass and showed it to the natives. They looked at the trembling needle, which they could see but not touch, on account of the glass, and were so astonished that they decided not

Pocahontas Saves Captain John Smith

to kill Smith at once, but to send him to Powhatan.

When Powhatan saw Smith, he was greatly pleased, and ordered him fed abundantly that he might be fat when the time came to kill him. Smith ate so much bread and deer meat and vegetables that he fell ill, and asked Powhatan to let him send word to his friends at Jamestown.

Smith wrote a note on a piece of bark, with a bit of burnt stick, and gave it to a messenger to take to the colony. The messenger quickly delivered the note, and came back with presents for Powhatan. But Powhatan said that any man who could make a piece of bark talk by merely marking on it was a magician, and should be put to death.

One day Smith was brought in before the old native Chief, bound and laid upon a stone, while the warriors prepared to beat him. This would have been the end of Captain John Smith if Powhatan's daughter, Pocahontas, had not rushed in and begged her father to spare his life. Old Powhatan ordered Smith unbound, and he was led away to continue his adventures in the wilds of America.

Chapter 10

Persecution of the Pilgrims and Puritans

When James I became King of England, he tried to enforce obedience to one Church, with all its forms and ceremonies and beliefs. Other kings had done this before him. Said he, "I will have one doctrine, one discipline, one religion in substance and ceremony."

This was very unwise in the King, for men should be allowed to worship God in their own way, and not in any king's way. But James cared little for the wishes of his people. "I will govern according to the common weal, and not according to the common will," was his haughty speech.

There were many people in England who were opposed to parts of the religious service and to many of the ecclesiastical ceremonies of the Church of England. They wished to purify the Church of its old customs, and so they were called "Puritans" by way of derision. The Puritans frankly refused to conform to the Church.

"I shall make them conform, else I shall harry them out of this land, or even worse," said King James, in anger.

Some of the Puritans, believing they had a right to think for themselves in the matter of religion, broke away from the Established Church, and quietly formed separate congregations of their own. One of these congregations met in the old Manor House of Scrooby, where lived a certain William Brewster, who was a staunch Puritan, Non-Conformist and Separatist. His followers were called "Non-Conformists" because they refused to conform to the

Established Church, and "Separatists" because they separated from it.

Every Sunday, numbers of people could be seen going to his house to listen to the sermon of their teacher and pastor. One of the most active of his congregation was William Bradford, whose home was near the old manor house. Bradford was only seventeen years old at the time he joined the congregation at Scrooby.

When King James heard of this meeting he was very wroth indeed. "They must conform to my Church and my service, or it shall be the worse for them!" he declared.

Therefore, some of the Puritans were taken and put in prison, others had their houses watched day and night, while still others were threatened with a loss of their means of livelihood. All of them lived in terror of the King and his agents. No wonder the Puritans resolved to leave the country, if possible.

Though the King said he would harry them out of the land, they now found it hard to get away. The King's officers were told to arrest any who attempted to go. Accordingly, they had to make their plans with great secrecy.

A large company of the Puritans hired a ship solely for themselves, and agreed with the owner to be ready on a certain day to board her with all their goods and chattels. After long waiting, much exposure, and many delays, the ship finally arrived one night, and the Puritans went on board, hoping to get to Holland.

Hardly were they gathered together before the Captain betrayed them into the hands of the King's officers. They were put into open boats, and were rifled of all their possessions. Even their shirts were torn open in the search for money. Their books and papers were taken away. Then the entire company was sent back to town, and put into prison, some for a month and others for even a longer time.

But the Puritans refused to give up their congregation, and they would neither conform to the King's Church nor bow to his will. After they were all out of prison, they secretly made an arrangement with a Dutch Captain to take them on board his vessel at a point agreed upon, far from any town.

The women and children were sent to this place in a small boat, which, arriving ahead of time, put into a small creek to wait. Unluckily the time came for low tide and they stuck in the mud. There was no way to reach them, nor could they get away until the tide rose and floated the boat. In the meanwhile, the ship arrived, ready for her passengers.

The men of the Puritan party had come and were walking impatiently along the shore. One of the ship's boats was sent to get them; for it was thought that the women and children could be taken up later. But just as these men were safely on board, an armed body of the King's pursuers was seen coming across the fields. The Dutch Captain, in great haste, weighed anchor, hoisted his sails, and made away.

The Puritans were in great despair over leaving their families to the mercy of the officers, but the Captain refused to go back, since he feared the wrath of his own Government at his thus defying the will of the King of England. Therefore, the men were landed in Holland.

But it was not long before the English King grew tired of the controversy. "Let them go; the country is well rid of them," said he, and gave orders to make no more arrests. Therefore, in a short while, the women and children and the rest of the Puritan Church joined the men in Holland, and began their new life in a strange land. It was now that they called themselves "Pilgrims."

For the next eleven or twelve years the Pilgrims lived in Holland. But it was hard to keep English customs in a foreign land. Their religion was too solemn and sober for the pleasure-loving Dutch. The young people were fast learning the Dutch language and customs. The elders saw more dangers to their religion from the Sunday pastimes of the people than they found in England from the wrath of the King. Besides, they were poor, and there was also a rumor of war coming on.

Therefore, the Pilgrims decided upon another change. The King of England granted them land in the New World, and let them know he would not molest them in their worship. Doubtless he was glad to put the ocean between him and the troublesome congregation.

Two vessels were engaged to take them across the Speedwell, lying at Delfthaven, in Holland, and the Mayflower, taking on supplies at Southampton, in England. The two vessels started out together, but the Speedwell sprung a leak, and had to put back into harbor. The Pilgrims, about one hundred and twenty in all, went aboard the Mayflower, and set sail for the shores of America, glad to turn their backs on the persecutions and hardships of the Old World, and knowing that they would find in their new home freedom to worship in their own way.

The Mayflower

Chapter 11

The Adventures of Miles Standish

Captain Miles Standish was an English soldier who, in his wanderings, came across the Pilgrim settlement in Holland. He liked the courage of these brave countrymen of his, and attached himself to their community, though he would not join their Church. When they began to discuss a plan for coming to America, he spoke up heartily in favor of it.

He was fond of adventure, and knew there were bears and wild creatures of all kinds in America to fight; and, since fighting was his main business and pleasure, he resolved to be among the very first to go over with the Puritans.

Accordingly, Miles Standish was among the colonial passengers on the Mayflower. For nine weeks, the little ship battled with wind and waves. It was a trying voyage, but Miles Standish was among those who did not lose courage. He strode the deck in the worst weather, and helped the sailors manage the ship. He had a cheerful voice and a kindly manner with his fear-smitten companions, all of which aided many a discouraged soul in standing the long voyage.

When the ship reached Cape Cod, Standish, with a few followers, went on shore, looking for a place to establish a settlement. Such a place was found almost at the very end of Cape Cod. The men went in single file for about a mile, when they saw five or six natives, with a dog, coming towards them. When the natives caught sight of the men, they ran into the wood and whistled for the dog to follow.

Standish and his men pursued the natives, but could not overtake them. When night came, they built a fire, set three men to act as sentinels, and slept on the ground until morning. By daybreak they were up and after the natives, but found no trace of them nor of any houses.

They next discovered some mounds of sand that looked like graves. These they dug into, and came upon bows and arrows. Other mounds contained baskets of corn, which the men very promptly carried away, since they were much in need of it for bread.

As they went through the woods, they came upon a deer-trap, which was such a curious contrivance that William Bradford examined it with much curiosity. Stepping upon the hidden spring, the trap closed on his leg so tightly that he called hastily for his companions to relieve him.

After wandering through the woods all day, they came to the shore, shot off their guns as a signal to the ship, and then were taken on board the vessel. This ended the first adventure of Miles Standish at Cape Cod.

After exploring the land several times for a place to found their colony, and locating none to suit them, the company spent about a month in the Mayflower, making the best of a very uncomfortable situation. At last, toward the end of December, they came to a place which John Smith, of Virginia, in one of his voyages along this coast, had named Plymouth. Here they landed and founded their colony.

Rough houses of logs were soon built, the spaces between the cracks of the logs being daubed with mud. Oiled paper was used instead of glass for the windows. The weather was now very cold, the snow covered the ground, and almost blocked the people in their homes. There was little fuel and scant food. The colonists suffered dreadfully.

Many of them died, including Rose Standish, the 'beautiful young wife of the brave Captain. But the Captain himself kept up staunchly, and went among the sick and dying, doing all he could to help them. At one time he and six others were the only well ones in the place. These well ones brought all the wood, made all the fires, cooked all the food, attended to all the beds, and even washed the clothes for the entire colony. When spring came, only fifty of the company were left alive. It was a dreadful winter, but the Pilgrims were not dismayed by this bad beginning.

During the spring they made friends with some of the natives, particularly with Massasoit, a native Chief, and with Squanto, another chieftain who knew how to speak English. Squanto was very helpful to the colonists. He taught them how to catch fish and how to tread eels out of the mud. He told them to plant corn when the oak leaf was as big as a mouse's ear, and to drop a dead herring in each hill for fertilizer. He informed the unfriendly natives that the settlers kept the plague in their cellars, beside the black thunder powder, and could let it loose whenever they chose. In fact, he saved the little colony from utter destruction.

At one time, Captain Standish had gone in a boat to buy corn from a tribe of natives down the coast. When he arrived, the natives formed a plot to

Miles Standish

kill him. One of them invited him to spend the night in his house. The wary Captain did not close his eyes. He could not understand what they said, but their actions were suspicious. Pacing to and fro, keeping his gun always ready, he watched through the long night for any sign of attack. "Why do you not sleep?" asked an native. "I have no desire to sleep in the house of a stranger," replied Standish. In the morning, Standish backed out of the house, making the native follow him to his boat, and even back to Plymouth.

The Massachusetts tribe formed a plot to destroy all the English at Plymouth. Massasoit sent word to the colonists that, if they would save their lives, they must kill the Massachusetts Chiefs. Standish, with eight men, undertook the mission. He went to their village, and pretended to trade for furs. The trade was very smooth, for smiling and fair words were spoken. But the natives said, "The Captain's eyes are watchful, and there is anger in his heart."

Then came a Chief, whetting his knife. He said boastfully, "By and by it shall see, and by and by it shall eat, but not speak." Then, turning to Standish, he said, "You are a great Captain, if you are a little man. I am not a Chief, but I have great strength."

Then Standish gave a signal, and sprang upon the native. Snatching the knife from the hands of the astonished man, he drove it through him, laying him dead on the floor. The companions of the Captain made an onslaught on the other natives, whereupon they all fled, shrieking to the woods. This ended the combat and the conspiracy. From that time on the name of Standish was enough to make the natives tremble with fear.

Chapter 12

Building a Canoe

The birch bark canoe was the most beautiful and ingenious of all the indigenous peoples inventions. It was so broad that it could float in shallow streams, so strong that it could shoot dangerous rapids, and so light that one man could easily carry it on his back.

To make such a boat they picked out a tall tree, with thick bark and with as few branches as possible. This they would cut down, care being taken to prevent it falling against other trees, thereby hurting the bark. The bark was then split along the length of the tree, and carefully peeled off in pieces the length and breadth of the canoe. They were very particular not to have any holes in the bark, which, during the season when the sap was in the tree, was firm and fine.

The bark was then spread on the ground in a smooth place, the inside downwards, and, in order to stretch it better, logs of wood or stones were placed on it. Then the edges of the bark were gently bent upwards to form the sides of the boat. Some sticks were fixed into the ground at a distance of three or four feet from each other, forming the curved line which the sides of the boat were intended to make. The bark was bent to the form which the boat was to have, being held firmly in position by the sticks thus driven into the ground.

The ribs of the boat were made of tough hickory, cut into long, flat pieces, and bent to the shape of the boat, the wider ones in the middle, and the narrower ones towards the ends. When thus bent and tied in position, the ribs were placed upon the bark about ten inches apart.

The upper edge of each side of the boat was made of two thin poles, the boat's length, and put close together with flat edges to hold the bark between. These long poles, firmly attached to the ribs, determined the shape of the boat. The edge of the bark was now inserted between the poles on each side, and was sewed to the poles by means of mouse-wood, bark, or roots.

The poles were now sewed together at the end, and the bark was made water tight where it was joined by pounded bark of the red elm. Bands were placed across the top of the ribs of the boat to prevent spreading or crushing in, and boards were laid across the bottom to step on. The boat was then ready for. use.

This was a frail structure, and had to be treated very tenderly. The sides were easily torn open by rocks and hidden branches of trees, and, therefore, the operator was always on the lookout for danger. The bottom could be easily crushed through; hence they went barefoot, and entered the canoe very gingerly.

But with such a canoe three or four persons could easily float, and in some of the war canoes even a dozen people could find space. With long paddles and strong arms, the natives forced their craft over the lakes and along the rivers with great ease and speed. It was strong enough to hold a heavy load, so long as it did not strike a rock or hidden tree. Such a boat could shoot down a dangerous rapid, if it was directed by skillful hands. When they wished to move from one lake to another, they lifted the canoe out the water, strapped it across the back of one man, who took it over the trail across country from one body of water to another.

Chapter 13

The Flight of Roger Williams

There was a young Puritan minister, named Roger Williams, who lived with his wife and two children in the town of Salem, Massachusetts. His congregation was small, but his labors, especially the comfort he gave to those who were sick or in distress, made him greatly beloved.

He at one time had preached at Plymouth, and had visited the Narragansett natives. He slept in the wigwams, and ate the food of his native friends. He went fishing and hunting with them, and learned from them many secrets of native woodcraft. After awhile he could speak their language, and for hours would sit around their camp fires and hear them tell their stories. In this way the natives became his firm friends, and he thus came to understand much about them he would not otherwise have known.

When Roger Williams went to Salem to preach, he became very bold in his opposition to many of the doctrines of his Puritan brethren. For instance, it was the Puritan law that everybody had to go to meeting on Sunday, whether he wished to or not. At the beating of the drum, or the ringing of the bell, or the sounding of the horn, everybody, who was not sick in bed, had to march out and proceed to the, meeting-house. In fact there was a captain who inspected the houses to see that nobody was in hiding.

Roger Williams thought this was wrong. "We should not compel people to go to church. If their own consciences do not urge them to attend worship, let them stay at home," he said.

When the Puritans heard of this, they were greatly shocked, and declared Roger Williams a dangerous member of society. To them it was a great crime to stay away from church.

Another rule of the Puritans was that every man had to pay a tax for the support of the Church. No matter whether he was a good man or not, he had to go to church and had to pay for the preacher.

Roger Williams thought this was wrong. "No man should pay for his religion unless he wishes to do so. His conscience and not the General Court should determine the amount," he said.

When the Puritans heard of this they were still more surprised and shocked, for by this time Roger Williams was becoming so bold that there were threats of sending him out of the community.

But this was not all, by any means. Roger Williams declared, "The King of England has no right to give away the lands in America. They do not belong to him, but they belong to the native people. They alone have a title to them, and it is from them alone that they can be bought."

This was more than the Puritans could stand. "It is dangerous to have such a man in our colony. He must be sent back to England," said the Puritan leaders, and they straightway ordered him before the General Court.

Little mercy did they show the brave minister. "Back you go to England in six weeks, or else you must stop preaching those dangerous doctrines," was what they told him.

"I shall not go to England. I came here to find freedom for my conscience and here I find nothing but persecution. You are trying to do in America the very thing for which we left England," replied Williams boldly.

So he went on preaching his own doctrines and the Puritans decided to seize him, put him on board a ship, and send him to England. The kind Governor Winthrop secretly sent him word that he had better escape, or else he would be arrested.

When Williams received the message, he hastily left his wife and children, and, taking a package of food and a heavy cane, committed himself to the wilderness. It was mid-winter when he started.

The ground was covered with snow, and he had only a small pocket compass to guide him through the forest. Fearing that the officers of the General Court would try to overtake him, he traveled only at night, hiding by day in caves or in the deep shelter of the woods.

Thus he wandered for fourteen weeks. At night he built a fire as best he could, and cooked the game he had caught in the snow. Oftentimes he had only acorns to eat. If it had not been for the wigwams of his native friends, which he found along his journey, he would have frozen to death; and but for their aid he would long since have starved.

At length he came to Massasoit, one of his oldest friends, "I have come to live with you. My friends have cast me out, and I am cold, hungry, and very tired," said he to the native Chief.

Massasoit took him into his own wigwam, laid him down on a couch of skins, and covered him up so he might be warm. Then Williams slept long, while Massasoit wondered what this friend had done that he was cast out of Salem. When Williams awoke he was given food to eat, a pipe to smoke, and warm clothes to put on.

When Massasoit heard his story he said, "Stay here until the snow has gone, and the spring has come. They shall not find you or hurt you." So Williams stayed in the wigwam of Massasoit until spring.

By this time, the Puritans decided to let him alone, provided he did not come back to them. Hearing this, Williams sent for his wife and children, and, with a few friends who joined him, journeyed to Narragansett Bay in the spring. He bought some land from Canonicus, and made a settlement.

"We shall call this place Providence, for the Lord has provided for us," said he. And so it is called to this day.

Massasoit took him into his own wigwam.

Chapter 14

Old Silver Leg

The Dutch took possession of the Hudson River settlements, and for forty years their Governor ruled over the colony at the mouth of the river. They called their town, New Amsterdam. Traders came from Holland to traffic with the natives, and to bring supplies to the merchants of the town. The fat old burghers sat on the door-steps of their quaint Dutch homes, and smoked their pipes of peace, perfectly satisfied with themselves and with all the world.

At last came Peter Stuyvesant from Holland to govern the colony. He had been a fine soldier, and had lost a leg by fighting in the West Indies. He had a wooden leg, of which he was so proud that he had silver bands put around it as ornaments. He used to tap it with his heavy stick and say, "I value this old wooden leg more than all my other limbs put together." The people called him "Old Silver Leg."

Peter was very high-tempered and obstinate. He made his own laws and had them obeyed; but they were very good laws and he was a

Winthrop and Stuyvesant

just old governor, even if he was cross at times. He had a Council of nine men, chosen by himself, but as they were self-satisfied and sleepy old merchants, all they did was to smoke their pipes and hear what Stuyvesant had to say.

If the people did not suit him, or quarreled among themselves, or disobeyed his laws, the irate old man would berate them with his heavy stick, and storm up and down the village streets. But as he was generally right in all he did and required, the people let him have his way, however much he belabored some of them over their backs. Meanwhile, the colony prospered, the natives were friendly, ships came and went, schools and churches were opened, and the people were contented and happy.

And so the years went by, until the English settlements, up in Connecticut, began to worry the Dutch. As a matter of fact the English still claimed the land the Dutch had occupied, because the territory had been explored by John Cabot, an Englishman, and because Henry Hudson was an Englishman, even if he did sail under a Dutch flag. At last the King of England boldly gave the Dutch colony to his brother, the Duke of York, and told him to go and take possession. This was not very just, but it was the way kings did things in those days.

Stuyvesant was in Boston when he heard of those high-handed plans, and he at once sent word to the Dutch to prepare for war. The Council met and decided to build defenses for their town; but as this cost money and as the people were very thrifty, and as the enemy was not in sight, the poor little city got no fortifications at all.

When the English fleet appeared off the coast of New Amsterdam, demanding the surrender of the town, the people ran to their houses and hid themselves, praying for the brave old Governor to come home and tell them what to do. When

Stuyvesant returned from Boston he was in a great rage because nothing had been done. He stormed and threatened the Council for not obeying his orders, and he swore he would not surrender his town.

The burghers listened with dismay. The English commander had told them to surrender, and they could live peaceably under the English flag. Otherwise he would destroy their town and drive them away. They did not care whose flag they lived under so long as they were let alone. English or Dutch, it was all one to the peace-loving merchants of New Amsterdam.

They showed Stuyvesant a copy of the summons to surrender. But he thrust it in his pocket, and told the Council to go home; he would defend the colony all by himself, he said. The burgomasters called a meeting of the people, who agreed to surrender the town, and a note was sent to Stuyvesant to that effect. He used the note to light his pipe, and made no reply.

Governor Winthrop of Connecticut wrote him a letter, advising him to surrender. The burgomasters came in a body to present this communication. But Stuyvesant tore it into bits, threw the pieces in the face of the nearest man, hit another over the head with his pipe, and kicked the rest down stairs with his wooden leg. "You are a pack of cowards," he called after them. "Out of my sight! I have done with you!"

In the meantime, the English had sent their own men among the Dutch, and had told them of the terrible things that would happen to them if they did not surrender. On the other hand, they were promised they would not be attacked if they quietly gave up their town.

And so the Dutch, who loved their stores, houses, gardens and cattle, and cared little for the Dutch flag, decided they would surrender anyhow. When Stuyvesant heard of it, he swore a great oath, but had to agree, for there was nothing else to do.

The treaty of surrender was brought to him to sign. He threw away the pen and tore up the paper. The next day the people gathered in a crowd before his house, and harangued him for three hours. They put the treaty on the end of a pole and thrust it up to his window. At last he signed it, threw it out, and closed the shutters. The British then entered the city, and changed the name from New Amsterdam to New York.

Stuyvesant retired to his farm on Manhattan Island, where he lived quietly the rest of his days.

CHAPTER 15

WILLIAM PENN AND THE QUAKERS

Among the religious sects which came to England about the time of the settlement of America were the Quakers, or, as they called themselves, "The Society of Friends." They believed that no special honor should be paid to anyone, and that all men should be addressed as "Friend." They even spoke of the King as "Friend James" or "Friend Charles." They would not take off their hats in the presence of anyone, not even the King himself. They always used the words "thee" and "thou," instead of the word "you" in speaking to a person.

Soon after Charles II was crowned King of England, William Penn, who had become a Quaker, was given an audience. When Penn entered the royal room, he found the King standing with his hat on, as was the custom; and all the courtiers were around him uncovered and vying in their efforts to flatter him and do him the most honor.

William Penn

Penn came up with his hat on. The King at once removed his hat and bowed very low to the approaching Quaker. "Why dost thou remove thy hat, Friend Charles?" asked Penn. "Because it is the custom of this Court for only one man to remain covered," explained the King, to the amazement of the courtiers.

The Quaker men dressed very simply in drab or gray clothes, with broad-brimmed hats. The women wore gray dresses, with simple white cuffs and collars. No matter how rich or poor, the Quakers wore costumes that cost about the same. They believed all men to be equal, and an honest man who tried to do right was entitled to as much respect as the King himself, and more so, if the King was not a good man.

In their meetings the Quakers had no music and no preaching. The people came in and sat silently, until someone was moved by the spirit to speak or pray. Not having any paid preacher, themselves, they believed no one should be paid to preach the Gospel, and so they refused to pay taxes to support the Church of England. Since the Bible said it was wrong to swear, they refused to take an oath in the courts of law, saying that a truthful man did not have to swear to what he said; if he were not a truthful man he did not mind swearing to a lie.

They did not believe in courts of law and quarrels, and they refused to go to law about anything, but settled their differences among themselves. Not believing in quarrels and bloodshed, they disapproved of taking a part in war. They were a people of peace, who believed in equality, brotherly love, and simplicity of living.

It was not long before the English Government made laws to prevent the spread of the doctrine of the Quakers. These laws forbade them to hold meetings. Many of the Quakers were thrown into prison and fined, some were publicly flogged, and all were hooted at and sometimes stoned upon the public streets. But the Quakers made no protest, and endured all these persecutions.

The Quakers attracted the attention of the young man, William Penn. He was the son of a famous English Admiral, Sir William Penn. When the boy was fifteen years old, he was sent to Oxford

University, where he met a Quaker who had great influence over him. At that time the students were required to wear long black gowns. Penn and some of the other younger men refused to wear these gowns, and even went so far as to tear them off of some of their fellow students. For this he and his friends were expelled from College.

His father was very angry, and sent William to Paris to indulge in the cheerful life of that city, hoping it would divert his mind. After two years, however, the young man returned to England unchanged in mind, and openly joined the Society of Friends. It was then that he began to preach their doctrines. For this his father disowned him, and the King ordered him thrown into prison.

While in prison he wrote many books and pamphlets on religious subjects, and sternly refused to change his faith. When he was released, he and his father were reconciled, just a short while before the old Admiral died, leaving William Penn his estate.

Penn now found himself a wealthy young man, and resolved to carry out his plan of founding a colony in America for the persecuted Quakers. It seems that the King owed Penn's father a lot of money he had borrowed from him. Penn proposed to the King to cancel the debt by receiving a grant of land in America. This was easy for the King to do, for it cost him nothing, and was a good way to get rid of the debt.

The King said to Penn, "I shall never see you again, William, for the natives will boil you in their kettle."

"Nay, nay, Friend Charles," replied Penn, "I shall be friends with the natives, and pay them for their lands."

The King was astonished, and asked Penn why he intended to buy lands that were the King's by right of discovery.

"Discovery!" exclaimed Penn. "Suppose a canoe full of natives had landed in England, would they own this kingdom by right of discovery?" To such a question the King made no reply.

Penn wanted his grant named "Sylvania," which means woodland. But the King would add "Penn" to the name in honor of the old Admiral, his friend. And so the future colony of the Quakers came to be called "Pennsylvania."

Chapter 16

The Charter Oak

When James II became King of England, he made a determined effort to overthrow the liberties of the American colonies. He was a tyrant who tried to work hardships upon his own people in England, and to discipline the colonists abroad. His idea was to take away the charters of the New England colonies, with all the rights granted them by former kings, and to make them submit to the arbitrary rule of governors whom he should appoint. Sometimes it seemed that the kings of England did everything they could to destroy the affection of the people of America.

King James sent one of his adherents, Sir Edmund Andros, to New England to be Governor-general of those colonies, with authority to take away their charters and to rule them according to his own and the King's will. Some of the colonies submitted, but those of Connecticut absolutely refused to surrender the precious document. Andros lived in Boston in the most arrogant style, and for a while Connecticut was left undisturbed.

After nearly a year had passed, and the charter of Connecticut still remained unsurrendered, Andros resolved to go after it. Therefore he made his appearance in Hartford with a body-guard of sixty soldiers, and marched up to the Chamber where the Assembly was in session, declaring boldly, "I have come by the King's command to order you to surrender the charter of Connecticut. I am henceforth to be the Governor of this colony, and to give you such laws as it pleases the King to grant. You will at once place the charter in my hands. It is the will of His Majesty, King James II."

Now, the charter allowed the people of Connecticut to elect their own Governor, and to have their own Assembly, and to make their own laws. Consequently, they did not wish to surrender it.

Nor were they willing to displease the King if it could be avoided. Therefore they showed much respect to the blustering Andros, and began to explain, entering upon a long and calm debate of why they could not place the charter in his hands.

Governor Treat, who was presiding, addressed Andros with respect and remonstrance. He said:

"Sir, the people of this country have been at great expense and hardship in planting this colony. Their blood and treasure have been freely poured out in defending it against those who have tried to drive them from their possessions. We came here by consent of the King, and His Majesty, Charles II., the brother of our most gracious King, granted us our liberties only fifteen years ago in a charter which we greatly prize. We beg you, therefore, to represent to the King that we are his loyal subjects and will remain faithful to him, but we earnestly desire to keep in our possession the rights and privileges granted us."

Thus the Governor spoke at great length, while Andros grew more and more impatient. He had not come to hear arguments; he had come to get the charter, and words were wasted on him. Night was drawing on, and still the members spoke, as if they would wear out the tyrant with their argument. At length Andros thundered forth,

"No more of this; I am weary of your words. Bring in the charter, or I shall arrest the Assembly."

Reluctantly, the box containing the charter was brought in and laid on the table. Candles were lighted and placed beside it so that it could be seen. It was opened, exposing to view the document the tyrant sought. Andros rose from his seat and advanced to the table to seize the precious papers, and thus end the whole matter, when suddenly someone threw a cloak upon the candles, completely extinguishing them, and leaving the room in darkness.

Amidst the confusion there was a sound of papers being rolled and of feet rushing from the hall. When the candles were re-lit, the charter had disappeared. It was nowhere to be found, and to all the threats and ravings of Andros the members returned a blank stare. No one knew what had become of it. It had disappeared as completely as if it had sunk into the earth.

What had happened? In the Chamber, a brave young militiaman, Captain Joseph Wadsworth, had thrown his cloak over the candles. He had then made a rush for the table, seized the charter and leaped out of a window. To the crowd assembled without he cried: "Make way for me. I have the charter, and it shall not be surrendered to a tyrant." The crowd cheered, and let him through. He disappeared in the darkness, just as the candles were being lit again inside the Chamber and Andros was raving in his disappointment.

Wadsworth sped onward, looking for a safe place in which to conceal the document. He came to a great oak tree, standing in front of the house of one of the colonial magistrates. There was a hollow in the tree, ample inside, but with an opening not larger than a man's hand. Into this Wadsworth thrust the charter, and concealed the opening with leaves and rubbish.

"Now, let Sir Edmund rave!" he said to himself. "This oak will keep its secret." And so the oak did. It became known as "The Charter Oak." It stood the storms of many winters, and was pointed out, for one hundred and sixty-nine years afterwards, as the place of refuge of the Connecticut charter. A tempest felled it to the ground in 1856.

As for Andros, he assumed control of Connecticut, charter or no charter, and ruled for a short while with an iron hand. The next year, however, the royal tyrant of England was driven from his throne, and Andros lost his power. He was thrown into prison in Boston, and shipped back to England. Then the precious charter was brought out of its hiding place by Wadsworth and a few others, who knew where it was, and Connecticut again had her rights and liberty.

The Charter Oak

Chapter 17

Bloody Marsh

When Georgia was settled by an English colony under Oglethorpe, and the town of Savannah was begun, the enterprise was met with protest from the Spaniards in Florida, because Spain claimed all the territory of America, clear to the Arctic Ocean. She had founded only one colony, that of St. Augustine, in Florida, but still she claimed the whole land.

Ten years after Georgia was settled, the Spaniards resolved to wipe out the colony, then march to Charleston, and so on as far north as possible. We shall see that they did not get very far.

A great fleet of thirty-six ships, with five thousand men on board, appeared off the coast of St. Simon's Island in Georgia. The Spaniards raised the red flag of war and landed their troops on the southern end of the island. Oglethorpe had hastily collected all the men he could, but at best he had only six hundred and fifty to oppose the great army confronting him.

Oglethorpe posted his scouts, and awaited the coming of the Spanish forces. He was determined to make his little army check the advance of the enemy as long as he could. One day a scout came into camp, and announced that the Spaniards were within two miles of Oglethorpe's camp. The General hastily called for a body of his own troops, skirted through the woods, and fell upon the advance forces with such fury that they were nearly all killed or captured. Oglethorpe took two prisoners with his own hands.

"That is a good beginning," he said to one of his captains.

"Now for the rest, before they can rally. We will lie in ambush for them." And so he did, along the road by which the Spaniards had to march.

Before long the enemy came in sight, halted where the ambush was, and stacked their guns. Some began to cook, while others lay down to rest, for it was July and the day was very hot. One of their horses noticed a strange uniform in the bushes, and by rearing and pitching gave the alarm. The Spaniards sprang to their guns, but it was too late. A deadly fire poured into them from an unseen foe, how many or how few they did not know! They fled in all directions, but were met by the bayonet of the English soldier. The ground was covered with their dead. Because of this victory and the great slaughter of the Spaniards, the place has ever since been called "Bloody Marsh."

The defeat drove back the advance force, but there was still the main body to be accounted for. Oglethorpe resolved to surprise it by night. He knew these soldiers were not accustomed to warfare, or to fighting in the tangled forests, and he was trying to demoralize them with fear before they could attack his small army.

He advanced within a mile of their camp, late in the night, and was making ready to attack, when one of his soldiers, a Frenchman, fired off his gun and ran into the Spanish lines. He was a deserter, and had fled to the enemy to give the alarm. Oglethorpe hastily retreated to save his little army.

He knew the deserter would tell the enemy of his real strength, and he at once devised a plan to thwart this purpose. He wrote a letter in French, urging this man by all means to persuade the Spaniards to attack, to speak of the smallness of his forces and the exposure of his position. He must not, however, mention the reinforcements which had arrived, but must induce the Spaniards to stay on the island so Oglethorpe could attack them in a few days.

Of course this was a decoy letter. He handed it to a Spanish prisoner, and said to him, "Take this letter to the man whose name is on it. He is a friend of mine in the Spanish camp. Say nothing about it to any one, and I will give you your liberty."

The man agreed, was handed the letter, and was set free. The deserter put the paper in his pocket, where it was found by the Spanish Commander, when he ordered the deserter examined. The Commander read the letter with alarm, and was at a loss to know what to do. He called a council of his officers and laid the facts before them He said, "This deserter is a spy in our camp, and this letter is the opposite of the truth. I believe the English are on us in great force." Thereupon he ordered his great army to get on their ships and sail away.

Thus did General Oglethorpe, with a few hundred men, outwit a force nearly ten times as large as his, and save the southern colonies from invasion by the Spaniards.

Chapter 18

The Saving of Hadley

King Philip's War was raging. Hundreds of the people of New England had fallen victims to the fury of the native peoples. Whole villages had perished, their inhabitants being slain or carried away as captives. The country was in a state of terror, for Philip, the son of Massasoit, was a ruthless foe.

The settlers were ever on the lookout. The farmer took his gun with him to the fields, and listened always for the sound of alarm from his cabin. The churches were guarded like forts, and men prayed with musket in hand. By night the villages slept with a watch posted at every avenue of approach.

Hadley, Massachusetts, was a frontier town at this time. It was on the northwestern edge of the settlements, and beyond were the forests full of Narragansett natives. One day, in the midst of summer, the people were gathered at church. The hour had been set apart for fasting and prayer, that the land might be delivered from the scourge of warfare. As the people prayed, the men clutched their muskets and the women cowered in dread.

Precaution was well taken. The natives had crept through the bushes and, under cover of the forests, had passed the guards and were upon the people before they knew of their danger. The men ceased their prayers and grabbed their guns. Hurrying out, they found the foe in the streets of the village, filling the air with terrible cries of ferocious triumph.

Confusion and terror reigned among the inhabitants. The

suddenness of the attack prevented the villagers from getting ready with their usual vigor, and it seemed that a panic would ensue, and everybody would be slain or captured. Hadley then would be one more of the towns wiped out by the natives!

Just at the critical moment, a strange man appeared among them. He was tall and stately, with long white hair, and dressed in the old-fashioned style of England. His face glowed with determination, his manner gave confidence, and his voice inspired the people to resistance.

"Here, get into line and order at once! The women and children must retire to the church! Come on, men, with me! Ready, march." He gave orders in a quick fashion, and the men, without question, obeyed at once. It seemed to them that God had sent an angel to deliver them from their trouble.

Inspired by the thought that God had answered the prayers which, only a short while before, they had offered up, and firm in the belief that an angel led them, they shouted with one voice, "Lead on! We follow to the last man." Their shout of determination matched the war cry of the Narragansetts themselves.

With remarkable vigor for an aged man, the stranger led the attack. The men of Hadley followed closely, and pressed vigorously upon the ranks of the natives. Seeing the sudden vision of a white-haired figure in a strange dress, the natives were dismayed, and began to waver.

"Make ready! Fire!" cried the leader, and raised his stick. The men of Hadley sent volley after volley into the terrified enemy, who turned and fled to the forest, pursued by the settlers until they were completely out of sight. They then returned to the town to thank their savior who had led them successfully through this dreadful disaster.

He was nowhere to be found. He had mysteriously disappeared even as mysteriously as he had come, and from that time on no man in Hadley ever saw him again, except the minister himself, the only one in all the town who knew anything about him.

To solve the mystery we must go back to England, to 1649, the year in which Charles I was executed. To his death-warrant there were signed the names of fifty-nine judges. After a number of years his son, Charles II., mounted the throne and swore he would behead everybody who had had anything to do with the murder of his father. As a result, many of the judges received the death penalty.

We have only to do with two of them – Whalley and Goffe, who, when they saw the fate that awaited them in England, fled to America and landed in Boston about thirteen years before the incidents occurred which are the chief interest of this story. Here they hoped to live in peace. But word came that they were wanted in England, so they moved to New Haven to escape capture at the hands of the King's men. The King had sent royal messengers to America to find and arrest the regicides, as they were called. He was resolved to put them to death.

These messengers found nothing but trouble in their path. The people, who knew Whalley and Goffe very well, would give no information whatsoever to the King's agents, but passed the two judges on from town to town, hiding them in cellars or attics, and even in caves in the woods, that they might escape. They lived for months, sometimes even years, in the houses of friends, and only a few people would know when they were in the village. At one time the royal pursuers passed over a bridge, while Whalley and Goffe were lying beneath it, only an arm's length from the horses' feet!

Once they dwelt in a cave, their food supplied by the people of a neighboring village, when the natives found their retreat. The poor fugitives feared the natives would betray them, so they hastened to find a new place of shelter. They made their way to Hadley, aided by many friends and traveling only by night. Here they were received by the minister of the village and given a refuge in his house. For twelve years, they lived comfortably here, never venturing outside, their presence quite unsuspected by the villagers. It was not until the natives attacked the village that one of them, Goffe, showed himself, and in the manner we have described!

After the attack was over, the mysterious leader disappeared from view and from history. What became of him and his companion will forever remain one of the mysteries of the period in our history when this country was very young.

Chapter 19

Sir William Phips and the Treasure Ship

This is the story of a poor boy who lived on a miserable plantation on the Kennebec River, in New England, yet who ended by becoming a nobleman of Old England. His name was William Phips, and he had twenty brothers and five sisters. In his early life he tended sheep, and learned the trade of a ship carpenter. He then went to Boston, where he learned to read and write and, later on, married a good wife. He settled down to hard work, and after ten years became Captain of one of the King's ships. Little did he know he was about to face the great adventure of his life, as we shall see.

These were the days when Spanish ships were seeking silver and gold and precious stones on the coast of Peru; when they were carrying their cargoes back to the old country, if they were fortunate enough to escape the pirates! Some of these cargoes went to the bottom in storms, or ran foul on dangerous reefs. Many were the stories of precious wrecks along the shores of the Bahamas.

On one of his trips to the Bahamas, Phips heard of a Spanish wreck "wherein was left a mighty treasure" at the bottom of the sea. He made up his mind to be the discoverer of that ship and to recover that treasure, if it was possible. Many a man would have laughed at the story, or would have hesitated over the task; but Phips was not like other men. He was born for great adventure, and herein he saw his chance.

Forthwith he sailed for England, and sought the wealthy people of the realm. He was a comely man, full of honesty and sincerity, and Royalty at Court listened to his smooth words with apparent confidence. For he came back to New England, Captain of his King's ship, and with full power to search the seas for silver and gold in sunken cargoes.

Phips's task was not an easy one. Fifty years had passed since the particular ship of which he had heard had sunk; hence the exact spot was not easy to find. All that was known was that it was somewhere near the Bahamas. But men have ventured in search of gold on far less certainty than this, and Phips was not one to be dismayed.

He took his crew to the Bahamas, and began his long and discouraging search. He dredged here and there; he questioned the old inhabitants along every coast; he used every means .of information and discovery. But without success.

At length his crew grew mutinous. They wanted to turn pirates, and to set sail for the South Seas. Accordingly, one day they rose, and marched with drawn swords to the Captain, saying, "We will have no more of this. Take us to more profitable waters under the black flag, or we will heave you overboard. We will be pirates henceforth, and will not search the bottom of the sea for ships, when there are plenty to be found on top of it."

Phips was aghast at this mutiny, and, besides, he was unarmed and helpless. Still he was by far the most powerful man on board, and was terrible in his wrath. Slowly he approached the ringleader, as if to parley with him. Then, with bare hands, he leaped upon him, knocked him down, seized his cutlass, and attacked the others with fury. So impetuous was the onset that in a short time the deck was strewn with wounded men, while many others fled in dismay, begging mercy of the infuriated Captain.

Soon after the mutiny, Phips sailed back to Jamaica in order to get a new crew, more disposed to do as they were told. The treasure-ship must be somewhere, and its riches haunted him day and night. He sailed to Hispaniola in search of information. He met a very old Spaniard who said he knew where the ship was sunk, and who told of the spot on a reef of shoals, a few leagues from Hispaniola, and not far from Port de la Plata which was so named because of a boat-load of sailors who landed there with plate saved from the sinking vessel.

This was enough for our hero. He needed more men and more money, so he bravely returned to England to beg for both. He had a hard time to convince any one of his story, but Phips was very plausible and the account of how he quelled the mutiny on his vessel won him many admirers. Such was not an easy task in those days of adventure. However, it was not long before Captain Phips found himself headed for the lost treasure on the quarter-deck of a new ship, well manned and equipped.

He reached Port de la Plata in due time. It was now about 1685. He set about getting ready a great canoe, hollowed out of the trunk of an enormous tree. The point selected by him for search was a terrible reef, known as "The Boilers," where the sea foamed over a sloping reef no man knew how deep. Phips anchored his ship near the perilous spot, made ready his divers and his diving-bell, got out the canoe, and set to work with a slow and steady resolve to see the undertaking through or else perish.

Days passed in vain search. The weather was calm and the ship's supplies were abundant. The men did not complain, but dived down, along the reef, looking everywhere for signs of a lost vessel. One day a boatman, gazing into the clear water, saw, growing out of what seemed to be a rock, what he thought was a beautiful sea feather, usually to be found in sea gardens. So a man went down after it and brought it up in his hands.

"That was not a rock, but a great gun you saw," said the diver to his companions in the boat.

"What do you say? Gun! Gun!" .they cried. "It must be what we are seeking! On board, all you divers!" There was intense excitement in the canoe.

Other men were sent down, and one of them came back with a lump of silver in his hands. It was a bar worth a thousand dollars. "I found it near the gun. There are other guns and other lumps like it, many, many!" he explained, his eyes almost starting from their sockets.

The sailors roared with joy. At last the place was found! Their search was over! They were masters of the silver-ship! Riches untold were in their possession! They marked the spot with a buoy, and rowed back to the ship to inform Phips of what they had found and to show him the bar of silver.

"Thanks be to God, our fortunes are made," cried the Captain, and at once repaired with his men to the spot marked by the buoy.

There was no indifference now on the part of the crew. Every diver went down and every sailor lent a hand. Bar after bar was brought up from the ocean's depths, and stored away, as well as cases of silver coin, gold in large quantities, together with pearls and precious stones. Never was there such treasure dug up from the bottom of the ocean, where it had lain for half a century. It was worth a million and a half dollars. The work continued until provisions were exhausted and the men were ill. Though the sunken ship held more, they had to leave it where it was. Phips sailed to England and showed his treasures to the King, and to his friends.

He was the most honest and generous man of his day, and paid his crew liberally. He gave his patrons a large share of his fortune, and his employees had naught to complain of. What remained to him after this still left him a very rich man, and for a time he was the most talked of man in England.

As for the King, he was so well pleased with the adventure, and with the admirable manners of Phips, that he made the latter a knight, which meant that he was called "Sir William" from that time on. And this is the story of how a plain country boy of New England came, through his his love of adventure, to belong to the aristocracy of England.

Never was there such treasure dug up from the bottom of the ocean!

Chapter 20

A Young Surveyor

When Washington was a boy, there lived in Virginia an old English nobleman, by the name of Lord Fairfax. He had come into possession of a large tract of land, but was by no means sure of its extent and boundaries.

The grandfather of Lord Fairfax, the famous Lord Culpepper, had, at one time, been Governor of Virginia. When he went back to England, he asked the King, Charles II, to give him all the land between the Potomac and Rappahannock Rivers, which the King, in his easy-going way, readily consented to do. It was a large and valuable estate, with but few settlers on it. Lord Culpepper, however, did not trouble himself much about it, and never came back to Virginia to see it.

When the old Governor died, this land descended to his daughter, and from her to Lord Fairfax. The latter was a fashionable young nobleman in London society; so he sent his cousin, William Fairfax, to look after his great estate in the wilderness of America, not caring a great deal at that time what became of it.

Now, it happened that Lord Fairfax fell in love with a beautiful young lady, and the two became engaged to be married. But she proved faithless to her promise, and, when a nobleman of higher rank presented himself, she promptly threw Lord Fairfax aside. This was a bitter blow to him, and he was so distressed and mortified that he determined never to marry anyone, but to move to America and live on his Virginia estate.

So he came across seas, and, with his cousin, dwelt in his fine mansion at Belvoir, not far from the Washington estate at Mount Vernon. Here he became a middle-aged man, tall, gaunt, and near-sighted, spending much of his time in hunting, of which he was very fond. His favorite companion on these hunting trips was young George Washington, who was a very active boy, fond of all outdoor life.

Lord Fairfax was so much attached to Washington that he decided to employ him as a surveyor for his great estate. George had studied surveying, and was anxious to undertake the work. The old man and the young boy, now sixteen years of age, talked the matter over carefully, and everything was made ready for the great survey.

Lord Fairfax's estate was large, his "grant" stretching between the Potomac and Rappahannock Rivers, and crossing the Blue Ridge mountains into the valley beyond. It was all wild country, with only a few settlers here and there. But it had to be surveyed and measured, and maps had to be drawn before any part of it could be sold. To make this survey and these maps was the task assigned to George Washington, the young surveyor.

It was in the early spring of 1748, that George Washington and George William Fairfax, son of the Master of Belvoir, armed with good guns, mounted on sturdy horses, and fully equipped with surveying instruments, started on their trip into the wilderness. The country in which they found themselves was beautiful. Lofty trees, broad grassy slopes, sparkling streams, and giant mountains lent variety and interest to their work. Spring was just beginning, and the birds, the early flowers, and the fresh sunshine made life very happy for the two boys entering upon their summer's excursion into the woods.

Their course led them up the banks of the Shenandoah, where

they measured and marked the land as they went, and mapped down its leading features. At night they found shelter in the rude cabin of some settler, or, if none was near, they built a fire in the woods, cooked the game they had killed, and lay down upon the ground to sleep. Thus they went on, day by day, till they came to the place where the Shenandoah flows into the Potomac. Then up the Potomac and across the mountains to a place called Berkeley Springs.

The two boys had no serious adventures. They met one band of natives, about thirty in number, painted and armed for war; but these paid no attention to the two surveyors and offered them no harm. At times life in the woods was hard; rains often soaked them, and the dampness prevented them from building a fire for cooking; it was also difficult to get warm in the chill nights of the mountains. They slept mostly in the open air, wrapped up in their great coats, and lying upon a bed of leaves or boughs. Often they cooked by merely holding bits of meats on sharp sticks before the fire; while chips or pieces of bark took the place of dishes. But the two boys enjoyed the work heartily. They were never sick and never dissatisfied.

The weeks passed by, and still they measured the land, located the marks, and made their maps. It was nearing summertime when they completed their

Young George Washington

journey, and turned their faces homeward. They rode over the mountains, and back to Belvoir, where they made their report to Lord Fairfax. The old nobleman was delighted with what they had done, and more than pleased with the wonderful estate they had surveyed.

Lord Fairfax left Belvoir, and made his home at Greenway Court, which was a hunting lodge he had built upon his estate. Here he spent the remainder of his life, surrounded by the great forests, in sound of the running waters, and in sight of the tall mountains. Here, an old and feeble man, the Revolutionary War found him still alive. When he heard of the victory of George Washington at Yorktown, he exclaimed, "I knew, when he was a lad surveying the wilderness for me, that boy would make a great man. Still, I am sorry he did not fight for the King instead of against him."

Chapter 21

The Adventures of Young Washington

When Washington was twenty-one years old, he was sent by Governor Dinwiddie, of Virginia, with a message to the French Commander in the Ohio Valley, directing him to withdraw from that territory, since it was claimed as an English possession. The place where Washington was to go was about five hundred and sixty miles away, through a tangled wilderness, beset by dangers of all kinds.

Washington, with a small party, started, in October, on his long journey. The winter soon settled down on the travelers as they toiled along. The snow fell thick and fast, the rain froze, and the sleet cut their faces like knives. Still, they were all strong young men, capable of enduring great hardship, and they bravely pursued their way.

When they reached the French settlement, they found the officer in charge busily engaged, preparing his fort. Washington delivered the letter from Governor Dinwiddie. The French Commander politely replied that he was a soldier, acting under orders, and that it was his purpose to stay where he was, until the Governor of Canada directed him to move. He

George Washington

wrote a letter to Governor Dinwiddie to this effect, and handed it to Washington; after which he treated the party with much consideration and kindness, until they were ready to depart.

Our story mainly deals with his return journey. It was now the dead of winter, and very cold. The long pathless forest, the steep mountains, the swollen streams, the hunger and cold, lay before Washington; but, with a few faithful native guides and a companion, named Christopher Gist, he prepared to start on his perilous way. The French were polite to the very last. They stocked his canoes with provisions, and gave him every thing he needed for his journey.

But Washington found the snow falling so fast that he sent a few men with the horses and baggage through the forest, while he took his own small party in canoes down the river. The way was most difficult. The channel was obstructed by rocks and drifting logs. Shallows and dangerous currents abounded.

"Many times," wrote Washington, "all hands were obliged to get out and remain in the water half an hour or more, while taking their canoes across the shoals. At one place, the ice had lodged and made it impassable by water; so we were forced to carry our canoe across a neck of land the distance of a quarter of a mile."

In six days they went one hundred and thirty miles, on a half frozen river, in frail canoes, to the place where they had planned to meet their horses and baggage. When they arrived, they found the outfit in a very pitiable plight.

Under these conditions Washington and Gist determined to proceed alone on foot, leaving the others to follow. With his gun on his shoulders, his knapsack on his back, and a stout staff to steady his feet, the brave adventurer started, followed by his faithful companion, similarly equipped. Leaving the regular path, they struck a straight course, by the compass, through the woods.

The journey was full of excitement. At one place, a native met them and agreed to show them the way. At the end of the first day, Washington grew very weary and foot-sore with the heavy traveling. The man, who had carried his knapsack, now offered to carry his gun also. This Washington refused, and the native fell back a few paces, his face scowling. They had proceeded a few miles further on when the man, who had dropped behind, suddenly stopped.

Washington and Gist looked back and saw the man aiming his gun at them. With a cry of alarm they both leaped aside, just as the weapon was fired, thereby escaping injury. But it was a narrow escape, and Gist was angry at this treatment; so he ran in pursuit of the him, who had taken refuge behind a tree. He seized him by the throat and was on the point of thrusting his knife into him, when Washington called out, "Don't kill him. It will do no good, and will only sound an alarm to bring other natives down upon us. Bind him, and have him go with us."

Gist accordingly bound the man and ordered him to walk ahead of the party for a day or more. Then Washington released him, and bade him begone to his home in the woods. The following night they reached the Allegheny River, where they were destined to meet with a most dangerous experience.

They had hoped to cross on the ice, but the river was not frozen hard enough; so they lay down on a bed of snow, and covered themselves up in their blankets, expecting that, by morning, the thick ice would be formed. But on rising, they saw, at a glance, that the ice was not yet to be trusted.

"We will make a raft, and rely on our good fortune to get us safely over," said Washington. Whereupon he and Gist began to cut down trees with their one small hatchet, and to bind the logs together with vines. It took a whole day to complete the raft, but, not caring to spend another night in the same place, they immediately launched their frail craft, and put out from the shore.

Before they had gone half across, the raft was jammed in the floating ice, so that it seemed as if they would be thrown into the water at any moment. Washington tried to hold the raft with his pole, in order to prevent it from drifting down stream. The result was most disastrous. The strength of the current was so great that Washington, powerful as he was, was jerked violently from the raft, and thrown into the icy current.

It was a dangerous moment for the future leader of the Revolutionary armies of America. By heroic effort, he breasted the cold water, pushed aside the floating ice, and caught hold of one end of the raft. Here, Gist assisted him to regain his place, dripping and shivering.

They had to abandon the raft and seek shelter on an island. All night long, without fire and food, his wet clothes freezing to his body, Washington waited for the hours to pass till morning. He kept alive by stamping his feet and beating his arms. When day dawned, the river was frozen over, thick and solid, and our two adventurers hastened to cross to the other side. Gist had his face and fingers frozen, but Washington escaped injury. They reached a trading-post where, after several days, they were completely recovered and ready to resume their journey.

The remaining portion of the trip was without adventure, though it was not without hardship. In due time, Washington reached the capital of Virginia and delivered to the Governor the answer of the French Commander. He had been absent eleven weeks and had traveled more than a thousand miles.

Chapter 22

How Detroit was Saved

At the close of the French and Indian War, also known as the Seven Years' War, the town of Detroit was garrisoned by about three hundred men, under command of Major Gladwyn. All appearance of conflict was at an end. The native people there seemed to be most friendly, and approached the soldiers for the purposes of trade and conference.

Pontiac, however, a noted native Chief, conceived a plan for capturing the fort, and murdering the garrison. He approached with a band of his men, and camped a short distance away. He sent word to the Governor, Major Gladwyn, that he would like to come into the fort to trade and to have a talk. The Governor replied that he would be glad to have so famous a Chief, and his warriors, pay him a visit; and he fixed the day for their reception. He had no idea that they meditated treachery, and was really anxious to secure their good-will and friendship.

The evening before the meeting, a native woman who had been employed by Major Gladwyn to make him a pair of moccasins out of elk skin brought them in. They were beautiful, and Major Gladwyn was so pleased with them that he thought he would like to give them to a friend. He therefore told the woman to take the rest of the elk skin, and make him another pair.

He then paid what he owed her, and dismissed her. The woman went to the door, but no further. She held back as if she had something more to say. Upon being questioned why she did not hurry home, she hesitated a while, and then replied, "You have been very good to me. You have given me work and have paid me for it. I do not want to take away the elk skin, for I may never see you again to give you the shoes you want me to make."

The Governor insisted upon knowing why she felt this way, and, after much persuasion and many promises that no harm should ever befall her, she confided to him that Pontiac, the chief of the Ottawa tribe, and his band had formed a plot to kill all the garrison, during the visit they were about to pay the following day; after which they planned to plunder the town.

She told the Governor also that the natives had shortened their gun stocks, so as the better to conceal them under their blankets. At a given signal, they were to rise and fire, first upon the Governor himself, and then upon every soldier in sight. Other natives in the town were to be armed likewise.

Major Gladwyn is warned of the attack.

This was a terrible story, and the Governor began at once to make preparations for thwarting the plans of Pontiac and his warriors. He sent the woman away, called out all the soldiers, and armed them heavily. He gave every man directions what to do, and told all the traders in town to be in readiness to repel any attack.

About ten o'clock, Pontiac arrived, his warriors covered with heavy blankets. The Governor and his officers received them cheerfully. Pontiac was surprised to see so many soldiers on guard, and gathered in the streets. So he asked why it was. The Governor replied, "I drill them every day to keep them ready for service." Pontiac was disconcerted by the number, but said nothing further

He then began his speech of friendship and goodwill, saying he never intended to harm the English any more, but always expected to live in peace with them. He desired his warriors to have free access to Detroit, promising no danger to the people. He was about to hand the Governor a belt of wampum, which was the signal for attack, but Gladwyn turned upon him suddenly, and said,

"You are a traitor, and are not to be believed; see this evidence of your deceit!" He tore aside the Chief's blanket, revealing the shortened gun concealed beneath it. The soldiers thereupon seized the blankets of the other warriors, and laid bare all the guns ready for their foul design.

The natives were thus taken by surprise, and gave no signal to their companions outside. The Governor told Pontiac that the English had means of discovering all their plots, and that everything they did was sure to be known at once. He then led the much astonished Chief and his band to the gates of the fort, and ordered them never again to return for trade or conference. He spared their lives, but the next time he promised there would be no mercy.

By evening all the natives had been driven out of the town, and the gates were closed and guarded. Pontiac never discovered that Detroit was saved by the timely warning of a grateful woman, but ever afterwards he believed that the English had a way of knowing whatever plan he made for their destruction.

Chapter 23

The Story of Acadia

Once upon a time, in a land of the far north, which we now call Nova Scotia, there lived a company of French people whose ancestors, in generations back, had come from France to make their homes in the New World.

They were very happy and peaceful, for they were industrious and frugal. In spring and summer there were bright flowers and abundance of fruits, while autumn brought a bounteous harvest. They desired nothing more than to be let alone in their homes, to pursue their daily labors undisturbed, and, on the Sabbath, to worship in their own way. They called their country Acadia.

So the dark-eyed children wandered through the woods and orchards in the bright sunshine, and through the fields when the grain waved, and over the meadows where the cows tinkled their bells. The fathers of these boys and girls worked in the fields or in their shops; and built little houses by the side of the streams. Their mothers took care of the homes, nursed the babies, and made clothing for the winter.

All day long the colony was very busy. Not a soul who could do anything to help was idle; even the children, when not in school, and even after their hours of play, had their appointed tasks to do. At night the families would gather on the doorsteps, or in winter by the fires, and tell stories of their ancestors who lived in France.

Because their grandfathers and great-grandfathers had left France to come to America, these people still loved the old country, and considered themselves to be French. They spoke French, dressed in French manner, and kept up the customs of the land in which their forefathers were born.

Thus, for a hundred and fifty years, lived these peasants in the happy valley of Acadia. There were about seven thousand of them, and to them the world, with its quarrels and wars, its rulers and conquests, was of no moment; they cared to have no part in it.

Times of trouble soon loomed up for the Acadians. The land in which they lived became an English possession, and the King of England was their lawful ruler. The simple Acadians, loving only the old France of their ancestors, refused to take the oath of allegiance to England.

"We are French people. Our great-grandfathers came from France. We speak French, and our priests tell us to love the land from which we sprang. We cannot forswear our beautiful France," they said to the British officers.

An English Governor was sent to rule over the country. The French and Indian War commenced, and it was feared the Acadians would send help to the French, even though they promised to be neutral.

"We are French born, and therefore love the French people. You say we are now English subjects by treaty and cession of our land to England. Therefore, we pray you to let us be neutral; we do not want to enter this war, for we would not care to take sides against our King and our people," replied the Acadians to their new Governor.

But the English were not satisfied with this, and decided upon the harsh measure of moving all the Acadians away from their homes. On the first day of June, 1755, a ship sailed into the Bay of

Fundy, and anchored within a few miles of Beauséjour, the only military post held by French troops.

It took short work to dispose of this fort. In a few months the troops were ready to carry out the order of the English government. The people were again asked if they would take the oath of allegiance to the British King, and again they said, "No."

It was now August, and the waving fields of grain betokened the industry and thrift of the people. The cattle were lowing in the meadows, and the orchards were heavy with the ripening fruit. The green slopes were dotted with farmhouses, from whose chimneys came the curling smoke of busy housewives, and around whose doors grew bright autumn flowers nodding to the laughter of little children.

A body of English troops encamped in the village of Grand-Pré. An order was issued for all the men to gather at the church on a certain day, in order to hear a decree of the King. The bayonets of the soldiers showed plainly that the men had to obey.

Clad in homespun, wholly unarmed, and innocent of impending misfortune, the men came, at the sounding of the bell and the beating of the drums. Without, in the churchyard, were the women, sitting or standing among the graves of their dead.

Then there arrived the guard from the ship, and the soldiers entered the church. The door was closed, and the men waited in silence to hear the will of the King.

The Commander arose, and held up a paper bearing the royal seal. Then he spoke: "You are convened by his Majesty's orders to be told that all your lands, dwellings, and cattle of all kinds are forfeited to the Crown, and that you yourselves are to be transported from this Province to other lands. Even now you are prisoners."

The men listened to the voice of the Commander as if they did not hear him. They were silent for a moment in speechless wonder. Then, when they understood the awful meaning of the order, louder and louder grew their wails of anger and sorrow. They rushed, with one impulse, to the door, but in vain; for the soldiers had barred the entrance and held it with their bayonets.

One man, a blacksmith, rose, with his arms uplifted and with his face flushed with passion. "Down with the tyrants of England! We have never sworn allegiance. Death to those foreign soldiers, who seize on our homes and our harvests!" he cried. But the merciless hand of a soldier smote him upon the mouth, and he was dragged to the pavement.

The order was carried out to the letter. In a few weeks, the population of the peaceful valley was launched upon the sea for unknown shores, while the lowing of cattle and the howling of dogs were the only sounds heard from the desolate homes that once were the scenes of peace and plenty.

Some of the people escaped to the woods and were not captured. The others were scattered among the English colonies all the way from Connecticut to Georgia. Many made their way back to Canada, while some few returned to their old homes in Acadia. A number found their way to Louisiana where, on the west bank of the Mississippi, their descendants may still be found.

Chapter 24

Blackbeard the Pirate

In the days before the Revolution, the high seas surrounding America were infested with robbers, called pirates. Their ships, manned by desperate men, and carrying cannon and arms for fighting, scoured the ocean highways, and attacked peaceable and slow sailing vessels, which they robbed of merchandise; often they killed the sailors and sank the ships.

These pirates had hiding-places along the coast, especially the inlets, where they landed for supplies, sold their prizes, or buried their treasures in secret. A pirate's life was full of adventure. So terrible was the menace from these robbers that every sailing vessel dreaded to meet them on their way across the ocean, or up and down the coast.

Among these pirates was a Captain whose real name was Thatch, but who was known as "Blackbeard." He wore a long black beard, of which he was very careful and proud, but which gave him a frightful look. Around his shoulders was a strap from which huge pistols hung, ready for use in case of battle.

The scene of his operations was around the shores of Virginia and North Carolina, and even as far south as the coast of Georgia. He had accomplices on shore, who bought his ill-gotten cargoes, supplied his ships with provisions, and his men with arms. He became so bold and terrible that the people of Virginia fitted out two ships to go after him and to destroy him, if they could.

Only vessels that could sail in shallow water near the coast were sent out, and these, under the command of Lieutenant Maynard. For many days the ships sailed around, looking for Blackbeard and his crew. After a while the pirate ship came into view, and hoisted her flag with the skull and cross bones, calling on Maynard to surrender. But instead, Maynard hung out his flag and dared the pirate to come on. Blackbeard drew near, and called out, "Give up your ship at once, I take no prisoners."

"I shall not surrender!"

Maynard replied, "I shall not surrender, and I shall not show you any mercy." With that the battle began.

Maynard, after sending most of his men into the hold of his ship for safety, ran alongside the pirate. Blackbeard fired a broadside into Maynard's vessel, and, seeing no men aboard, thought that every one was killed. He therefore ordered his own crew to take possession. When the pirates came aboard, swords in hand, Maynard's men sprang from the hold of their vessel, and desperate fighting began on the deck.

Blackbeard was shot five times, besides being wounded with sword cuts. He fought bravely, calling so loudly to his men, that his voice was heard above the roar of the battle. His pistol was soon emptied, and, seizing another, he leveled it at one of Maynard's men. Just then, however, he received a wound through the head and was instantly killed. His men were taken prisoners and the battle was ended.

Maynard hung the pirate's head before the bow of his ship, and sailed back to Virginia, where the people made a great celebration in honor of his victory.

Chapter 25

The Adventures of Daniel Boone

Daniel Boone was one of the first settlers in Kentucky. He had to fight wild animals, but he liked it. He loved adventure, and went forth to find a home for his family in the deep and unbroken forest. He came to Kentucky, in June, 1769, with five companions. We will let him tell his story in his own words:

"We found, everywhere, abundance of wild beasts of all sorts through the vast forest. The buffaloes were more numerous than cattle in the settlements, fearless because ignorant of the violence of man. Sometimes we saw hundreds in a drove, and the numbers about the salt springs were amazing.

"As we ascended the brow of a small hill, near the Kentucky River, some natives rushed out of a thick cane-brake upon us, and made us prisoners. They plundered us of what we had, and kept us in confinement seven days. During this time we showed no uneasiness or desire to escape, which made them less suspicious of us. But, in the dead of night, as we lay in a thick cane-brake by a large fire, I touched my companion, and gently woke him. We improved this favorable

Daniel Boone

opportunity, and departed, leaving them to take their rest.

"Soon after this, my companion in captivity was killed, and the man that came with my brother returned home by himself. We were then in a dangerous, helpless situation, exposed daily to perils and death. One day I took a tour through the country, and the beauties of nature I met with expelled every gloomy and vexatious thought. I laid me down to sleep, and awoke not until the sun had chased away night.

"I returned to my old camp, which was not disturbed. I did not confine my lodging to it, but often slept in the thick cane-brakes to avoid the natives, who, I believe, often visited my camp, but fortunately in my absence. In this situation I was constantly exposed to danger and death. In 1772, I returned safe to my old home, and found my family in happy circumstances.

"I sold my farm and what goods we could not carry with us, and, in company with five families more and forty men that joined us, we proceeded on our journey to Kentucky. After two weeks, the rear of our company was attacked by a number of natives, who killed six men and wounded another. Of these my eldest son was one who fell in the action. This unhappy affair scattered our cattle, and so discouraged the whole company that we retreated to the settlement on Clinch River.

"Within fifteen miles of where Boonesborough now stands we were fired upon by natives, who killed two and wounded two of our numbers. Although surprised and taken at a disadvantage, we stood our ground. Three days later we were fired upon again, and two men were killed and three were wounded. Afterwards, we proceeded to the Kentucky River without opposition, and began to erect the fort at Boonesborough, at a salt lick, about sixty yards from the river on the south side.

"In July three girls, one of them my daughter, were taken prisoners near the fort. I pursued them with only eight men, overtook them, killed two of the party, and recovered the girls. Shortly afterwards, a party of about two hundred natives attacked Boonesborough. They besieged us forty-eight hours, during which time seven of them were killed. At last, finding themselves not likely to prevail, they raised the siege and departed.

"In October, a party of natives made an excursion into the district called the Crab Orchard, and one of them, who was advanced some distance before the others, boldly entered the house of a poor, defenseless family, in which was only a man, a woman, and her children. They attempted to capture the man, who happily proved too strong for him and threw him on the ground; in the struggle, the mother of the children drew an ax from a corner of the cottage, and cut his head off, while her daughter shut the door.

"The other natives appeared, and applied their tomahawks to the door. An old rusty gun-barrel, without a lock, lay in the corner; this the mother put through a small crevice in the door, perceiving which the natives fled. In the meantime, the alarm spread through the neighborhood. The armed men collected, and pursued them into the wilderness. From that time they did us no mischief.

"I can now confess that I have proved true the saying of an old friend, who, on signing a deed for his land, remarked, 'Brother, we have given you a fine land, but you will have much trouble in settling it.' Many dark and sleepless nights have I been the companion of owls, separated from the cheerful society of men, scorched by the summer's sun, and pinched by the winter's cold, an instrument ordained to settle the wilderness."

Chapter 26

Sunday in the Colonies

All the Colonists were strict in the observance of worship. Sunday was a severe day, and everybody had to be on his best behavior. The first building used for church purposes was the fort, to which every one marched in a body, the men fully armed to protect the congregation from the natives. Before the fort was finished, the people worshiped under trees, or in tents, or anywhere they could find a place. Many of the earliest meeting-houses were log huts, with mud between the cracks, and with thatched roofs.

These early churches had oiled paper in the windows. When glass was brought over, it was set in by nails, for there was no putty. Neither was there any paint, so the outside of every house was left to turn gray with the weather, or to become moss-covered from the dampness of the grove in which it was usually placed.

All sorts of notices were posted on the church doors, so that everybody might see them announcements of town meetings, of proposed marriages, of cattle sales, of rules against trading with the natives; in fact the church door took the place of the newspaper of today for spreading the news. It was the only means of advertisement.

In front of the church stood a row of hitching-posts and stepping stones, for nearly everybody rode to meeting. On the green, in front or to one side, were often placed the pillory, stock, and whipping-post.

There were many ways of calling the people to church, such as beating a drum, ringing a bell, or blowing a shell. Many of the churches had a drummer, who went up and down the streets, or else stood in the belfry and drummed. After the signal was given, a man went the rounds of the village, and looked in all the houses, to see that everybody who was able had gone to church. Woe betide the man who was late, or the boy who had skipped away to the woods!

The inside of a Colonial church was simple enough. Overhead, the rafters usually opened to the thatch or clapboard roof; the floors were of earth, or rough boards; and the pews or benches had straight backs and were hard. The pulpit was usually a high desk, reached by a staircase or ladder, with a sounding board over it. There was no heat in these early churches, for a heating stove was unknown. The chill of the building, dark and closed all the week, and damp from the shadowed grove, was hard for every one to stand. To keep from suffering during the long service, the women put their feet in bags, made of fur and filled with wool. Dogs were allowed so that their masters might put their feet under them. In fact, churches appointed dog whippers to control the dogs or to drive them out if they became noisy and unbearable. Some of the women and children had foot stoves, which were little metal boxes on legs, with small holes in the top and sides, and with hot coals inside.

The services were very long, no matter how cold it was. The snow might be falling and the wind blowing, but the people had to wrap up in their furs, snuggle down in the benches, and listen to a sermon two or three hours long. Sometimes a single prayer lasted an hour, while the people knelt on the bare floor. When a church was dedicated, the sermon generally lasted three or four hours. We might well wonder what the preacher could find to say, that it took so long a time to say it!

There was a tithing-man, whose duty it was to maintain order, and also to keep everybody awake. The men sat on one side of the church, the women sat on the other, while the boys and girls were made to sit near the pulpit. The tithing-man kept close watch for sleepers. He had a long stick, with a rabbit's foot on one end and a rabbit's tail on the other. If a man nodded, or a boy made a noise, the tithing-man struck him a sharp blow on the head. If an old lady closed her eyes, the tithing-man gently tickled her nose with the rabbit's tail. He was generally kept pretty busy toward the end of a long sermon!

During the noon intermission, in the winter time, the half frozen congregation went to the nearest house or tavern to get warm, and to eat a simple Sunday meal. In summertime, they sat on the green and talked in low, solemn tones. After two hours' intermission, the congregation assembled again, and the dreary service was resumed. The singing was very doleful. There were few books, so the deacon or leader gave out the hymn, a line or two at a time. Often, the singing of these psalms or hymns lasted a half-hour, during which the people stood. Altogether, we can easily see that a Sunday service, morning and afternoon, would last seven hours.

In all the Colonies, Sunday was strictly observed. Any unseemly conduct was punished by whipping or by fire. It was forbidden to fish, shoot, sail, row a boat, or do any kind of work on that day. Horses were used

A Colonial Church

only to drive or ride to church. There was little or no cooking, but everybody ate cold food on the Lord's Day. No one was allowed to use tobacco near any meeting-house. The Sabbath began at sunset, on Saturday, and lasted until sunset, on Sunday.

After the Colonists grew better off, they built larger and better churches, sometimes of stone, or brick, and often beautiful in their stately architecture. Many of these churches are preserved at the present day, with their high pulpits, and their big, stiff back benches, or box pews, for the whole family. In all of them, however, the same severity of worship was observed, for it was thought thereby to make a God-fearing and God-serving people.

Chapter 27

The Salem Witch Trials

In olden times nearly everybody believed in witches. These witches were supposed to have sold their souls to the devil, and to have received from him power to ride through the air on broomsticks. With "the evil eye," they could make people ill, they could destroy cattle by mysterious diseases, they could blight the crops, and do other impossible and dreadful things. They were supposed to have meetings at night, when the devil came and they received the witches' sacrament. Consequently, everybody was afraid of a witch, and nobody wanted to be called one.

The witches were blamed for everything that went wrong. If children fell suddenly ill, if a horse became lame, if a house burned down, if the butter would not churn, if the cart stuck in the mud, the explanation always was, "A witch did it."

Generally, women, or old men, or deformed persons were accused of being witches; but sometimes suspicion fastened upon younger persons, and even upon those in high authority. To test whether a person was a witch or not, pins were stuck into the body to find a place where it did not hurt. These were supposedly spots where the devil's hands had touched the witch. Another test was by water. The accused witch was thrown into the water; if she sank and was drowned, she was innocent; if she floated, she was assuredly a witch and must be burned.

The belief in witchcraft and in the punishing of witches was nowhere stronger than in Salem, Massachusetts. The least suspicious circumstance was sufficient for an accusation. A young girl, thirteen years of age, accused a laundress of having stolen linen from the family. The mother of the laundress rebuked the girl severely for this false charge. The girl became immediately bewitched, or said she was, which amounted to the same thing. Others in her family began to act strangely. Some grew deaf, then dumb, then blind. They barked like dogs and purred like cats if anybody came near.

The town went wild with excitement over the bewitched family. The poor mother of the laundress, who was nothing but a harmless and illiterate old woman, and who had tried to defend her daughter from the charge of stealing linen, was accused of being a witch. She was tried, convicted, and executed.

Shortly afterwards, the child of the minister, nine years old, and his niece, twelve years old, began to act strangely and to suffer great pains. There was nothing the matter with them that a little medicine would not have cured, but they chose to think themselves bewitched. A woman servant in the house, was also accused, and, being whipped, she tried to secure her release by confessing that she was really a witch. Of course she was not, but the poor creature would say anything to save herself from torture. The two children were the two most conspicuous figures in the village; they had "fits" and everybody came to the house to see them. They were generally accommodating to all beholders!

An epidemic of witches now broke out in the village. Anyone who desired notoriety, or who wished to wreak vengeance upon another, would fall down in a fit and cry out, "Witch! Witch!" The excited town folk would set upon the poor accused one, throw him in prison, and often string him up on the gallows.

An old farmer, who did not believe in witches, cured his servant by a good beating. "I'll flog the witch out of you," he cried; and before long the servant was perfectly well. But this brought down the people's wrath upon the old farmer. They said, "He is a witch himself, for he rebukes the disease in others." And forthwith the farmer and his wife found themselves in the common jail.

So it went, until nineteen persons were put to death on the accusation of being witches. One poor old man, who stoutly maintained that nobody was a witch, was pressed to death between two doors!

One-hundred-and-fifty people were thrown into prison; so many indeed that the jail was full to overflowing. Two hundred and more were accused and left outside the jail for lack of room. It seemed as though everybody in Salem, sooner or later, would have to stand trial for being a witch.

At last, when they began to accuse persons of high rank, such as one of the Judges, the wife of the Governor, and the wife of the minister himself, it brought the people to their senses. Suddenly it

The Salem Witch Trials

occurred to them what fools they had been. Then the jails were opened, and the poor people inside were set free, and allowed to go about their business. The children who pretended they were under a spell were punished; and soon there was nobody under accusation.

Since then, no one has really believed in witches. There never was, nor ever can be, such evil beings, and the people in Salem would have been spared much folly and misery if they had known it. In Salem, there stands to this day one of the old houses, and it is pointed out as "The Witch House."

Chapter 28

Traveling by Stage-Coach

In early Colonial days, the pioneers had to walk or go by canoe from one village or settlement to another. Later on, the trails were improved to the extent that horses could be used; and for a long time this was the only means of travel. Women and children usually rode on a pillion, or on cushions behind a man. Sometimes pack horses followed, carrying the household goods, or provisions for the journey.

One way by which four persons could ride, at least part of the distance, was known as the "ride-and-tie system." Two of the four persons started ahead on foot. The other two, mounted on the saddle and pillion, rode about a mile past the two who were walking, dismounted, tied the horse and walked on. When the two, who had first started, came to the waiting horse,. they mounted, rode on past the walking two ahead of them for a mile or more, dismounted, tied the horse and again proceeded to walk. In this way, all four rode half the distance, and the horse had a rest every few miles.

The mail, what there was of it, was carried by post-riders on horseback. The postage was very high, and was paid for by the person receiving the letter, if he ever received it! It took about a month to send a letter from New York to Boston, and to get a reply. The mail generally lay in the post-rider's house till he had enough to pay for the trip. When the mail was delivered, it was laid on the table at an inn, and any one could have his letter by paying the innkeeper the postage.

After the Revolution, the roads were widened and made better than the old trails. Hence, wagons, or stage-coaches, came into use for transportation. Traveling by stage-coach lasted until the time of the railroads, and indeed still later in some places in the West. The stage between New York and Philadelphia made the trip in two days, provided the weather was good. From New York to Boston took a week's hard riding.

A passenger from Boston to New York thus describes his journey:

"The carriages were old and shackling, and much of the harness made up of ropes. One pair of horses carried us eighteen miles. We generally reached our resting place for the night, if no accident interfered, at ten o'clock, and, after a frugal supper, went to bed, with a notice that we should be called at three next morning, which generally proved to be half past two. And then, whether it snowed or rained, the traveler must rise and make ready, by the help of a lantern and a farthing candle, and proceed on his way over bad roads, sometimes getting out to help the coachman lift the coach out of a quagmire or rut, and arrived in New York after a week's hard traveling, wondering at the ease, as well as the expedition, with which the journey was effected."

On good days, in the spring and summer, travel by stagecoach was not disagreeable. The horses were generally good and strong, and the coach rattled along fairly well. The driver had a long horn which he blew when he approached a stopping-place, so as to let the people know the stage was coming. The stops were frequent, and when the coach drove up to a tavern or inn, the passengers would get out for a meal, or else stretch themselves by taking a short walk.

Some of the turnpikes were beautiful and splendid roads. The way from Albany to Schenectady, New York, ran in a straight line, between rows of poplars, with many taverns along the route. Relays of horses were provided every ten miles; teams were changed in a few minutes; and with blowing of horns the coach would merrily depart. It was not at all unusual, over the fine roads, to make one hundred miles in twenty-four hours.

But all the roads were not good ones; some of them were very bad indeed. And all the weather was not spring time! In the dead of winter, over a bad road, a stagecoach was anything but pleasant to ride in. There was no way of heating it, and the passengers had to endure hours of freezing cold, with much jolting and hard pulling over bad places. Sometimes, the coach stuck hard and fast in the mud, when all hands had to get out and pull and dig until the wheels were released.

Sometimes the driver had to call to the passengers to lean out of the carriage, first on one side and then on the other, to prevent it from overturning or sticking in a ditch. "Gentlemen, to the right," he would call, upon which all the passengers would rush to the right and lean out of the windows to balance things. "Now, gentlemen, to the left," he would say, and the same thing would be done on the left side.

Along the road were inns or taverns for the travelers. Here, the weary passengers could take their meals, get warm by the fire, and find a bed at night. The cooking was good, the food abundant, and

Traveling by Stagecoach

the beds usually comfortable. The charge was not high. One can well imagine how welcome these wayside taverns were to the cold, hungry, and tired folks, when they drove up at dark on a winter's day, to find a blazing fire in the big front room with its raftered ceilings, a hot supper ready on the table, and a warm bed to sleep in. What matter if they did have to rise by candle light, and be on their way! Nobody traveled for pleasure, anyway, in those days, and so necessity made the hardships endurable.

Many of these taverns had very curious signs hanging outside, with names upon them, such as "The Red Horse," "The Bear and Eagle," "The Anchor," "The Blue Jay," "The Twin Bogs"; and often these signs would be painted to represent the name itself. Even the rooms were sometimes named, instead of being numbered, as in modern hotels. Such names as the "Star Chamber," "Rose Room," "Sunrise Room," "Blue Room," and even "Jerusalem Room" were common.

As one journeyed south, the roads were not so good and the taverns less frequent; because few people traveled by stages in the southern country. Those who traveled at all went in their own coaches, or by horseback. But there were some coaches going over the rough highways, and it was the universal custom for the planters to open their doors for meals and lodging. Eager for news and company, they would invite the passers-by to come into the house to be entertained.

Gone is the old stage-coach, with its picturesque history! Nowadays we speed at the rate of a mile a minute over smooth rails, and lay down to sleep to find ourselves several hundred miles away when we awake in the morning.

CHAPTER 29

KING GEORGE AND THE COLONIES

We must not get the idea that the Colonies in America were disloyal in their allegiance to the mother country. On the contrary, they loved the Old England from which their fathers came, and looked forward to a happy development under the British flag.

It was not the English people, but the English King, George III, who caused all the trouble. He had ascended the throne when he was twenty-two years of age. He was nearly forty when the Revolution began. He was obstinate and short-sighted in dealing with his subjects. He believed in the right of kings to have their own way and to him the will of the people counted for nothing as against the will of the King. Whatever George III wanted, he proposed to have people or no people, Colonies or no Colonies. Kings do not act that way nowadays, but then it was different.

When he came to the throne his mother said to him, "George be a king." She taught him to think that he owned his people, and that they should always do his will.

Instead of choosing the

King George III

wisest and best men in the kingdom to be his advisers and ministers, George III turned to the weaker men, who flattered him and who were ready to do his bidding. It was always one of the "King's friends" who proposed in Parliament the obnoxious measures against America. Finally, the King succeeded in getting a Prime Minister, Lord North, who was willing, in all things, to do as his sovereign wished. In fact, someone has said that, while North was in office, "the King was his own Prime Minister."

In spite of the protest of some really great men in England, who knew the Colonists were illtreated, the King went blindly and obstinately to work, until the Colonies in America were in complete revolt.

To see how poorly the great mass of the people of England was represented in their Parliament, we should know that, when George III came to the throne, there was a most unequal distribution of seats in the House of Commons. For two hundred years, no changes had been made in the allotment of seats according to the number of the population.

Some very large cities, like Manchester and Sheffield, that had grown up in the meantime, had no representatives at all, while some very small and old places had several representatives. One town, named Old Sarum, went on sending members to Parliament long after it had ceased to have any inhabitants at all.

The result was that many members represented only a handful of voters, many seats in Parliament were bought and sold, and some were given away, as favors. This made an assembly of representatives that did not truly represent the great body of the people, and it, therefore, became easy for the King to secure such laws as he and his friends wanted.

Was it not natural that a corrupt Parliament should do George III's own bidding? He united, with the ruling class, to suppress public opinion in England, and self-government in America. He began to rule the Colonies by royal orders, and sent instructions, over his own signature, to be obeyed in America; otherwise, so he threatened, military force would be used to make the people obey. Colonial assemblies were dissolved, unusual places of meeting were appointed, orders were issued, lands were granted or taken away, and by many other acts the Colonists were treated without consideration.

But the Colonists had many friends among the English people, who sympathized with them in their opposition to the tyranny of the King and his Parliament. They were still English people and English subjects, though their home was across the sea, and they had rights that their relatives and friends in England thought should be respected. So there were many in the old country who believed that the Colonists were right to oppose the King; some voices in Parliament even spoke out bravely in their defense.

One great Englishman, William Pitt, who was the Earl of Chatham, declared in the House of Lords, "This kingdom has no right to lay a tax upon the Colonies. I rejoice that America has resisted." After the Revolutionary War had begun, and the King had been forced to hire about 20,000 German troops from the Duke of Brunswick, because the English simply would not enlist for this unpopular war, Pitt said, in another speech,

"My Lords, you cannot conquer America. In three years' campaign, we have done nothing and suffered much. You may swell every expense, accumulate every assistance you can buy or borrow, traffic and barter with every little pitiful German prince, but your efforts are forever vain and impotent, doubly so from this mercenary aid on which you rely, for it irritates to an incurable resentment. If I were an American, as I am an Englishman, while a foreign troop was landed in my country, I would never lay down my arms, never, never, never."

While the Stamp Act was being debated in Parliament, Colonel Barre, who had fought by the side of Wolfe at Quebec, replied to the statement that the Colonies were children "planted by our care, nourished by our indulgence, and protected by our arms," by exclaiming with great eloquence,

"They planted by your care! No, your oppression planted them in America. Nourished by your indulgence! They grew up by your neglect of them. They protected by your arms! Those sons of liberty have nobly taken up arms in your defense."

The expression, "Sons of Liberty," became a popular rallying cry of the Patriots in America.

The quarrel between King George III and the American Colonists grew into the Revolutionary War. During that War, the Colonists had many friends in England, especially in the city of London. As he walked through the streets, William Pitt was loudly cheered for the part he took in defending the cause of the Colonists. When the war was over, many in England were secretly rejoiced that the Colonies were independent, and that the will of the foolish King was at last broken.

Chapter 30

Patrick Henry and the Parson's Cause

Among the noted men in the history of the struggle of the American Colonies against the tyranny of the King of England, none occupies a more striking position than Patrick Henry, the great orator of Virginia.

His father was a magistrate, of an old Scotch family, whose lack of means kept his son, Patrick, from an education in college. However, young Henry studied at home, and acquired a fair education. He seemed to be ill-fitted for business of any kind. He kept a country store and failed; he tried farming and failed; then he went back to keeping a store and failed again. He became discouraged and idle, and began passing his time fishing and hunting and telling humorous stories to idle companions around the village inn.

Finally, he turned to the law. After studying for a few weeks, he was examined, and allowed to begin practice. It was four years, however, before he gave any evidence to the world that he possessed those marvelous powers of oratory that have made him famous.

Now, let us see how Henry won reputation in the Parson's Cause. From the beginning, the Colonists of Virginia were accustomed to pay the preacher's salary in tobacco. Each parish minister received so much tobacco out of the amount raised by the tobacco tax. If the price of tobacco was high, the minister had the benefit of the high price. If the price was low, he suffered accordingly. For a long time the ministers took their chances on the tobacco market, and lived in abundance or in want, as the market price went up or down. At best, however, their salaries were never munificent.

In the year 1748, an Act was passed, fixing the annual salary of each parish minister at 16,000 pounds of tobacco. This Act was approved by the King, and became the law in Virginia. Each minister was allotted his tobacco salary, which he sold at whatever price he could get. This went on for a while, until the Legislature passed another Act, paying the minister's salary in paper money, at a fixed price per pound for tobacco. This fixed price was always lower than the market price, and reduced the minister's salary very much.

The Act was clearly unconstitutional, for it did not have the consent of the King, and, therefore, could not be law. Besides, it was manifestly unjust to the ministers who were employed under a tobacco contract, and not under a paper money contract. However, the people did not care, for the ministers were unpopular. And as for the King and his consent the Colonies were rapidly becoming rebellious of his authority.

The ministers had to take paper money for their salaries, or receive none at all. They complained to the Legislature, but could get no hearing. They complained to the Governor, but he gave them no consolation. They sent some of their own number to England to lay the matter before the King's Council. There they were told that their cause was just, and that they had a right to sue for damages in the Courts of Virginia. Whereupon they returned home to begin their suits.

One of the cases was brought by Rev. James Maury into the Court of Hanover County. The Judge promptly decided that the Act, paying the salaries in paper money, was no law, and that the ministers were clearly entitled to damages to be fixed by a special jury. The case of the people against Maury seemed hopeless, especially as it was very easy to calculate the difference between the value of the tobacco and the value of the paper money paid. However, a jury was drawn, and the desperate cause of the people against the clergy was committed to Patrick Henry, then almost unknown as a lawyer and advocate. Indeed, no other counsel or lawyer would take the case, as they said it was a hopeless one, and the people had better pay and be done with it.

Now comes the story of how the world found out the marvelous powers of oratory possessed by Patrick Henry. On the day of trial, the courtroom was crowded with people, the clergy being there in force to witness the triumph of one of their number. On the bench sat Henry's father, the presiding Judge of the trial, who looked with much distrust upon the ability of his son to defend the people's cause.

No one had heard Henry speak before a jury. He was considered an idle young man, of twenty-seven years of age, without learning or ability. He was badly dressed, and appeared ill at ease. When he arose to speak, he did so very awkwardly, and began in a stammering and hesitating manner; so much so that the ministers smiled, the people looked disappointed, and his father sank back in his chair mortified.

But wait, let us see what happened! In a few minutes, the young orator forgot his awkwardness, and ceased his stammering. His form straightened up, and his eyes began to flash, as he unrolled his invectives against the King, and narrated the grievances of the Colonies. He did not hesitate to call the King a tyrant, who had forfeited all right to obedience. His face began to shine with a nobleness and grandeur which no one ever saw before, and his eyes seemed to hold the lightning of wrath and power. His actions were graceful, bold, and commanding. For an hour he spoke, while the crowd listened as if under the spell of some enchantment. One of them said, "He made my blood run cold and my hair stand on end." As for his father, such was his surprise and joy that, Judge though he was, he allowed tears of happiness to run down his cheeks.

When Henry had finished his great oration, the jury was so overwhelmed by his arguments that they voted Rev. Maury just one penny damage whereas his suit had been for many pounds. In this way did Patrick Henry begin that marvelous career which made him one of the greatest orators this country has ever produced.

Patrick Henry Argues the Parson's Cause

Chapter 31

Paul Revere's Ride

On the night of April 18, 1775, in a suburb of Charlestown, just outside of Boston, stood a strong and keen-eyed man beside a restless horse, ready at a moment's notice to mount and ride hard upon some secret mission. His eye was fixed upon the distant steeple of a church, scarcely to be seen in the darkness, as if he expected some signal to make him spring into instant action.

He had not long to wait. Into the night there suddenly flashed the rays from two lanterns; as soon as he saw them, he grasped the reins of the bridle, leaped into the saddle, and rode swiftly away. The man's name was Paul Revere. The signal was from the steeple of the Old North Church, in Boston, and it had been placed there by a friendly hand to let Revere know that the British troops were moving silently out of Boston to capture the military stores which the Patriots of the Revolution had at Concord, about nineteen miles away.

Swiftly his horse bore Revere past Charlestown Neck. Suddenly two British officers appeared in his path.

"Halt! Who goes there?" was the stern command.

Revere made no answer, but turned his horse's head, and went flying back to seek another road. The officers started in swift pursuit, calling out, "Halt, or we fire!"

Revere paid no attention to them, but, spurring his horse onward, turned into Medford Road. One of the officers tried to intercept him by a short cut across the field, but, in the darkness, he fell into a clay-pit, where Revere left him as he went thundering by.

On he went, mile after mile, intent upon arousing the people. At every house he stopped, rapped furiously on the door, or called out from the roadside, "Get up, and arm yourselves. The Regulars are marching to Concord!" And then he would dash away, leaving the occupants to rise and hastily dress themselves.

The British marched out of Boston about midnight. Just at that hour, Revere rode into Lexington with a great clatter of hoofs upon the streets. He galloped up to the house of the Reverend Mr. Clarke, where Samuel Adams and John Hancock, two leading Patriots, were asleep.

"Don't make so much noise," called out the guard in front of the house, "you will awake the inmates."

"Noise!" exclaimed Revere. "You'll have noise enough before long. The Regulars are coming!"

At that moment, a window was thrown open, and John Hancock, looking out, inquired what was the matter. Recognizing Revere, he directed the guard to open the door, and admit the messenger, who soon told his startling tale. Hancock and Adams quickly dressed, and, while Revere set out again on his journey, these two Patriots left Lexington to avoid capture.

Revere was now joined by another rider, named Dawes, who had left Boston at the same time by a different route. Upon these two was put the responsibility of arousing the people. From every house the good men of the countryside rushed out when they heard the news. The Minute Men began to gather, with such guns as they had, and by two o'clock in the morning over a hundred of them had met upon the green in Lexington. As no foe was in sight, and as the air was cold, they disbanded to assemble again at the sound of the drum.

Meanwhile, Revere and Dawes rode toward Concord, six miles off. On their way, they fell in with Dr. Samuel Prescott, to whom they told their story as the three rode along. Suddenly, a group of British officers appeared in the road before them, and laid their hands upon Revere and Dawes, who were a little in advance. This occurred so unexpectedly that escape was impossible for those two. But Dr. Prescott urged his horse over a stone wall, and was well away before he could be stopped. He alone bore the news to the people of Concord.

When Prescott arrived, at about two in the morning, he at once gave the alarm. The bells were rung, and the people rushed toward the center square where Dr. Prescott addressed them.

"The Regulars are on their way to capture the stores in the warehouse," he declared. "They may now be in Lexington, and it is certain they will be here before long. Revere and Dawes brought me word. We must remove the stores before the British arrive."

This was enough. It did not take the people of Concord many hours to put the precious stores in a place of safety.

Meantime, the British had come to the outskirts of Lexington. It was about daybreak, and the drum-beat called the Colonists together on the village green. There were about one hundred stern and determined Patriots, facing five or six hundred British troops. The moment was one of intense excitement, for both sides knew it meant war if a shot was fired. Captain John Parker, in command of the militia, said to his men:

"Stand your ground; don't fire unless fired upon; but if they mean to have a war, let it begin here."

The British Commander, Major Pitcairn, drew his pistol, and, pointing at the Patriots, cried out:

"Disperse, you villains! Lay down your arms, you rebels, and disperse!"

The Patriots did not move. The British came nearer, as if to surround Parker's men. A shot, fired from the British line, was answered immediately by the Patriots. Then Major Pitcairn drew his pistol, and discharged it, calling out, "Fire." The British then fired upon the Minute Men, killing four of them, after which the others retreated. This was the opening shot of the Revolution, and we shall see how England paid dearly for it.

The British moved on to Concord, reaching there about seven o'clock. They were too late, however, for most of the stores had been removed. They did what damage they could, by knocking open, sixty barrels of flour, injuring three cannon and setting fire to the court-house.

About midday, the British began their retreat. The Patriots had gathered in haste from the neighboring towns, and were preparing to harass the enemy along the road. Concealing themselves behind houses, barns, roadside walls, and trees, they poured a galling fire into the retreating British. The Red Coats, as the British were called, began to run in order to escape the deadly fire of the farmers, with their rifles and shotguns. The six miles from Concord to Boston were one dreadful ambush. Reaching Lexington, a number of the British fell exhausted on the ground, their tongues parched from fatigue and thirst.

Here they were joined by a large number of fresh British troops, and the whole force proceeded to Boston, pursued by the Patriots up to the very entrance of the city. Altogether, they lost about three hundred men, while the Americans lost only one hundred.

Such was the beginning of the American Revolution. The midnight ride of Paul Revere was a very good beginning for the cause of American freedom.

Paul Revere's Ride

Chapter 32

The Green Mountain Boys

Between Lake George and Lake Champlain, there once stood a famous old fort, known as Fort Ticonderoga. At the beginning of the Revolution, it was feebly garrisoned by English troops, but was well supplied with arms and ammunition. The Patriots needed these arms and ammunition, so as to carry on the war which had just begun at Lexington. We shall see how the fort was captured.

As soon as the mountaineers of Vermont heard of the battle of Lexington, they dropped their axes and plows, and, seizing their rifles, banded together for a march on Ticonderoga. Ethan Allen, a rugged and brave mountaineer, was their leader. In order to meet the expenses of the expedition, funds, amounting to fifteen hundred dollars, were collected from the people of Connecticut.

As the expedition advanced, one of the Connecticut agents, named Noah Phelps, went on ahead to find out the condition of the fort. Disguising himself as a countryman, he entered the stronghold on the pretense that he wished to be shaved. Hunting for the barber, he kept his eyes and ears open, asking questions like an innocent farmer, until he found out all about the garrison and its equipment.

When Allen and the Green Mountain Boys neared their goal, they were joined by another force under the command of Benedict Arnold, who was then a brave officer in the American army, though he afterwards proved himself a traitor. The two parties approached the fort, one moving at daybreak, a farmer's boy, who lived near, acting as their guide.

The stockade around the fort was reached. The gate was open, since the English Commander suspected no danger. The sentry tried to fire his gun, but it failed to go off; whereupon he ran inside and gave the alarm. The attacking party was close upon his heels. Before any of the garrison could be awakened from their sleep, Allen and his men had taken possession, and resistance was useless. The capture was made by surprise and without bloodshed.

Allen compelled one of the sentries to show him the way to the quarters of the Commander, Captain Delaplace. Reaching his room, Allen called upon him in loud tones to surrender. The Commander sprang from bed, surprised and alarmed at the unusual demand.

"By whose authority?" he asked, in his half awake condition.

"In the name of the Great Jehovah and the Continental Congress," replied Allen, in a loud voice.

Delaplace made no reply, but hastily dressed to see what the madman from the mountains meant.

He soon discovered. Outside he heard the shouts of the

Ethan Allen and the Green Mountain Boys
Capture Fort Ticonderoga

Patriots, and saw the movement of men taking possession of the stores. When he came from his quarters he realized that the fort had been occupied by a force, superior to his, and that it was surrendered without a shot being fired or a blow exchanged.

The captured stores consisted of a large number of cannon and ammunition, besides small arms much needed by the Patriots in the great war which was to last for some years.

Chapter 33

The Father of His Country

Let us learn something of the kind of man George Washington was the man whom we have long known as the "Father of his Country." To look at, he was a fine type of man and soldier, the type that would attract attention anywhere. He was tall, and held himself as straight as an arrow. He was six feet, two inches high, and weighed two hundred and twenty pounds. Wherever he went, in whatever company, he was distinguished for his splendid height and erect figure. His eyes were light blue, and so deeply sunken that they gave him a serious expression. His face was grave and thoughtful, though his disposition was full of cheer and good-will.

In his young days, he was very athletic, with a strong right arm. It is said that he once threw a stone from the bottom to the top of the Natural Bridge, in Virginia, a height of over two hundred feet; and that he threw a piece of slate, rounded to the size of a silver dollar, across the Rappahannock River, at Fredericksburg, a feat no other man had ever been able to accomplish.

In fact, during the Revolution, though some of the backwoodsmen in the army were men of great size and strength, yet it was generally believed that Washington was as strong as the best of them. One day, at Mt. Vernon, some young men, who boasted of their power, were throwing an iron bar to see who could cover the greatest distance. Washington, watching them, said, "Let me try my hand at this game." Without taking off his coat, he seized the bar, and, to the amazement of the party, threw it a considerable distance further than any of the others had done.

He was a fine wrestler when he was a young man. At one time, he was witnessing a wrestling match, and the champion challenged him to a trial of strength. Washington turned, and, without a word, seized the strong man, and, to the great amusement of the crowd, threw him flat on the ground. The defeated champion said he felt as though a lion had grabbed him, and, when he hit the ground, he expected every bone in his body to be broken.

Washington was also very fond of parties and dancing. He often rode, on winter nights, a distance of ten miles, to attend a dance, and would reach home just in time for breakfast. He kept this up. until he was sixty -four years old, when he had to write to a friend, "Alas! my dancing days are over." He liked to dress well, and was very fussy about the quality of cloth and the fit of his garments. He wore ruffled shirts, silver and gold lace on his hat, scarlet waistcoats, blue broadcloth coats, with silver trimmings, and marble-colored hose. In fact, the "Father of his Country" was something of a dandy, and kept it up to the end of his life.

Like most soldiers, Washington Vas fond of horses, and was a splendid and daring rider. As he rode at the head of his troops, he was a conspicuous figure. Lafayette once said of him, "I never beheld so superb a horseman." Jefferson wrote, "Washington was the best horseman of his age, and the most graceful figure that could be seen on horseback."

Washington was very methodical in his habits, and thrifty in business. He kept a diary, putting down daily happenings of his life, and keeping an accurate account of what money he received and how it was spent. He became wealthy, and, at the time of his death, was worth a half million dollars. He was then the richest man in America. His estate at Mt. Vernon covered eight thousand acres. His orders were, "Buy nothing, you can make yourself." Hence, he was the greatest farmer of the day. He made all his own flour and meal, and even the flour barrels. The cloth for the house and for the farm hands was woven on the premises. Like all rich Virginia planters, he kept open house, and there was rarely a time when his table was without one or more guests. He said his house was more like a tavern than anything else.

George Washington

He was very correct in his habits. He ate carefully and slowly, and the simplest of food. He was grave and dignified, and seldom laughed, though he was not of a gloomy disposition. In almost every relation of public and private life, his character is worthy of study and of emulation.

Chapter 34

Nathan Hale

Washington's army had been defeated in the battle of Long Island, and, only by a narrow chance did the troops manage to escape to Manhattan Island. The British were threatening New York, and Washington was almost in despair. The one thing he needed most was information concerning the plans of the enemy.

"If I could have someone to go into the enemy's lines, and find out their strength and purpose, I might save my army," he said to one of his officers. "Get me the man if you can."

The officer called his associates together, and put the problem before them, but, one by one, they refused the dangerous task. They knew the perils of the life of a spy. They knew he had to wear the enemy's uniform, or no uniform at all; had to pretend friendship with the foe, to keep an eye on everything, to find out what he could, to draw plans of forts, to secure important papers and keep them hidden, until he could slip back within his own lines. He needed quickness of mind and wit, a heart of courage, and nerve of iron, for he would be surrounded by danger every minute, and if lie were caught, his fate would be certain death.

At last one officer heard what Washington wanted, and at once said, "I will take any risk for Washington and my country. I am ready to go." His name was Captain Nathan Hale. Hale had been a school teacher before the war. He was young, athletic, brave, and much admired by all who knew him. He was a famous runner, and, when a student at Yale College, held the record for the longest standing jump. When he came to Washington and asked for instructions.

"My boy, I have little to say. Go into the enemy's lines, find out how many troops they have, where they are placed, and what they intend to do. That is all. Bring me word if you can. If you never get back, remember you are serving your country!"

Hale saluted and departed. He took off his uniform, and put on a brown suit and a broad-brimmed hat, the dress of a Quaker school teacher. He went on board a sloop late at night, and was landed near the British outposts. He spent the next day with a farmer nearby, and then, in the afternoon, walked boldly into the enemy's lines.

What he did for the next two weeks no one will ever know. He acted his part very well, however, for he was not suspected of being a spy. He told the British he was a Quaker, who did not believe in war, and that he wanted to teach school. But he was learning all he could. His eyes were alert and watchful, without seeming to be so. He listened to conversations and, occasionally, when close, he would make drawings of the forts and camp. All his notes were written in Latin, so that they could not be easily read.

At last Hale learned all he thought was necessary. Gathering his material together, he ripped open the soles of his shoes and carefully hid the precious notes therein. Then he was ready to start for home. Washington was looking for him, and, by previous arrangement, was to send a boat for him to take him into the American lines. There was a little tavern at Huntingdon, near the place where the boat was to come. Hale walked into the tavern one day, and sat down, waiting until the time arrived for him to meet his friends.

As he sat there, a man came in and looked him over closely. Hale paid no attention, and the man went out. But Hale had been recognized by someone who knew him, and the man was on his way to the British to report that the school teacher was also an American officer, known as Captain Nathan Hale. After an hour or two, Hale left the tavern, and walked down toward the shore to meet his boat. But instead of his own boat at the landing, there was a British boat. The officer called out, "Surrender, you spy, or I fire."

Hale knew he was caught, and held up his hands in token of surrender. He was carried to the British Commander, and made no effort to conceal his name or his purpose. They tore open his shoes and found the papers. Then they condemned him to be hanged at sunrise the next day.

It was a beautiful Sunday morning, and Hale was led out before the gallows, which was nothing but the limb of a tree. "Have you anything to say?" asked the British officer. The brave young patriot looked up into the sky, and then at the rope, which already was around his neck, and slowly replied, "I only regret that I have but one life to lose for my country."

Statue of Nathan Hale

A few moments later Nathan Hale was dead. His body was probably buried there, under the tree, but nobody to this day knows.

Chapter 35

The Bravery of Elizabeth Zane

This is a story of the attack on Fort Henry, a small frontier settlement near where Wheeling, West Virginia, now stands. It was in the summer of 1777, when Simon Girty, one of the worst characters that ever appeared on the stage of American history, led a band of four hundred natives in assault upon the fort. Colonel Sheppard was in charge of the fortification, with only forty men. As soon as the movements of Girty and his band became known, the inhabitants of the little town of Wheeling, then composed of about twenty-five log huts, hastened to the fort for protection.

A reconnoitering party was sent out by Colonel Sheppard to discover the whereabouts of the enemy. They fell into an ambush, and more than half of them were victims of the rifle and tomahawk. Another party went to their relief, but most of them also were killed by the natives. This reduced the fort to a small garrison. Inside were the women and children, and outside raged a band of four-hundred natives, led by a desperate and skillful commander. The situation of Fort Henry was indeed perilous, and all those within seemed doomed.

Colonel Sheppard was not a man to surrender easily He would rather die by rifle shot, than be burned at the stake. Calling his men around him, he said:

"We must defend this fort to the last man. If we surrender, it means sure death to us all by slow torture, and the women and children will suffer most. Let each man do his full duty, and the women must help."

Gladly they began their desperate defense. The women cast the bullets, measured out the powder from the scant supply, and loaded the rifles. Among them was Elizabeth Zane, the sister of two of the defenders of the fort. She had recently returned from school in Philadelphia, and knew very little of border warfare, but she had a brave spirit, as we shall see.

Early one morning, Girty and his followers came before the fort with a white flag, and demanded its immediate surrender.

Colonel Sheppard hurled back the defiant reply, "This fort shall never be surrendered so long as there is an American left inside to defend it."

Girty was infuriated, and, blind with rage, called out, "Then we shall force you to surrender, and not a man or woman shall be left alive in this town." Turning to his followers, he ordered them to attack the fort.

Unfortunately, some of the log huts of the inhabitants were sufficiently near to afford protection to the natives, so that they could begin their assault under cover. They ran into these huts, and opened fire, but with little effect, for the defenders kept well out of sight. The brave Patriots within were all sharp-shooters, and had no powder to waste; every shot they fired meant the death-knell of someone who had exposed himself.

After six hours, the natives withdrew from the houses to a place nearby, and, for a while, there was quiet. It was fortunate, for, just at that moment, someone brought word that the powder of the fort was nearly exhausted; it would not last an hour longer, and then the Patriots would be at the mercy of their foe.

Ebenezer Zane looked at his own house, about sixty yards away, and said, "There is a keg of powder yonder. If we could get it, we would be safe; but someone will have to go for it."

"Powder," cried Colonel Sheppard, "we will have to get it, no matter what the risk. One of us must go at once."

Who should undertake the dangerous mission? The natives were in easy gunshot, and it meant death to any one showing himself outside the fort. Colonel Sheppard would not order any person to go, but instead, called for volunteers. Every man instantly offered to go; not one held back. But just as they were deciding, a woman stepped forward, and said:

"No man can be spared now. We have too few to defend this place. I am the one to go. Unbar the gate and let me out."

Colonel Sheppard looked at her with great admiration, and, after & few moments, said, "God bless you, my girl, and may you return in safety. Perhaps your going will throw the natives off their guard. Unbar the gates, men, and let her pass."

The gate was opened, and she walked steadily and quickly across the open area toward the house where the powder was. The natives looked on in wonder, thinking she was coming to them as a captive. But the girl sprang into the house, seized the keg, and reappeared at the door, on her way back to the fort. There was now no time for leisure. She ran as fast as she could with the precious keg in her arms.

With a yell of defiance, the natives sprang in pursuit, and opened fire upon the fleeing girl. She ran like a deer, swift and straight toward the open gate. Not a shot touched her, though bullets struck the ground about her feet and went flying around her head. In a few moments, she had reached the fort, and fell into the arms of her friends, who raised a great shout as the gate was barred and the powder was safely in their hands.

"We have a heroine in this fort, and will now conquer or die," cried the men, as they hastily prepared to meet the next attack. Suffice it to say that they did defend the fort, until help came and the natives were driven away. And, to this day, the people love to tell the story of how Elizabeth Zane saved the fort, and the lives of those who afterwards helped build a great city.

"Unbar the gate and let her pass!"

Chapter 36

Capturing the Hessians

It was a cold December night, and the little army of General Washington stood upon the banks of the Delaware River, getting ready to cross its icy waters. The men were cold and hungry, tired and discouraged. It seemed as if the war would be lost for lack of men and supplies. The whole country was downhearted.

Not so General Washington. He knew that one victory would raise the hope of the troops and the country, and he proposed to start winning it that night. Over at Trenton were a thousand hired Hessian soldiers, celebrating Christmas. Washington determined to be on hand at the celebration.

"Courage, my men," he cried. "Tomorrow will be a great day, if you can stand this night."

The men got into the boats, and took the oars. Blocks of ice floated by over the frozen river. The wind blew keen and cold. The men shivered and shook, as they steered their boat amid the perils that surrounded them.

At last they were over. What stamping of feet and blowing of hands to keep warm! Then came the long march of nine miles to Trenton, through a blinding snow-storm. Hour after hour passed, while the men stumbled and fell and got up and trudged on and on. No soldiers, except those fighting for home and country and freedom, could have endured through that march. But at last the almost exhausted army came to Trenton.

In the meantime, the hired soldiers of the King of England had been having a great time, drinking and feasting and boasting of what they would do to Washington's army when next they met. The Hessian Commander at Trenton was named Rail. He had made his headquarters in the house of a merchant, one Abraham Hunt. Rail was very fond of drinking and playing cards. On Christmas night, he and Hunt were in a warm room, before a big fire, with plenty to eat and drink at hand; a game of cards was in progress. Just at this moment Washington's army was crossing the Delaware, amid the snow and ice.

A servant came in and handed Rail a note. He thrust it into his pocket, saying, "I will read it later on." But it so happened that he forgot the note, and went on playing cards and drinking. Late in the night, he went to bed and slept, and all the while Washington was drawing closer and closer through the blinding snow!

The next day, Washington was before Trenton. The sun was shining, and his troops were eager and ready for battle. Bursting

Just at this moment Washington's army was crossing the Delaware amid the snow and ice.

upon the unsuspecting Hessians, the great battle of Trenton began. It did not last long. All the Hessians, one thousand in number, surrendered, after a hundred had been killed. Washington lost four men, two frozen to death and two killed.

Rail was mortally wounded, and borne to a tavern nearby. It was then that he thought of the note in his pocket, and asked for it. When it was opened it was found to contain a warning of the plans of Washington, which had been sent by a Tory, and delivered to a servant in Hunt's house. What a difference in the history of our country, if the note had been read in time for the Hessians to have met Washington on his way to Trenton!

It was a great American victory, and brought a happy Christmas season to the Colonies when it became known.

CHAPTER 37

HOW LAFAYETTE CAME TO AMERICA

Lafayette belonged to the highest rank of the French nobility. When he was only thirteen years old, he was left with large landed estates, and the title of Marquis. He went to college in Paris, and, while there, met the King of France, Louis XV, who took him as a page into the royal household. When he was fifteen years old, he was given a military commission through the influence of the Queen.

Soon after this, he was married, and was stationed as Captain of Dragoons, at a fort on the German border. At dinner, one day, he heard someone talking about the Americans and the Declaration of Independence. He listened very attentively, and then said:

"If what you say of those Colonies is true, they deserve their liberty, and I, for one, would like to help them."

Shortly after this, he heard of the American victories at Trenton and Princeton, and, hastening to the American agents in Paris, he said to them, "I desire to aid America in her fight for freedom. I am willing to go in person, if you can find a way to send me."

But Lafayette was only nineteen years of age, and belonged to the

Lafayette

French nobility. France and England were at peace. If he should try to come to America, there might be trouble with the English government, and, besides that, his own King probably would not let him undertake so foolish an enterprise. So the agent said:

"Marquis, you are very brave and you are very wealthy. We cannot help you even if we would, for America has no ships on this side of the ocean. If you desire to go to America, it must of necessity be at your own expense. We shall be glad to know that you have decided to go."

Lafayette, thereupon, went about getting ready. His preparations were made secretly, for fear the King of France would forbid his going on account of the existing friendship with England. At his own expense, he purchased a ship and fitted it out for the voyage. While the vessel was being prepared, Lafayette paid a visit to London so as to remove suspicion from his design.

While he was in London, the British Ambassador at Paris in some way learned of his purpose to go to America, and procured orders for his arrest. Accordingly, when Lafayette reached his ship, and was about to sail, he was arrested by order of the King. Letters were sent to him by all his noble relatives, telling him how foolish he was, and urging him to abandon his purpose. His wife wrote to him, however, not to give up his enterprise, but to go to America if he could find a way to do so.

Lafayette was not to be stopped by orders from the King or any one else. So, while the arresting party was on the way to Paris, the bold young nobleman donned a disguise and slipped past the guards.

After a few hours, the guards discovered the trick played upon them; a great stir and commotion followed. Swift horses were saddled, and men went galloping in the direction the escaping

Marquis had taken. But Lafayette had three hours start, and was driving the best horses that could be found. He was headed for the border of Spain, after passing which he would be safe from arrest.

In spite of the furious pursuit, Lafayette at last was safe; in a short while he was on board his own vessel and ready to set sail. With him were eleven officers bent on the same mission. His departure created a great sensation in France and England, but Lafayette cared very little for that.

The Captain of his vessel did not know where he was bound, until Lafayette ordered him to steer for the shores of America. The Captain was alarmed and said, "I dare not do so. The English will capture us." To which Lafayette replied, "If you do not do as I tell you, I shall put you in irons. This is my vessel, and I will order it wherever I desire." Thereupon the Captain steered the ship for America.

The voyage was long and stormy, but at last Lafayette and his party arrived one night near Georgetown, South Carolina. At first they were taken for the enemy, but, as soon as it was known who they were, the people of Georgetown and Charleston entertained them with great hospitality. Their arrival in America created a greater sensation than their departure from Europe, for the fortunes of the American army were at a low ebb just at this time, and the people were much discouraged.

Lafayette and his party proceeded by land to Philadelphia, where Congress was then in session. Upon his arrival, he wrote a letter to the President of that body, asking leave to enter the army as a volunteer, and to serve without pay. But Congress had no idea of letting so brave a man take such a low position; he was at once given the rank of Major-General.

He then lacked one month of being twenty years old. Those who saw him, at the time, described him as tall and slender, very graceful in his movements and gracious in his manners. He talked rapidly, with many gestures, and, when he spoke of liberty for the Colonies in America, his eyes shone very brightly and his face expressed his great emotion.

Soon afterwards, Lafayette met Washington at a dinner party in Philadelphia. The two men looked at each other with interest. Washington was tall, dignified, and forty-five years of age. Lafayette was hardly more than a college boy, slender and enthusiastic. After the dinner was over, Washington took him aside and said:

"Sir, I thank you for the sacrifice you are making for the cause of America. I shall be glad to have you a member of my military family."

Thus began the intimacy between these two great men, which was never for a moment interrupted. Washington loved Lafayette as a son, and learned to trust him as a General of ability and courage. He served in many battles with distinguished gallantry.

When Lafayette went back to France to get more aid for America, he was forgiven for running away, and was received everywhere with great enthusiasm. France became the ally of America in the War for Independence, and Lafayette raised large sums of money for the Colonists. The head of the French Ministry laughingly said:

"It is a fortunate thing that Lafayette did not take it into his head to strip his Majesty's palace of all its furniture to send to his dear Americans for I verily believe the King now would refuse him nothing."

Chapter 38

The Patriotism of Lydia Darrah

When the British occupied Philadelphia, the Adjutant-General of the British Army had his quarters in the home of a Quaker, named Darrah, and his wife, Lydia. The two were stanch Patriots, who little liked the private conferences of the British officers, frequently held in their house at night.

One cold and snowy day in December, 1777, the Adjutant-General told Mrs. Darrah to make ready the upper back room of the house for a meeting of his friends, which he intended for that very night.

"Be sure your family are all in bed early, for my friends may stay until a late hour. When they are ready to depart, I will call you that you may let them out, and extinguish the fire and the candles."

She set about doing as she was bid. At the same time, she was so impressed with the mystery of it all, and so suspicious of the purpose of the officer, that she resolved to find out what was going on.

When night came, she saw that her family were in bed, and, after the officers arrived, she bade them good-night, saying she would also retire to her room. So she did, but not to sleep.

After a while she quietly stole, in her stocking feet, along the passage until she came to the room where the officers were in consultation. She placed her ear to the keyhole, and listened intently to what was being said inside.

One of the officers was reading a paper, which was an order

from Sir William Howe, arranging for a secret attack on the forces of General Washington. The British troops were to leave Philadelphia on the night of December 4, and to surprise the Patriots before daybreak. The plan was carefully made, and these officers were receiving their instructions.

Mrs. Darrah had heard enough. She went quietly back to her room, and lay down on the bed. In a few minutes, steps were heard along the passage, and there was a rap at her door.

"Come, wake up, Mrs. Darrah, and let us out," demanded the Adjutant-General.

Mrs. Darrah pretended to be asleep, and the officer rapped more loudly and called again. Yawning, and in a sleepy voice, the patriotic woman answered. Then she arose and let the men out of the house. She slept no more that night, for she knew that Washington must be warned; her thoughts were busy with some plan to convey him the information she had.

By dawn she was out of bed and ready for action. She knew that flour was wanted for her family, and so she told her husband that she was going to Frankford to get the needed supply. This was not an unusual thing, since the people in those days depended on the Frankford Mills for their flour, and delivery wagons were not heard of.

The morning was cold, and snow covered the ground. Frankford was five miles away, and Mrs. Darrah had to walk the entire way, and bring back the flour on her shoulder. Bag in hand, the brave woman started on her journey afoot. She stopped at Howe's headquarters to get a passport to leave the city. It was still early in the day when she reached the Mills, and left her bag to be filled with flour. From the Mills she pushed on toward the headquarters of General Washington.

After walking a few miles, she met Lieutenant-Colonel Craig, one of Washington's officers, who had been sent out in search of information. It did not take her long to tell her story to him. He returned rapidly to his own lines, while she walked leisurely back to the Mills, as though there was nothing on her mind. She shouldered her bag of flour, and trudged home through five miles of snow. But she had the satisfaction of realizing that Washington now knew the plans of the enemy.

Lydia Darrah giving warning

On the night of December 4, the British troops moved quietly out of Philadelphia, and advanced to attack the supposedly unsuspecting Americans. Just before daybreak, they arrived in front of the American lines, and, to their surprise, found everything ready to receive them. The Patriots were armed and prepared for their foe. In much dismay, the British turned quietly around and marched back to Philadelphia, having gone miles through the cold and darkness for nothing.

The Adjutant-General could not imagine how Washington had found out the plans for the attack. The next day he said to Mrs. Darrah:

"It is strange how Washington discovered our purpose. You and your family were all asleep when I gave the orders to the officers, and yet some one found out. We marched miles and miles to find the Americans under arms, with cannon, ready, and then we had to march back like a parcel of children. I wonder who told him we were coming?"

Mrs. Darrah could have enlightened him on this point, but she kept her counsel. It was some months after the British had left Philadelphia before she mentioned to any one the way in which she had outwitted General Howe and saved the Americans from surprise.

Chapter 39

Captain Molly Pitcher

The British had left Philadelphia, and were in full retreat across Jersey on their way to New York. Washington was right behind them, the front ranks of the American Army fighting the rear ranks of the British. It was a long, running fight. At last they came to Monmouth, and there a battle was begun. General Charles Lee, in charge of the American forces, acted so badly that the issue of the fight was long in doubt.

When Washington saw the disorder of the troops, he was angry, and rebuked General Lee so harshly that the officer turned as white as a sheet. He was afterwards tried by court-martial and dismissed.

Then Washington took charge himself. Orders flew thick and fast. Aids scurried in every direction, putting cannon in position, and getting ready for the renewed attack which was sure to come. Soon the guns roared, the heat of battle became terrible, and smoke covered the entire field; the dust and dirt were blinding. The men were suffering for lack of water. It was then that Molly Pitcher, the wife of one of the gunners, called out, "Go on with the firing. I will fetch water from the spring."

The men waved their hands to her; she ran down the hill, drew water in a canteen, and carried it back and forth to the soldiers. She passed from cannon to cannon, while the men drank and kept on with their deadly work.

How many times she did this no one knew, but, as she was coming once with her supply of water, a shot from the enemy struck her husband in the breast, and he fell beside his smoking cannon. Molly ran to him, and knelt down by him; one look was enough to convince her that he was dead.

As she sat there in speechless grief, an officer rode up, and said to some soldiers, "Take this cannon to the rear; there is now no one to serve it."

When Molly heard this, she sprang to her feet, and cried out, "Stop! That cannon shall not leave this field for lack of some one to serve it. Since they have killed my poor husband, I will take his place, and avenge his death."

With that, she seized the rammer from the hands of her dead husband, sprang to the muzzle of the piece, rammed home the powder, and stepped back, saying, "Ready!" Then the cannon blazed again, carrying death and dismay to the ranks of the enemy.

Molly Pitcher stood at her post as long as the battle lasted. Black with smoke, covered with dirt and dust, blinded by the heat, she did the work of a man. She never flinched for a moment, nor did she stop until the order came to cease firing.

Then she sat down on the ground by the side of her poor dead husband, took his head again in her lap, and gave way to her tears and grief.

Washington had seen her with her cannon during the battle. He admired her courage and patriotism, and sent for her to come to headquarters. He told her what a splendid deed of heroism she had done, and conferred on her an officer's commission. After that, she wore an epaulet, and everybody called her "Captain Molly."

She seized the rammer from the hands of her dead husband, sprang to the muzzle of the piece, rammed home the powder, and stepped back, saying, "Ready!"

Chapter 40

Marion, the Swamp Fox

The army of the American General, Gates, had crossed the Pee Dee River, in South Carolina, and was pushing forward to encounter the British who were overrunning that portion of the country. On the march, there suddenly appeared a body of twenty men who asked that they might join the army. It was a sad lot of ill-clad and badly-equipped men and boys, all mounted on the worst looking horses you can imagine. The soldiers of the regular army broke into laughter when they saw this motley crowd of volunteers. And yet this very band was destined to become famous, for its leader was Francis Marion, the "Swamp Fox" of South Carolina.

Marion himself was small in size and thin-faced; a modest man, of no better equipment than his men, and riding a horse of which no one could be proud. But his eye flashed with a brave spirit, and he had the manner of a man of high adventure.

General Gates gave no welcome to this ragged soldiery, and, when Marion modestly offered some advice about the best methods of dealing with the British in the South, the conceited General told him he needed no assistance in that line, which

Francis Marion

was far from the truth.

Governor Rutledge knew Marion, and realized what his service would mean; so a commission as Brigadier-General was given him, much to the delight of his men, who were glad to be under so brave a leader. With this commission, and with his force increased to a hundred or more men, he rode away to carry on warfare according to his own ideas.

The swamps were his headquarters. In their impenetrable thickets, he found hiding-places for his men, from which they could emerge at any time to strike stinging blows at the enemy; and into which they could retreat, safe from attack. No force dared follow them into the dangerous morasses. His little company was constantly changing, at one time numbering several hundred and then shrinking to a mere handful.

The swamps could not feed a large army; still there were game in abundance, and fish to be had in the streams. The nearby farms afforded grain for the horses, and occasional food for the men. The camp was in the middle of some swamp, on dry land, surrounded by thickets and cane-brakes; the paths leading in and out were known only to the men themselves. It was a safe retreat, from which the little band could saunter forth like a drove of hornets, whose blows struck deadly terror to the foe.

A young British officer was sent from Georgetown to treat with Marion for the exchange of prisoners. Marion was glad enough to be rid of prisoners, because he had to guard and feed them. The British officer, by Marion's command, was blindfolded, and led through the swamp to the camp of the brave patriotic leader. When he arrived, and the bandage was removed, he was amazed to see the hiding place of Marion and his men, with great trees around, and deep swamps on every side. In their rough uniforms, the men, lying about, looked more like a band of outlaws, than a camp of soldiers.

He was still more surprised when he saw Marion himself. Instead of a burly giant, there stood a small, quiet man, of polite manners, roughly clad and poorly equipped. Little in his appearance would indicate that he was the dreaded leader, who had spread terror throughout the South among the enemies of his country.

The business of exchange having been arranged, Marion turned to his guest, and said,

"My dear sir, I should be glad to have you dine with me. It has been some time since you have had food, and you will feel better for having eaten. Our dinner is nearly ready."

The officer readily consented, and looked forward to the enjoyment of a meal for which he was quite eager. In a few minutes, a log was brought, upon which the officer and Marion took their seats. Then the cook appeared, carrying a large piece of bark, upon which there were some roasted sweet potatoes.

"Help yourself," said Marion. "This is all we have for dinner today," and, taking a large potato he broke it in two, and placed it before his guest.

"Surely, you have more food than this!" exclaimed the astonished soldier. "This cannot be your ordinary fare."

"Yes, indeed," said Marion, "only we have more than usual today, there being a guest to serve!"

The officer ate his potato in silence. On returning to Georgetown, he resigned his commission, saying that a people who could live on such simple fare in order to gain their liberty should be allowed their independence.

For many years, Marion and his men carried on their effective warfare, and, in the end, did such valuable service to the American cause that the large armies of General Greene were enabled to drive the British from the Southern States.

Chapter 41

Outwitting a Tory

During the Revolution, the soldiers of Sumter and Marion in the South were very annoying to the British Commanders. The most notorious of these Commanders was Colonel Tarleton, and many are the stories of his cruelty. He was active in plundering and burning the homes of the sturdy Patriots. Tarleton liked nothing better than to destroy the fields and harry the family of some patriot soldier who happened to be away with Marion or Sumter.

Not all the inhabitants of the country were Patriots. Some still adhered to the British cause. These were bitterly hated by their neighbors, and were called Tories.

During one of the raids of Colonel Tarleton, a young Scotchman named MacDonald, one of Marion's soldiers, decided to play a trick upon a man living in his neighborhood whom he suspected of being a Tory. As soon as MacDonald heard that Tarleton was near by, he put on a British uniform, and, early one morning, calling at the house of the man, said to him:

Colonel Tarleton

"The compliments, sir, of Colonel Tarleton, who sends you his respects as being one of the friends of the King."

"Come in! come in!" cried the Tory, much delighted to have a visit from a British officer. "You say that Colonel Tarleton sends me his compliments, and knows that I am a friend of the King? Why, indeed, I am, and am ready to show it at any time. Tell the Colonel so."

"That I will," replied MacDonald. "But Colonel Tarleton is already in need of your aid, and desires me to beg of you one of your fine horses for him to ride. He will use it in driving these rebels out of the country."

"One of my horses!" cried the old Tory. "That I will, gladly. He shall have the best in my pasture. I shall get him at once. I am honored to furnish the Colonel with a horse!"

Whereupon the Tory called his servant, and gave orders that the best horse in his stable should be brought out and made ready for the British officer to take away with him. While the servant was gone, the Tory brought out rich food and wine, and spread it before MacDonald, who did not hesitate to eat and drink to his heart's content.

When the horse arrived, a beautiful young animal, the sly old Tory said,

"Now, you tell the Colonel I send this with my compliments, and, if I find he can ever do me a favor, I shall come to ask him."

"That I shall, the very next time I see him," said MacDonald, and rode away on the full-blooded steed. But, instead of going to the headquarters of the British Army, MacDonald rode off to the swamps, where Marion and his men were in hiding. Here he told them how he had fooled the old Tory. They laughed a long time over the story.

"Of course we could have taken the horse anyhow, but I wanted to be sure he was a Tory, and then, I enjoy a joke. I would like to hear what he will have to say when he finds out his mistake," declared MacDonald to his companions.

The next morning the old Tory went to see Colonel Tarleton, and presented himself with a smiling face. Tarleton received him coldly, and inquired his business.

"How do you like the horse I sent you yesterday?" asked the smiling Tory.

"What horse?" demanded Tarleton. "No one sent me a horse yesterday or any other day."

"Why, a British officer came to my house, and said you sent him for one of my fine horses; I gave it to him, with a saddle and blanket, a pair of silver mounted pistols, and a rain coat; and he had, heavens knows how much, food and drink," cried the bewildered Tory.

"Somebody has been fooling you, old man. I have not seen or heard of your horse," said Tarleton, turning away.

The Tory now realized the trick that had been played upon him. He swore roundly that he would get even with those rascally rebels, if it took him the rest of his life. He then went home in a great rage; but he never saw his fine horse again.

As for MacDonald and his new friend, they became inseparable. It was a beautiful horse, sixteen hands high, with the eyes of an eagle, and a proud spirit in his veins. The road was never too long for him, and the run never too swift. He learned his master's voice and whistle, and, when he heard the call, he came like the wind, bearing him swiftly into battle, or safely beyond the reach of his enemies.

Chapter 42

Supporting the Colors

Among the heroes of the Revolution, none were more famous for their adventures than Marion's men. They lived in the woods and swamps, sometimes a large body, and sometimes a small body, but always ready to sally forth under their leader, Francis Marion, to punish the enemy.

The best known of all these men was Sergeant William Jasper. He was very brave, and in no way did he seem to fear for his life. At the battle of Fort Moultrie, Jasper was busily engaged. While the struggle was at its height, with danger at its greatest, he saw the flag of the fort fall outside the works. It had been carried away by a shot from the enemy.

Without a moment's hesitation, he leaped over the walls of the fort, jumped down into the ditch, and picked up the flag where it lay on the ground. Coolly fastening it to a rod, which was used for wiping out the cannon, he leaped back on to the wall of the fort, and stuck the rod in the sand of the breastworks.

Shot rained thick around him, and it seemed every moment as if he would be killed. But he finished his work, left the flag waving defiance to the enemy, and quietly took his place in the ranks with his men.

General Moultrie was so struck with admiration by this deed that he unbuckled his own sword, and handed it to Jasper, saying, "Take this, and wear it. You have committed a deed of great bravery, and I honor you for it."

When the soldiers were hiding in the woods of South Carolina, Jasper was often sent into the British lines to find out what the enemy was doing. He was a good scout, and could so change his appearance that nobody recognized him. His favorite amusement was to pretend to be a simple-minded countryman, who had something to sell. In this guise he would find his way into the British camps. There he would abuse the Americans and praise the British, but his keen eye meanwhile learned a great deal that would be of value to his Commander.

Upon one of these risky visits, Jasper and a friend, named Newton, saw a body of American prisoners brought in. The wife of one of them had come along, carrying a little child. She was crying, and seemed in great distress, for she knew her husband had once been a soldier on the British side, and had deserted to fight for his own country. This meant quick trial and certain death for desertion.

Jasper felt sorry for the couple, and resolved to rescue them, if he could. The prisoners started, under escort, for Savannah, where they would stand trial. Jasper and Newton quietly left the British camp, and went in an opposite direction, after pretending that "the scoundrels ought to be shot."

Soon, they turned, and made their way back toward Savannah. The two had no guns, nor weapons of any kind, but they were determined to rescue the unfortunate prisoners, if they could.

Within two miles of Savannah, they stopped on the edge of a forest, near a spring; there they hid themselves, awaiting the arrival of the prisoners and their guard. It was not long before the party, consisting of ten British soldiers in charge of the prisoners, came into view.

The soldiers were tired. The spring looked cool and inviting, and the day was warm. Leaning their guns against the trees, they took off their knapsacks, drank freely of the water, and lay down to rest. Two soldiers only were left in charge of the guns and the prisoners. The latter sat on the ground, and Jasper could see the woman near her husband, with the baby asleep in her lap.

"Now is the time," whispered Jasper to Newton. At the word, the brave men sprang from the thicket, seized the guns from the trees, and shot down the two sentinels. The others cried out in dismay and sprang to their feet. But it was too late, for they found their own guns levelled at them, by two very brave and determined Patriots. "Surrender at once, or you are dead men," cried Jasper.

The British threw up their hands, and became the prisoners of those whom, a short while before, they had been guarding. The party then turned about, on their way now to the American camp.

Not long after this, Jasper was among the troops that assaulted Savannah, trying to capture it from the British. The column to which he belonged had pressed forward over ditches and parapets, and had planted the flag of South Carolina on the works of the enemy.

A storm of shot and shell drove back the Carolinians, and cut down the staff that held the flag. Jasper saw that the flag would fall into the hands of the British, and ran back to get it; in doing so he received a mortal wound.

He was borne from the field, and carried to his death-bed. He exclaimed, "I have at last got my furlough."

Pointing to his sword, he said to those around him, "That was presented to me for my services in defense of Fort Moultrie. Give it to my father, and tell him I have worn it with honor. If he should weep, say to him that his son died in the hope of a better life."

A little later, they brought him the flag he had rescued. Looking at it, he smiled.

"Tell Mrs. Elliott," he said, "that I lost my life supporting the colors which she presented to our regiment."

As death drew near, the brave officer began faintly to recall many scenes of battle in which he had taken part. He sent a farewell message to his Commander and his men, and to the prisoners he had rescued at the spring. His last words, breathed to a friend nearby, were, "I am glad to have saved their lives, and I do not mind losing mine; for I was supporting the colors."

Jasper saw that the flag would fall into the hands of the British, and ran back to get it

Chapter 43

Nancy Hart, the War Woman of Georgia

Among the remarkable women of the Revolution was Nancy Hart, the sturdy wife of a farmer. She lived in a log cabin, in one of the counties of Georgia. She hated the Tories, who were the American sympathizers with the British, and never lost an opportunity to show her feeling for them.

There are many stories told of the courage of Nancy Hart. One evening she and her children were sitting around a log fire, over which a pot of soap was hanging. Nancy was stirring the boiling soap with a big ladle, and was telling the children some exciting adventures of the war. Suddenly, one of the children heard some one creeping up to the house, and noticed an eye peeping through the cracks between the logs. "Tories, mother, Tories," whispered the child.

Nancy nodded, but went on talking and stirring the soap, while she kept a sharp lookout for the eyes. Suddenly, she dashed a ladle of the scalding soap through the crack full into the face of the eavesdropper, who, taken by surprise and blinded with pain, roared at a great rate!

Nancy soon had him bound, hand and foot, and hastened to turn him over to the Patriots.

When the Tories were overrunning Georgia, Nancy one day heard the tramp of a horse rapidly approaching her cabin. It was a Patriot riding for life, pursued by a party of British. She let down the bars of the fence before her cabin, ordered the man to go around to the back, and disappear, if he had time, in the woods. She then put up the bars, closed the door of her cabin, and waited.

In a few moments some Tories rode up, and called out noisily to her. She wrapped her head up in an old shawl and, opening the door cautiously, asked, in a complaining voice, why they wanted to disturb a sick, lone woman.

"Have you seen or heard anybody on horseback pass this way?" they demanded.

"No," replied Nancy, "but I saw someone on a sorrel horse turn into the woods a little way up the road."

"That is our man," they said, and rode away in search of him.

"What fools!" exclaimed Nancy. "If they had looked at the ground, instead of at me, they could have seen the tracks of a horse coming up to my house, and leading around to the swamp."

Not long afterwards, a party of five or six Tories, who had been on a murder expedition in a neighboring county, reached Nancy Hart's cabin. Entering boldly, they demanded food. Nancy's husband and the other members of her family were away at work in the fields, and Nancy was alone, except for one little girl.

She replied, "I never feed the King's men. The villains have stolen my chickens and killed my pigs, so that I can hardly feed my own family. I haven't anything but that old turkey."

"Well, that you shall cook for us," said one of the Tories; and, raising his gun, he fired at the turkey, which fell dead. Another Tory brought it to the house, and soon it was clean and ready. So Nancy put it on to cook, and sent her little daughter to the spring for water.

"Tell your father and the others to come quickly; there are Tories in the house," she whispered to the child.

Soon the turkey was ready to eat. The Tories began drinking and singing, and boasted of their exploits in killing several Patriots a few days before. Nancy recognized the names of these victims as persons she knew, and her blood was hot with rage. The soldiers had stacked their guns in one corner, and now drew near the table, ready for the meal. Nancy waited on them, frequently passing between them and their guns in the corner.

Suddenly, the brave woman seized one of the weapons, and pointed it at the party. They sprang up in terror, while she swore she would shoot the first man that moved a foot. One of them started forward, and, true to her word, she fired and killed him where he stood.

Suddenly, the brave woman seized one of the weapons,
and pointed it at the party.

By this time the little girl had returned from the spring, and Nancy called out to her, "Go, call your father and the neighbors. Tell them I have caught some base Tories." The child ran to the fields, while the men, in alarm, tried to seize the intrepid woman. She fired again, and another man fell badly wounded.

Before the others could escape, Nancy's husband and some of the neighbors rushed in, and bound the Tories hand and foot. The neighbors would have shot them, but Nancy said, "No! shooting is too good for the base murderers. They must hang for their crimes!"

This was enough. It was not long before they were all hanging to a tree, which was pointed out to passersby, for fifty years afterwards, as the spot where Nancy Hart avenged the death of her countrymen.

Chapter 44

Mad Anthony Captures Stoney Point

Anthony Wayne was about thirty years old. He was a handsome young officer in Washington's army, and fond of fine uniforms and military equipment. He was a very dandy in his appearance, but, when his spirit was aroused in battle, he forgot all his fine manners in reckless daring. His men spoke of him as "Mad Anthony."

Indeed, he was about the hardest fighter of the Revolution. In battle, his eye would blaze with fury, and his face flashed with the glory of conflict that was wonderful to see. He was afraid of nothing, and counted his own life as naught when it came to winning a fight.

Washington's army was in New Jersey, near New York. The British held a large part of the Hudson River, and had fortified Stony Point, only thirteen miles below West Point. This position controlled the King's Ferry, where troops and supplies were ferried across to support the Patriot army.

The fort was on a bluff nearly two hundred feet high, jutting out into the river, a half mile from shore. A marshy neck crossed by a causeway separated it from the mainland. The top of this rocky point was strongly protected with cannon that defended it in all directions.

Along the causeway, and in the marshes, the British had driven logs, sharpened on ends which pointed outwards so as to form what, in military terms, is called an "abatis." These logs were supposed to make a barrier that would stop the advance of enemy troops long enough for the guns of the fort to annihilate them completely.

Washington decided to attack Stony Point, and chose "Mad Anthony" for the purpose. He rode out, one day, to look over the situation.

"There is no one who can take that fort better than Wayne," said Washington, "but it requires all his skill and daring. Ten minutes warning to those troops in the fort would blast all our hopes."

The Commander-in-Chief gave orders to kill every dog within three miles of the camp, in order to prevent them from barking when the time came for the Americans to approach the fort. He also ordered all stragglers arrested or kept away.

One Captain reported: "Arrested the widow Calhoun, going to the enemy with chickens and vegetables."

In this way did Washington plan. And now it was time for Wayne to act!

About thirteen hundred picked men were chosen for the attack. They were lined up for inspection, with orders to be in marching trim, fully armed and provisioned, "fresh-shaved and powdered." After inspection, they marched away, instead of returning to camp. Not one of them had an idea of his mission, or of the danger of the enterprise upon which he had started.

"If any soldier loads his musket, or attempts to fire, or tries to shirk his duty in face of danger, he must be put to death by the officer nearest him. This is a struggle in which I take no risks, and absolute quiet is necessary," were the commands of Wayne.

One man started to load his gun. The officer called sharply to him to desist, and gave him warning. "I cannot fight without firing my gun," replied the soldier, and continued to put in the powder charge. The officer then ran his sword through the soldier's body, and left him dead on the road. He had to do this, so as to save the lives of the other men, and to carry out successfully the plan of attack.

All the hot July afternoon the men marched along the rough roads, through swamps and ravines, until they came to a place about a mile from Stony Point. Not a sound was heard. The soldiers sank upon the ground, and, in silence, ate their supper of bread and meat.

Then Wayne passed the word what he intended to do. It was the first notice the troops had had of what was before them. It seemed a hopeless task to attack a strong fort, across a swamp, protected by an abatis of heavy logs. But "Mad Anthony" was to lead the charge, and Patriots were his soldiers.

At half-past eleven came the quiet order: "Fall in! Forward march!" Every man pinned a piece of white paper or cloth to his cap, that he might be distinguished in the darkness from the enemy, and not be killed by his own men. Not a sound was uttered, every footstep was quiet, and not an equipment rattled as the men started forward. The watchword was "The fort is our own."

An old man, named Pompey, who had been selling fruit to the British, was engaged as guide. He knew the short cuts through the woods, and the road across the swamp. At midnight, the silent band of Americans reached the edge of the swamp, and waded in.

"Steady! Make no noise! Let the men with axes go first, so as to cut down the abatis. The rest of you rush in and follow me," were the whispered orders Wayne passed down the column.

The water was waist deep in places, for the tide was in. The marsh was six hundred feet across. The night was dark, and the danger very great. The column moved as if on parade. Yard by yard they silently crossed the marsh, and, at last, found themselves close to the outer defenses of the British.

"Halt! Who goes there?" cried a British sentry. No answer from the steadily advancing Patriots! The sentry, catching sight of troops, fired his gun for a general alarm. The sleeping British leaped from their beds. The "long roll" was sounded, calling the men to fall in and repel an attack. They were taken by complete surprise, and the battle was on before they had time to think.

The Patriot axmen rushed forward, and cut away the logs, while the bullets whizzed over their heads. The main columns of Americans climbed over the wall and formed in line on the other side. A small attacking party made a detour around the fort, and opened, a brisk fire on that side. The British guns were turned upon them, and a British force was sent down to engage them, thinking they were the main body of the enemy. But the small attacking force withdrew, leading off their prisoners, while the main body of the Patriots rushed in and took the fort, crying out, "The fort is our own! The fort is our own!"

The Storming of Stony Point

Wayne was shot by a musket ball, and fell to the ground. "Take me into the fort and let me die at the head of my troops," he said to the officer near him. It turned out to be only a flesh wound, and so "Mad Anthony" was able to enter the battle again.

The bayonet did its grim work of death. The British fled, crying out, "Mercy! Mercy! Quarter! Quarter! We surrender!"

In thirty minutes it was all over, and Stony Point was captured. Only one British soldier escaped. He leaped into the river, and swam a mile to a British ship, and here he told of the exploits of "Mad Anthony Wayne and his terrible men."

AMERICA FIRST: UPDATED EDITION

CHAPTER 45

THE EXECUTION OF MAJOR ANDRE

Major Andre was a British officer, who bargained with Benedict Arnold for the surrender of West Point. The agreement was made at a meeting between Arnold and Andre, and would have resulted in serious calamity to the American forces, if Andre had not been captured on his way to New York, and the tell-tale papers discovered hidden in his boots.

Major John Andre

Andre was declared a spy. The fact that he was a brave young officer, whom every one admired, could not save him from the fate of all spies, caught within the enemy's lines. He was tried by court-martial, and condemned to be hanged. Andre had hoped that the Court would order him to be shot, as befitted his rank, but this was not to be!

When the time arrived for his execution, he received the news without emotion. All present were deeply affected, but Andre kept a cheerful countenance, and talked in his usual manner with those around him. His servant came into the room, and Andre noticed tears in his eyes. Seeing this, he exclaimed, "You must not give way thus. Leave me till you can show yourself more manly."

His breakfast was sent him from the table of General! Washington. Every day during his confinement this had been done. He ate as usual; then shaved and dressed. Placing his hat on the table, he said to the officers, "I am ready at any moment, gentlemen, to wait on you."

The fatal hour came at last! A large body of troops was paraded, and an important gathering of citizens assembled. Many generals and field officers were present. Washington did not attend. The scene was solemn, and gloom pervaded all ranks. Major Andre walked from the stone house, where he had been confined, between two soldiers, showing the greatest dignity and composure.

He smiled as he approached the scaffold, and nodded to several acquaintances as he passed them. When he saw that he was to be hanged, and not shot, he was visibly moved, and said, "I am reconciled to my death, and shall bear it as a brave man should, but I had hoped to be shot as a soldier rather than hanged as a felon."

As soon as things were in readiness, he stepped quickly into the wagon, drawn under the gallows, and took two white handkerchiefs from his pocket. He then grasped the rope that hung from the gallows, and slipped the noose around his own neck. He gave one handkerchief to the provost-marshal to bind his arms behind him, and, with the other, he bandaged his own eyes.

"It will be but a momentary pang," he said to those around him. "I pray you to bear me witness that I meet my fate like a brave man."

The wagon was then drawn from under him and, in a few moments he was dead. He was dressed in his royal regimentals and boots, and was buried at the foot of the gallows. Thus died, in the bloom of his life, the gallant Major Andre, pride of the Royal Army!

Chapter 46

How General Schuyler was Saved

During the latter part of the Revolution, the war was carried on mainly in the South. Still, the people of the North were frequently attacked by parties of Tories, who had recruited the natives, descended upon the small towns and outlying houses, carrying off all the plunder they could find.

At this time, General Schuyler was living in his own home, near Albany, just outside the wall, or stockade. It was a tempting bait for the Tories and natives. A party of them resolved to capture the General and his family, and to plunder the house.

When the marauders were on the way, they found out from a Dutch farmer whom they had taken that the General's house was guarded by six soldiers, three by day and three by night. They told the Dutchman they would punish him if he mentioned seeing them, or if, in any way, he warned the General of their approach. They then let the Dutchman go; and, as soon as they were out of sight, he ran as fast as he could to tell the General of the attack.

The Schuyler family were all seated in the wide hall downstairs. The doors and

General Philip Schuyler

windows were open, for it was a hot day in August. The guard was outside under the shade of the trees. Nobody was suspicious of danger. In fact, the General was dozing in his chair.

A servant entered the back door, and said, "There is a man outside who wishes to speak to the General." The General ordered him to be shown in. The Dutchman entered, and told of his meeting with the party of Tories and natives. In fact, hardly had he delivered his message before a scuffle in the yard showed to the dismayed family that the enemy had actually arrived, overpowered the guard, and bound them hand and foot.

Schuyler hastily barred the doors and windows, and retired with his family to the upper rooms. The Tories and natives approached the house, and tried the doors. Then, running to a window, they smashed the panes of glass, and made an entrance to the house. Schuyler, up-stairs, with his gun in hand, stood ready to defend himself and his family. At the other end of the room, the women were huddled in fear, weeping and praying.

Just as the natives entered, Mrs. Schuyler cried out, "My baby! My baby! I have left him downstairs in his cradle." She made a rush for the stairs. Her agony was extreme, and only the strong arms of her husband kept her from going downstairs to rescue her child, General Schuyler held her, and told her it would be death for both her and the baby if she should carry out her purpose. As they were thus hesitating, one of their daughters said, "I will go after my little brother. They will not see me." With that, she slipped past her mother and father, and, in a moment, was down in the hall.

It was dark because the doors and shutters had been closed. The natives were in the dining-room, devouring food, breaking china and furniture, and quarreling over their spoils. The girl darted by the open door, and reached the cradle where the baby lay asleep. Seizing the child in her arms, she started on her way upstairs, when she was discovered by one of the Tories.

He thought she was a servant-girl, and called out to her, "Here, where has your master gone?" The brave girl, half-way up the steps, turned and replied,

"My master has gone to the town to alarm the people. He will be here any moment with some troops."

When General Schuyler heard his daughter make this brave retort, he went to an open window upstairs, and fired his pistol several times. He then called out in a loud voice,

"Come on, my brave men! Here they are inside the house! Surround the buildings, and let no one escape."

He then made his men put their heads out of the windows, and utter loud yells of defiance. The natives and Tories recognized Schuyler's voice, and, hearing all this noise outside, thought that surely troops had come to the rescue. They broke out of the house more quickly than they had broken in, and ran away much faster than they had come, pursued by shots from the General's rifle.

"My brave little girl," said Schuyler to his daughter, "you have had courage to do a brave deed, and wit enough to get us out of trouble."

Chapter 47

How the Northwest was Won

It was the evening of July 4, 1778, and a merry dance was taking place at Kaskaskia, in that region afterwards known as the state of Illinois. It was a cheerful party, for the people were light-hearted and, having little else to do, were passing the time in dance. All the village girls were there, and most of the citizens and soldiers as well. They were dancing away at a happy rate, to the music of a fiddle, played by a man who sat on a chair. An native lay on the floor, watching them with sleepy eyes.

Kaskaskia was a British fort, but most of the people who lived there were French. Though the war of the Revolution was going on in the East and South, the inhabitants of this wilderness fort of the West cared little for a conflict that was being waged a thousand miles off. They thought themselves secure from attack, for surely no one would attempt to travel so great a distance for so small a prize. In this, they were much mistaken, however, as we shall see.

As the dance went on, a tall young man stepped into the room, and leaned against the door, watching the dancers. He was dressed as a backwoods-man, and had evidently come a long and difficult way. It was plain that he was not French, and that he was a soldier. The native was the first to see him, and to raise the alarm. His yell broke up the dance, and every one gazed upon the stranger with fright. The women screamed, the men sprang for their guns. The stranger raised his hand, and said very quietly,

"Do not be alarmed. I shall not hurt you. Go on with your

dance. But remember, you are dancing under the flag of Virginia, and not under the flag of England."

As he uttered these words, a crowd of Patriots, dressed as he was, stepped into the room, seized all the guns of the soldiers, and thus occupied the fort. The young man's name was John Rogers Clark. The fort had been captured without a blow or a shot.

This is how it happened. John Rogers Clark, who had been living for some time in Kentucky, saw plainly that the English were stirring up the Native Americans of the West for an attack on the English settlements. So he determined to put a stop to it. Besides, he wished to capture the western forts for his own country. He went to Virginia, and asked Patrick Henry, who was then Governor,

"Give me permission to raise a body of soldiers, and march West for the protection of Virginia and Kentucky."

Patrick Henry looked into the brave eyes of the young man, and said, "Go, my dear sir, raise your companies, and I will make you a Colonel. You will do this for the defense of Virginia and Kentucky."

It was not long before Clark had his soldiers, and was on his way. They floated down the Ohio River, landed fifty miles from Kaskaskia, marched through the woods, and entered, as we have described, the open and undefended fort.

This ends the first part of the story. There is a second part, however, not so easy as the first. Far to the South, on the Wabash River, in what is now Indiana, stood another fort, called Vincennes, one hundred and fifty miles away. This was also a French fort, held for the British. Colonel Clark wanted to capture Vincennes, as he had captured Kaskaskia. He did not have enough men to take it by force. So he sent a French priest to Vincennes to tell the people that the Americans were their best friends, after all, and to advise them to haul down the British flag, and raise the American flag in its place. Otherwise, Clark and his men would be down on them in short order.

The French agreed to do as they were ordered, and Vincennes became, for the time being, an American fort. Thereupon, Clark and his men went back to Kentucky, much pleased with the success of their expedition.

But the British were not to be dispossessed of their territory so easily. The British Commander at Detroit, Colonel Hamilton, marched down to Vincennes, took the fort back again, and threatened to march upon Kaskaskia and then even into Kentucky. When Clark heard of this, he resolved to go at once to Vincennes, recapture the place, and hold it!

It was a terrible task, for winter was at hand. The Wabash River had overflowed its banks and, for hundreds of square miles, the country was under water. Vincennes was in the center of a vast shallow lake, or swamp, of freezing water. Hamilton thought himself safe until the spring, anyhow.

Clark set out with his men,

"Wade in and follow me!"

dressed in hunting shirts, with fur caps on their heads, which were ornamented with deer or raccoon tails, and carrying long rifles. Then came cold days and steady rains. Every night they had to build fires to warm by, and to dry their clothes. They trudged on through the cold water, glad of any little island to rest upon or any dry place to sleep. Sometimes the water was ankle-deep, then knee-deep, and then waist-deep. Still, they went on, knowing they must plunge ahead or go back.

At last, they came within four miles of the fort. The water was waist-deep and very cold. "Wade in," cried Clark, "and follow me!" Seizing a drummer-boy, he placed him on his shoulders and told him to beat his drum. Then the brave leader plunged into the ice-cold water. With a shout, the men followed him. After a few hours' hard riding, they crossed the flood, and were before the fort of Vincennes.

Colonel Hamilton was amazed when he saw Clark and his. men at his very door. "They are mad, or else they had wings to cross at such a time," he said. But he resolved to defend his fort, and the fight began.

For hours the Kentucky and Virginia riflemen, with their unerring aim, poured shot into the loopholes of the fort. They were deadly riflemen, and every shot told. At the end of the day, Hamilton surrendered, and the flag of England was again hauled down. In this way did all that great Northwest Territory pass into possession of the Americans. Out of it the great states of Ohio, Indiana, Illinois, Michigan, Wisconsin, and part of Minnesota were afterwards formed.

Chapter 48

Benjamin Franklin

Benjamin Franklin was the youngest member of a family of seventeen children. His father was a poor man, who made his living by boiling soap and making candles. He went to school barely two years, though all his life he was a hard student. There was never a boy more fond of books than he; he borrowed them from anybody who would lend them to him, and, oftentimes, sat up all night reading. In this way, he became one of the most learned men in the country.

He began life by working for his brother in a printing office, where he soon became an expert type-setter. He read all the articles printed in his brother's paper, and decided he could write better ones. He slipped his own articles under the door of the printing office, without signing them. His brother was so pleased with them that he printed every one. One day, he said, "Ben, whoever writes these articles has plenty of sense. I wish I knew who he was." But Franklin never told his secret.

After a while, Franklin and his brother had a quarrel, and they separated. Franklin tried to get work in Boston, but was refused everywhere, because his brother had sent the printers word not to hire him. Then he went to New York, but with no better success. Finally, he made his way to Philadelphia in search of his fortune.

He arrived with only a few pennies to his name, his clothing rumpled and soiled, and his pockets stuffed with his extra stockings and shirt. It was a most unpromising beginning for a great career.

Many people turned in the street to look at him, for he was an awkward country boy.

Being hungry, he went into a baker's shop, and bought several rolls. He held them in his hands, and went along the street, munching one after another. A young girl, standing in the doorway of her home, laughed at Kim as he passed by, for he was indeed a comical sight. Her name was Deborah Reed. Years afterwards, she became the wife of this poor boy.

After several years of hard work in printing offices, and wandering back to Boston and even once to London, Franklin finally settled down in

Philadelphia, in business for himself. He began printing a newspaper, which was the brightest journal in America. He also published a book each year, called "Poor Richard's Almanac," full of wise and witty sayings, as well as containing useful information.

Franklin was one of the most practical men of his day. He had many good ideas for the public welfare. He established a public library in Philadelphia. He invented the open Franklin stove, which stored up much of the heat that once was wasted up the chimney. He suggested paving the streets, in order to save the wear and tear on vehicles, and to gain more speed in going about. He also proposed lighting the streets with lamps at night in order to help belated citizens find their way home.

Every one has seen the flash of lightning and heard the roar of thunder. For a long time, people did not know that the lightning in the sky and the electricity made by an electric machine were the same thing. And nobody could think of a way to find out, until Benjamin Franklin undertook the problem.

After studying the electric machine, he came to the conclusion that lightning and electricity were the same in nature. To test it, he made a large kite of silk, tying the string to the metal frame. The part of the string near his hand was tied to a silk ribbon, and a metal key was fastened just above the ribbon. The silk was used to keep the electricity from passing into Franklin's body.

Franklin supposed that the electricity would come down the wet kite string when it rained during a thunder-storm, and would collect on the key. He calculated that it could not reach him because of the ribbon in his hand. Silk, he knew, was a non-conductor of electricity. He waited for a rainy night when the lightning was flashing. He did not wish to be bothered by people watching him in the daytime. The kite shot up in the air, and soon was lost to sight in the darkness. Franklin let out the string as far as it would go, so as to be sure the kite was well up in the clouds. He held on to the silk ribbon, and stood under a shed so as to keep off the rain. He had a lamp with him to watch the kite string and the key.

The lightning flashed, the rain came down, the string was wet, and the kite was pulling hard in the strong wind. Franklin held on to the silk ribbon with one hand, and carefully put out his other hand to touch the key at the end of the string beyond the ribbon. Instantly, he felt a shock that almost knocked him down. He tried it several times, until he was afraid to do so again. He then knew that he had drawn the lightning from the clouds, and had proved it to be the same as the electricity made by the electric machine.

One day, he had his kite in the air, and was trying various experiments with the electricity on the string, when he thought he would see what effect it would have on a turkey. He walked carefully around, following the turkey, but could not get sufficiently close to the bird for the string to touch it. At last he came near enough, as he thought, but, just as he reached over to bring the string to the turkey's head, his own hand touched the key, and, before he knew what had happened, he was knocked down and nearly stunned.

When he recovered from his surprise and shock, he said, "Instead of killing a turkey, I came near killing a goose."

It was Franklin's experiments with his kite that led him to invent the lightning-rod which protects our homes during a thunder-storm.

Franklin became one of our greatest American statesman, noted for his wisdom and learning. He was sent abroad to gain the friendship of France in the War of the Revolution. When he appeared at Court, dressed in his plain, old-fashioned way, with his long, gray coat, big spectacles, and fur cap, he attracted a great deal of attention. The people soon learned to admire his humor and good sense, and everywhere he was greeted with enthusiasm.

After the Revolution, he helped form the Constitution of the United States, though he was over eighty years of age at the time. When he died, four years afterwards, it was said that twenty thousand people attended his funeral.

Franklin let out the string as far as it would go.

Chapter 49

Nolichucky Jack

John Sevier rode over the mountains from Virginia to see what kind of home he could find in the new settlements for himself and his family. Alone through woods and across the steep mountains he made the journey. At last, he found the very place his adventurous spirit liked, and there he brought his wife and children to join the settlers on the Watauga River, in what is now the State of Tennessee.

Life was rough in this pioneer settlement. James Robertson commanded the fort, and John Sevier, after a while, became his Lieutenant. Close by, clustered the cabins of the settlers, with their gardens and fields of corn. The soil was fertile, the woods were full of game, the rivers had fish in abundance, and the native people, at first, were friendly. All went well with the Watauga settlement until the Revolution.

Then the British began to arm the natives with guns, and to reward them for bringing in scalps and captives. The peace of the little frontier settlement was disturbed, and it looked as if they intended to make a general attack upon these pioneers.

One day the cry went through the village, "Natives! They are on the war path. Everybody to the fort!"

The men and women hastily gathered behind the barred gate and prepared for defense. There were forty or fifty resolute men, well-armed and on their guard. They were not altogether unprepared, for a friendly native woman had already warned them to be on the lookout for danger.

In the early dawn, the natives crept out of the forest, and stole up to the fort. But the settlers had kept watch during the night and were not to be surprised. When the natives were within reach of the guns, through the loopholes a deadly fire was opened on them, and many were killed as they tried to pass the open ground. Then they escaped back into the woods, glad to be out of reach of the aim of the Colonists.

The stockade was too strong to be taken by assault, so the natives decided to starve the settlers out. Three weeks passed, with the warriors lurking in the woods, outside of danger, but ready to descend on anyone who dared leave the protection of the fort. Food ran short and rations were reduced to parched corn – all they had.

The Colonists became very tired of confinement. Sometimes the natives would disappear for hours at a time, and then they would return and fill the air with hideous sounds. The settlers grew weary of inaction, and, from time to time, someone would venture forth, heedless of warning. In this way three or four men were shot by the natives, and one boy was carried off.

The water in the fort was giving out. One of the young women, named Kate Sherrill, took a pitcher and went to the river to fill it with water. No natives had been seen for several hours, and she thought she was safe. She was a tall, graceful, and beautiful girl, and very courageous. After she had gone some distance from the fort, several natives sprang out of the forest and dashed toward her.

She knew her danger was great and turned swiftly to flee for safety. She was a good runner, and her life was at stake. On came the blood-thirsty natives, with tomahawks uplifted ready to strike. On sped the brave girl, swift as a deer. Those in the fort cried out in terror, "Run to the palisade! Never mind the gate! We will pull you over!"

Guns were leveled at the pursuing foe; but they escaped the flying bullets. The cries of the men at the fort did not stop them; they sped all the faster after the flying feet of the girl.

At last she reached the palisade, as the nearest native was ten feet away. She made one desperate leap, caught the top pickets with her hands, and was pulled over the top just as a bullet killed her pursuer in his tracks. The other natives sullenly returned to the forest.

As Kate Sherrill fell over the pickets, completely exhausted, she landed in the arms of John Sevier.

The end of the story is that John Sevier, whose wife had died some time before, fell in love with the beautiful girl whom he had saved by his lucky shot, and persuaded her to marry him.

The natives gave up the siege after a while and returned to their villages. This left the Watauga settlement in peace for a time, but the friendly relations between the natives and the colonists were not restored for several years. John Sevier was constantly leading war parties against the natives. It is said that he fought thirty-five battles and was known as the greatest native fighter in the southwest.

Kate Sherrill is saved by John Sevier

Sevier became the leading man of the Colony. He lived in a big, rambling, one-story house, on Nolichucky Creek. It consisted of two separate wings, connected by a covered porch. In one part he lived with his family; the other part was given up to his guests. He kept open house for everybody.

Here, to all comers, his hospitality was abundant. Rarely was he without friends who sat around his plentiful table, gathered by the big open fires in the winter, or on the wide porch in the summer, and talked over the battles with the natives, and the coming of new settlers into the country.

At weddings, or on other great occasions, Sevier was accustomed to gather all the people of the community together, and to feast them at a great barbecue, in which an ox was roasted whole over a fire and basted with the richest sauce. The board tables were loaded with forest game and field produce, and the people drank cider.

In this way, Sevier became greatly loved by everybody. He was known far and wide as Nolichucky Jack. His wife retained her beauty and grace and was called "Bonnie Kate." Even the natives grew to like the stern old fighter, for he was always fair with them, though at times he punished them severely.

Everywhere in Tennessee, when word came that "Chucky Jack" was in town, crowds went out to meet him and shake his hand. When Tennessee became a state, he was elected the first Governor.

When he was eighty years old, he headed a party of surveyors to mark the boundary line between the State of Georgia and the lands of Tennessee. The labor was too great for his worn body, and he died in his tent, surrounded by a few soldiers and natives.

To this day, the people of Tennessee tell their children the story of how Nolichucky Jack fought the natives and the British, and how he helped build up their great State.

Chapter 50

Eli Whitney Invents the Cotton Gin

When we read about the millions of bales of white cotton raised in the South every year, it is hard to believe that cotton itself was considered only a garden plant until after the Revolution. A plantation of thirty acres of cotton near Savannah yielded what was then a very large crop. Just after the war with Great Britain, eight bags of cotton were shipped to England, and were seized by the Custom House officials, on the ground that so much cotton could not be raised in the United States.

The cotton which grows in the uplands of the South is known as short staple cotton, and its lint adheres very closely to the seed. At first this lint had to be picked off by hand, which was a slow process. A man and his family could hardly clean more than eight or ten pounds a day. In case of a large crop, there were not hands enough to separate the lint from the seed. Therefore, cotton was not profitable, and, in consequence, not much of it was raised. In the year 1791, only three hundred and ninety-one bales were exported from the United States.

In 1792, a young man, named Eli Whitney, was living in Georgia, at the home of Mrs. Nathanael Greene, a few miles from

Eli Whitney

Savannah. He was born in Massachusetts, and had just graduated from Yale College. He had come to Savannah to practice law, and to eke out his income by teaching school. Mrs. Greene had invited him to live at her plantation, and to help her with the education of her children.

Whitney had always shown a certain skill in making useful articles, and in mending broken things. Nothing was needed around the Greene house or farm that Whitney could not make; nothing that he could not fix. Mrs. Greene said to him one day, "Mr. Whitney, I believe you can make anything. Sooner or later, you will hit upon a fortune."

One day some visitors expressed their regret that it was such a hard matter to clean the upland cotton; they said it was a pity there was not a machine for that purpose.

Mrs. Greene replied, "There is a young man here who can make anything. His name is Eli Whitney. I believe he could invent a machine for cleaning cotton."

Whitney was sent for, and listened to stories of the trouble the Southern farmers were having with the cotton seed. He had never seen any cotton up to that time, but he cheerfully undertook to work up some scheme. He watched the seed-pickers, and brought some of the ripe cotton-bolls to his room, where he began to pick out the seed himself. He soon thought of a plan for a machine, and set to work building it. It was a hard task, for he had to make his own tools, wire, and nails.

Whitney toiled for several months on his invention, and at last had ready for its trial test his cotton engine, or cotton-gin, as it is called for short. It was a simple device, consisting of a revolving cylinder, covered with short teeth that passed through a stationary comb. The teeth caught the lint, and dragged it through the comb, leaving the seed behind. It was very crude, but even this first gin could do more work than twenty men. All the machines made since that day have adhered to the same idea, though the modern ones are a great improvement on the ones first made.

Mrs. Greene and another friend were the only ones allowed to see Whitney's first gin. They were so delighted when they witnessed how fast this little hand-turning machine could clean the seed, that they could not keep the secret. Others soon heard of it, and one night Whitney's shop was broken open, and his model machine was stolen and carried away.

This was a great blow to Whitney, for, before he could make a new one, and get it patented, other machines, based on his invention, were in operation. In after years, this gave him a great deal of trouble, and, in fact, kept him from making a fortune out of his gin.

A patent was secured for the Whitney cotton-gin in 1794. Soon, others began to claim that they had made gins before Whitney's appeared. Many lawsuits began to dispute Whitney's rights, and the juries did not give the poor inventor much satisfaction. In fact, he spent much money, with little benefit to himself.

At any rate, the world knows that Whitney invented the cotton-gin. As soon as gins could be bought, the farmers began to plant cotton plentifully. By using the gin, they could clean a thousand

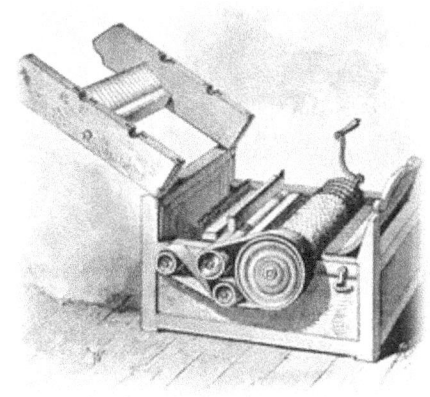

Eli Whitney's Cotton Gin

pounds a day, instead of only eight or ten pounds, as before. Everybody planted cotton, land was cleared for cultivation, machinery was made to help the farmer, and a great industry was opened to the people of the South, through the genius of this young man. He had studied the needs of the situation, and had applied his good sense to solving the difficulties.

Chapter 51

Thomas Jefferson

Thomas Jefferson was born near Charlottesville, Virginia, April 13, 1743. His father was a sturdy backwoods surveyor, of giant size and strength, whom his son always remembered with pride and veneration. His mother belonged to one of the prominent families of Virginia, and from her young Jefferson inherited his love for nature, music, and books.

Jefferson's father owned a farm of nearly two thousand acres, on which he had thirty slaves; he raised large crops of wheat and tobacco. He was a stern, though kind, just, and generous man. He often said to his son, "Never ask another to do for you what you can do for yourself." He died when Thomas was fourteen years of age.

From early childhood, Jefferson was a bright boy. He had his mother's gentle and thoughtful disposition, and, by nature, took readily to reading. His love of outdoor sports saved him from over-study. He became a keen hunter, was a dead shot with a rifle, a fine dancer, and rode a horse with great skill.

He entered William and Mary College, at Williamsburg, the capital of Virginia, when he was seventeen years of age. The college stood at one end of the main street, the old capitol at the other. On the same street there was situated an inn, known as Raleigh Tavern, in which was a room called "The Apollo," used as a dancing-hall. Here Jefferson was one of the leaders. He was described as a tall, thin young student, "with red hair, a freckled face, and pointed features," whom everybody liked, and who was brilliant at the college.

After graduating, he began to study law. When he became twenty-one years of age, he celebrated the event by planting an avenue of trees near his home. Some of those trees are still standing, a memorial to his love of nature and his desire to make things beautiful.

Among the friends of Jefferson, at this time, was a jovial young fellow, noted for his "mimicry, practical jokes, and dancing." Nobody thought he amounted to much, for he was most always frolicking. He and Jefferson became bosom friends, and spent much of their time together. They saw in each other qualities of mind of which the world did not yet know.

One day, while Jefferson was standing at the door of the capitol, a member of the House of Burgesses was delivering a most eloquent address. Everybody was amazed at the wonderful oratory of the man. Jefferson recognized him as his friend, Patrick Henry, who was making his famous speech against the Stamp Act.

Thomas Jefferson

Jefferson never forgot the scene. The sublime words that poured from Henry's lips took his breath away, and he listened as one enraptured. He resolved, from that moment, that he too would serve his country, and at once redoubled his studious habits, often spending as long as fifteen hours a day over his books. The result was, Jefferson became one of the most accomplished scholars in America. He was a brilliant mathematician, and knew five languages besides his own.

At the age of twenty-four, Jefferson began to practice law. His voice was not strong, and he was never a good speaker. His manner was hesitating and embarrassed, and his ideas did not find easy expression in spoken words. But he was a great writer and thinker, and, in a few years, he was known as the best lawyer in Virginia.

Jefferson was also a farmer. He loved to look over his broad fields and to attend to his growing crops. He once said, "No occupation is so delightful to me as the culture of the earth, and no culture comparable to that of a garden."

He delighted in experimenting with new things, and imported a large number of trees and shrubs to beautify the grounds of his home which he named "Monticello." He was as proud of being a successful farmer as he was of being a great lawyer.

Jefferson wrote the rules which he considered essential for a practical person to follow:

1. Never put off till tomorrow what you can do today.
2. Never trouble another for what you can do yourself.
3. Never spend your money before you have it.
4. Never buy what you do not want because it is cheap.
5. Pride costs us more than hunger, thirst, or cold.
6. We never repent of having eaten too little.
7. Nothing is troublesome that we do willingly.
8. How much pain we have suffered from the evils that never happened.
9. Take things always by their smooth handle.
10. When angry count ten before you speak: if very angry count a hundred.

His manners were plain and simple. When he was President of the United States, he did not stand aloof from the people, as other great men of the day did, but he encouraged everybody to be on familiar terms with him. He did not have the splendid parties and balls at the White House that other Presidents had, but lived quietly and without much display.

Jefferson's great fame lies in the fact that he wrote the Declaration of Independence. He was then thirty-three years of age, and one of the youngest members of the Continental Congress. It is among the greatest of our national documents. He secured legislation in Virginia, exempting taxation for the support of any church, and was the founder of the University of Virginia.

At "Monticello," he entertained with lavish hospitality, sometimes having as many as fifty guests in his house at one time. Some of these visitors stayed for months, imposing on his hospitality, with the result that in his old age he was much reduced in his circumstances.

Jefferson's home, Monticello

Chapter 52

The Burning of the *Philadelphia*

For many years the Moors, in Africa, were pirates, and preyed upon vessels in the Mediterranean. The weaker nations of Europe agreed to pay a tribute annually if these pirates would not molest them on the seas. Those nations that did not pay suffered dreadfully in consequence. The United States paid tribute for a while, but grew tired of it, and declared war against Tripoli, the boldest of these piratical countries.

During the war which followed, an American vessel, named the *Philadelphia*, while pursuing an enemy craft, ran aground on a reef, and was captured by the Tripolitans, who floated her and refitted her for service in their own navy. She lay in the harbor, a beautiful and tantalizing sight to the American vessels just outside the range of the guns of the fort that protected her.

Lieutenant Stephen Decatur volunteered to capture or destroy the *Philadelphia*, with the aid of a recently captured vessel, called a "ketch," which was named the *Mastico*, but had been rechristened the *Intrepid*. He had a crew of seventy-six men, and one night in July, 1804, he slowly drifted into the harbor of Tripoli on his perilous adventure.

The ketch, which was innocent enough as it made its way slowly along, looked like a belated coaster making its way into the harbor. All the men, except about a dozen sailors, were lying on the decks, hidden from view. The moon had set, and the lights of the town gave a dim outline to the big ship toward which they were purposely drifting.

At last, the gliding ketch came close to the *Philadelphia*, upon whose decks soldiers and sailors were plainly visible. An officer aboard hailed the ketch in the Tripolitan tongue, and inquired,

"What vessel is that, and where are you from?"

"This is the *Mastico*, from Malta," was the reply in the same language.

"Be careful or you will run afoul of us," was the warning.

To this the ketch replied, "We have lost our anchors in a gale and should like to tie up to you for the night."

The Tripolitan agreed to this, not suspecting for a moment that the ketch was otherwise than represented. The Moorish soldiers looked on lazily, and with idle curiosity. As the ketch came down, a boat was lowered with a line that soon was made fast to the forechains of the frigate. Another boat from the frigate was lowered to take a line from the stem of the ketch. Thus it was proposed to tie the two boats together.

When all was made fast, the American sailors slowly drew the ketch closer and closer to the side of the frigate. Suddenly, the officers of the frigate, seeing the anchors of the ketch still aboard, took alarm and cried aloud to cut her loose. It was too late. In a moment, grappling irons had fastened the two boats, and all the men aboard the ketch were swarming with drawn swords over the side of the frigate.

It was short work to disperse the crew of the frigate, most of whom leaped into the water and began swimming for the shore. In ten minutes, the *Philadelphia* was again in the hands of her former owners, and not a Moor was left on board alive.

There was no chance to carry the vessel off, since her sails were not set, and there was almost no wind. Besides, it would be only a few minutes before the swimmers would reach the shore and give the alarm. Therefore, Decatur determined to set fire to the frigate,

The *Philadelphia* was doomed

and to escape before armed boats could come to the rescue and defeat his purpose.

It took but a few minutes to spread fire from the hold to other places of the dry ship. The men barely had time to escape from the decks before vast volumes of smoke were issuing from the port holes, and the *Philadelphia* was doomed. The *Intrepid* now swung clear of the burning vessel, and left her to her fate. The men on board gave a great cheer as the flames burst forth to the rigging. Soon the boat was one mass of flames, from hull to peak, lighting the entire harbor with a deep red glow.

In spite of firing from the shore batteries and from several armed vessels, the *Intrepid* made her way out of the harbor, impelled by sweeps in the hands of the crew, and aided by a light wind. In a short time, Decatur had joined his American fleet, and was greeted with congratulations for his daring exploit.

Chapter 53

The Expedition of Lewis and Clark

The purchase from France, in 1803, of the great territory between the Mississippi River and the Rocky Mountains, known as Louisiana, gave to the United States a vast domain almost unknown to the colonists.

At that time, there were but two large towns in the whole area. New Orleans had, perhaps, eight or ten thousand wooden houses. The streets were dirty and ill-paved. The population numbered eight or ten thousand people. St. Louis was a fur-trading post, of not more than a thousand souls, many of whom were boatmen or traders among the tribes of the West. There were a few scattered villages along the rivers, but the great body of the territory was filled with Native Americans. So far as the country was concerned, very little was known about it.

President Jefferson resolved to find out more about this vast domain which had doubled the territory of the United States, and which had cost only fifteen million dollars to purchase. He looked about for the man to send on a mission of exploration. He selected his own secretary, Captain Meriwether Lewis, who invited Captain William Clark, the brother of George Rogers Clark, to join him.

Both were young men, who had seen service on the border; both were Virginians; and both entered into the enterprise heart and soul. They were directed to note carefully every detail of the country, and to find out all they could about the tribes.

The journey was a long one two thousand miles at least, and

most of it had to be covered on rivers unknown to the explorers. With a party of forty-three brave men, they started from St. Louis, in May, 1804, on their toilsome way up the Missouri River.

It was a pleasant time of the year, and for days the party sailed or rowed their boats up the yellow stream, enjoying the beautiful country through which they were passing. Great trees, hanging their branches to the water's edge, meadows filled with flowers, thickets full of birds and game, were passed day after day.

At night, they would tie up to a bank where there was a spring, or clear stream of fresh water; then they would build a big camp fire of driftwood, cook their evening meal, station sentries on the lookout for wild beasts, and lie down to sleep.

Late in July, the Platte River was reached. Selecting a shady and comfortable camp, the explorers sent messages to the natives to come to a friendly meeting. A great crowd arrived, and received presents of flags, tomahawks, knives, beads, looking-glasses, red handkerchiefs, and gaudy coats; they vowed eternal friendship to them. Why should they be at war with those who brought them such beautiful gifts?

The party continued on its way. The summer was passing, and the autumn was coming on. Great herds of buffaloes came down to the river to drink; great flocks of white gulls passed them overhead, while the woods were full of plums, grapes, and berries. Game and fish were to be had in abundance. The travelers fared well, and were very happy, though the nights were getting cold, and the camp fires on the banks had to be kept going all the time.

In the autumn, they reached the country of the Mandan tribe, where they decided to spend the winter. Friendship was soon established by the gifts of beads and looking-glasses. The time was spent in hunting, fishing, and talking. One night, by the camp fire, an old Chief rose and said,

"Far to the setting sun, my brother will find a deep gorge cut through the mountains. Down this gorge pours the mighty river with a roar like the thunders. Over it stands always a deep mist. High up in a dead tree, an eagle has built his nest. My brother cannot go there by the big canoe. Stay here with us."

But Lewis replied, "The great father has sent me to see beyond the mountains, and to find the big water of the sea. In the spring, I must go, and those with me must go also. When the snow melts I

"The great father has sent me to see beyond the mountains, and to find the big water of the sea."

shall be gone." So, when the flowers bloomed, Lewis and Clark made ready to move.

Leaving their friends, the party pushed on. But now the real troubles began. The navigation of the river became more and more difficult. Sometimes they had to drag their canoes along by towlines, or carry them around the shoals and shallows. Their hunters kept them supplied with bear meat, venison, and other game.

They reached and passed the Yellowstone. In May, they came in sight of the Rocky Mountains. The river grew swifter and smaller, and traveling became more and more difficult. Lewis and Clark went scouting in every direction, climbing the bluffs to get a view of the country. Often they saw great herds of buffaloes feeding on the prairies.

At evening, they always halted, the events of the day were noted down in their diaries, the difficulties of the journey discussed, and plans for the next day decided upon. Fresh logs were piled upon the blazing fire, sentinels were posted, and the men stretched themselves upon the ground for sleep. By daybreak they were up and moving.

In June, Captain Lewis saw in the distance a thin, cloudlike mist, rising out of the plain. He did not doubt but that it was the Great Fall, of which the Mandans had told him. In a few hours, the party stood upon the brink of the chasm, and saw the river pour its great flood through the gorge. Even the eagle's nest was there, just as they had told him.

There were thirteen miles of cascades and rapids. The Missouri rushed headlong over precipices and through canons a thousand feet deep. It was a sublime sight.

The boats were abandoned, for the river was now too narrow

and wild for navigation. No natives could be found anywhere to guide them across the mountains, so the party took to a well-beaten trail, which at last gave out high up in the mountains.

Lewis left the party in camp, and set forth alone to find his way over the mountains. It was a terrible task, beset with danger on all sides, but at last he crossed the divide, and came upon a village of the Shoshone or Snake tribe, to whom he told his story. They were amazed that he could have crossed the mountains without a guide, and on foot.

Going back with these natives to direct him, Lewis at last brought the whole party over, and the journey was resumed. It was now winter again. The snow fell and the water froze. There was little to eat, and the men grew discouraged. Their food consisted mainly of dried fish. When a horse gave out, it was killed and eaten. They learned to eat dog-meat, and to be glad to get it. This was the hardest part of their journey.

At last, ragged, half-starved, and footsore, the explorers came out on the other side of the mountains, more like fugitives than conquerors of a great wilderness. They had traveled four hundred miles on foot, through the tangled forests and over mountains.

But their troubles were over. After resting with a friendly tribe, they built canoes and embarked upon the stream that led into the Columbia River. More and more villages appeared, more and more game was to be found, and the streams were full of fish. So they fared well.

Finally, they entered the Columbia River, and, late in the fall, their canoes floated into the mouth of that great river in view of the Pacific Ocean. They had reached their goal at last!

Here the winter was passed. In March, 1806, the explorers

began their journey home, which, after many adventures, was safely reached. They had been gone two and a half years. Everybody had given them up for lost or dead. Hence, there was great surprise and joy at their return.

Chapter 54

Pike Explores the Arkansas Valley

Lieutenant Zebulon M. Pike was a bold young adventurer, who, when twenty-seven years of age, undertook to explore the country between Arkansas and the Red Rivers, in the same way that Lewis and Clark had explored the region of the Missouri River.

In July, 1806, Pike and his men, full of courage and high spirits, left St. Louis in row-boats. They were prepared for the usual hard journey that awaited explorers of the far west, with all its dangers and discomforts. Their boats made about fifteen miles a day. They lived on deer, turkeys, and bears which they easily killed in their hunting trips along the banks of the river.

They turned into the Osage River, and, about the middle of August, reached some native villages where they were welcomed by the dusky Osage warriors, and refreshed after their tiresome trip.

Here Pike mounted his men on horses, and made ready for his long journey by land.

Their first destination was the Pawnee villages far away on the Platte River, where a tribe of natives lived whose friendship for the Americans was uncertain. On September 1st, the party drove away full of hope and confidence. With them rode a band of Osage warriors

Zebulon Pike

for a short distance, to show them their goodwill and to do them honor.

In a few days the party rode across the dividing ridge, and the prairies of Kansas spread before them. Far as the eye could see, the rich land stretched, level and beautiful, covered with tall grass and low-growing bushes. A few hills, here and there, broke the monotony of the landscape. Occasionally, a group of trees could be located, and there, beneath the branches the Native Americans buried their dead to keep the bodies from the devouring wolves and coyotes. It was a wonderful country, which in future years was to be the greatest grain-growing section of the world.

At last, Pike came to the Pawnee villages. The reputation of these natives boded no good to his mission of friendship. He was far from home, and his band was few in numbers. Just before he arrived, a body of three hundred Spanish soldiers, from New Mexico, had been there, and sown distrust and enmity for the Americans. When Pike arrived, with his twenty-three men, the natives did not try to conceal their disdain.

"Our friends, the Spaniards, have many warriors, on strong horses, and bring many presents. You are nothing beside them, and we do not fear you," said the Chief to Pike.

Pike replied, "There are few of us here, but there are many of us where I come from. The Spaniards are many here, but few at home. We bring friendship and peace."

After leaving the Pawnee villages, Pike's party continued its westward journey, going up the Arkansas River, looking for its source. Toward the beginning of winter they reached the Spanish Peaks, where the river, growing smaller all the time, finally was lost among the hills. They were now in the land that afterwards became

Colorado.

Before them lay a lofty peak, which Pike determined to climb, that he might get a better view of the country. Day after day he struggled through the tangled brush, over gullies, and up the steep sides of the mountain. Every night brought him and his men nearer the top. Amid many difficulties, he reached a great altitude, and at last, on the very summit, saw the wonderful plains and prairies of Colorado spread before him.

The high point was afterwards named "Pike's Peak," in honor of the intrepid explorer. Today, a railway track is laid to the top of the same mountain, and in summer many visitors take, in perfect comfort, the same wonderful climb that Pike and his men took with such hardship.

Winter now set in. The rivers began to freeze, the snow fell and covered the trails, the wood became too wet to burn, and Pike and his men endured untold misery. Trying to find his way back to the head waters of the Red River, he missed his way, and the party wandered like lost men through the hills, without shelter and often without food. Men with less courage and strength would have perished in the terrible hardships they endured.

At last they built a block-house for shelter, and settled down to wait. Pike sent one of his men to hunt for Santa Fe, the Spanish town, and to bring succor. When the messenger reached Santa Fe and told his story, the Spaniards listened with some distrust, but sent a squadron of horse to find Pike and his men.

Reaching the brave little party, the Spaniards arrested Pike for being on Spanish territory; they suspected him of having designs on New Mexico. Pike was glad enough to be rescued, no matter what the Spaniards thought of him. Here is how he, himself, describes what befell him and his men, when they reached Santa Fe:

"When we presented ourselves at Santa Fe, I was dressed in a pair of blue trousers, moccasins, blanket-coat, and a cap made of scarlet cloth, lined with fox skins, and my poor fellows in leggings, breech-cloths, and leather coats. There was not a hat in the whole party. Our appearance was extremely mortifying to us all, especially as soldiers. Greater proof cannot be given of the ignorance of the people here than their asking if we lived in houses or in camps like the natives, or if we wore hats in our country."

After a brief detention, as prisoners, and largely because of satisfactory explanation on Pike's part, the explorers were sent back to the United States under an armed escort, though Pike's papers were taken from him, so that he had to supply the details of his explorations as best he could from memory.

Chapter 55

How the Pumpkins Saved a Family

When the Moore family moved to Ohio, about a hundred years ago, they had to carry with them everything they needed. They went in a covered wagon, with all their household goods, a long supply of provisions, guns, axes, implements with which to cultivate the farm and garden, and seeds to plant. Like all other pioneers who went into the wilderness of the West, they were prepared for almost any emergency. There could be no sending back home for anything!

The Moores built a log cabin by the side of a stream, and not far from the cabins of other pioneers like themselves. Around them was the deep forest, full of game. In the rivers and lakes there was an abundance of fish. The soil was very fertile and grew anything that was planted. Their cabin had but one room, with a big fireplace in which all the cooking was done. The boys slept in a loft, which they reached by a ladder from the inside.

The first winter was hard. It was cold outside, but Mr. Moore had cleaned up his land, and there was plenty of fuel; so that, when the wind roared and the snow fell, the family sat about the big fire and talked of the people back East, or discussed the plans for the spring planting. After the coals had been pulled over the embers, in order to have fire in the morning, the family went to bed, and covered themselves with the heavy robes they had bought from the natives. During the day, the boys trapped rabbits, and shot other game in the woods. So the family had plenty of meat to eat, though they had to be sparing of the meal and flour they had brought with them.

After the snow had melted, the ground was soft and ready for plowing and planting. Among the seed which Mr. Moore had brought were some pumpkin seed, and one of the boys, named Obed, was careful to plant them in a good place so that the pumpkins would flourish. He had not forgotten Halloween and Thanksgiving.

The crops did marvelously well. There was plenty of wheat, and corn, and potatoes, and the way those pumpkins grew was something to be proud of! Spring and summer passed, and winter came on again. There was now an abundance of food, ample wood for the winter, and everybody was well. The Moores were as happy and prosperous a pioneer family as one could find anywhere.

The only thing that gave any fear at all were the natives. Mrs. Moore had always been kind to them, and Mr. Moore had often given them tobacco and medicine. There was no reason why the Moores should be afraid of their native neighbors, but still they were, and Mr. Moore never left the house without misgivings.

On the Monday before Halloween, Mr. Moore set out for the nearest village on a two days' journey, to buy some things he needed for the winter. "Take care of the mother and the children," he told the boys, Joe and Obed, "and keep a sharp lookout for the natives." With that he mounted his horse and rode off down the trail.

Joe and Obed went into the garden, and brought in two immense pumpkins. With these they began to make jack-o'-lanterns, just as they did before they came to their new home in the West. They cut out the eyes and nose and mouth, and scooped out the inside of each pumpkin, making places for the candles. They were particular to make two as hideous heads as possible, though they had no idea what they would do with them afterwards.

Hardly had they finished the lanterns, than a man came riding up to the door. "They are coming! The natives are coming! Close your doors and get ready for an attack," he cried. "They are marching this way. Give me a fresh horse, for mine is broken down."

The boys quickly handed him over one of their horses, and led his exhausted animal into their barn. They barred the door and windows, put out the lights, for it was now dark, loaded their guns, and crouched down by the fireplace to wait. "If father were only here," whispered Joe to Obed. "Never mind," answered Obed, "we will give a good account of ourselves."

The two boys heard a sound in the yard. Even though it was dark, the snow had fallen that morning, so one could see fairly well. Cautiously peering through the windows, Obed caught sight of figures moving across the yard toward the cabin.

"They are coming," he whispered. "Give me the rifle."

Joe turned to get the gun, and his eyes fell on the two jack-o'-lanterns he and his brother had made. A great idea flashed through his mind. "It is worth trying, anyway," he said to himself. Then he seized a burning coal from the fire, and blew it into a blaze. Then he lighted two candles, and put them inside one of the pumpkins. He did the same thing with the other pumpkin.

"Here, Obed," he cried, "we will scare them."

Seizing one of the lanterns, with the light gleaming hideously from the great mouth and eyes and nose, Joe threw open the blind, and held the pumpkin in the window. Obed followed his brother's example.

By this time, a dozen natives were in the yard, making ready for

the attack. Seeing the hideous monsters at the windows, and hearing a loud groaning noise which Joe and Obed made, they were overcome with terror. The lanterns bobbed up and down, turned this way and that, and appeared to glare furiously at the intruders. Then the two boys let forth a hideous whoop, and fired off a gun.

This was too much for the natives. With loud yells, they fled into the forest, and did not stop running until they were miles away. Joe and Obed never tired of telling their friends how two pumpkins saved the Moore family from destruction.

Chapter 56

Old Ironsides

The good ship *Constitution* was built by order of Congress to fight the pirate ships of Algeria. She was built in Boston, and was designed to be a little bigger and a little better than any other fighting ship of her kind afloat.

The *Constitution* was made of the best material and with the greatest care. Workmen searched the lumber-yards of the South for oak, cedar and pine. Paul Revere, who made the famous midnight ride, furnished the copper. It took three years to build the frigate, and, when she was done, her timbers had seasoned until they were hard as iron.

The *Constitution* played her part in the war against the pirates of the Barbary Coast in Africa. For two years there was plenty of fighting, in which the frigate seemed to bear a charmed life. She never lost her mast, nor was she ever seriously injured in battle or in storm. She never lost a commanding officer, and only a few of her crew were killed.

It was during the War of 1812 that the *Constitution* won her chief glory. Her most remarkable feat was her escape from a British squadron.

At daybreak, toward the middle of July, 1812, off the New Jersey coast, the frigate found herself surrounded by a fleet of British ships that had crept up in the night. They were waiting for dawn to begin the attack. Captain Isaac Hull was in command of the *Constitution*, and had no idea of surrendering his ship. He thought only of means to escape from his danger.

Not a breath of air ruffled the water, and the sails of all the ships were useless. One of the British frigates was being towed by all the boats of her squadron, so as to get her near enough to the *Constitution* to open fire. The boats then expected to bring other frigates into position, and thus begin a general battle. This would seal the doom of the *Constitution*. Without wind, there was no chance for her to get away. But Hull was not to be caught. He thought of his anchor and windlass.

"How much water have we under this ship?" he shouted. Upon being told he had twenty fathoms, he cried out,

"Bring up the anchor and all the spare ropes and cable. Then all hands to the boats!"

The order was quickly obeyed. Putting the anchor into a boat, it was carried a mile ahead and dropped into the ocean. The ropes and cables attached to it were still fastened to the windlass.

The men on the ship began to wind up the windlass, and gradually drew the boat along to the place where the anchor was dropped.

Then the anchor was moved ahead another mile, and the boat drawn up again. In this manner, slow progress was made through the water, but it was better than not making any headway at all.

The pursuit was kept up for two days. But slowly the *Constitution* gained on her pursuers, until, after a two days' chase, the enemy was four miles astern.

A squall gave Hull his chance to open sails and hide behind the rain and cloud-banks. In a few hours, the weather cleared, and the British were almost out of sight. They soon abandoned the chase,

The *Guerriere* was a helpless bulk in the water.

and Hull took his frigate into Boston harbor, amid the cheers of the people.

In less than two weeks, he was out again, searching the ocean for British craft, and ready to give battle to any vessel he might meet. The British had a fine frigate, named the *Guerriere*, commanded by Captain Dacres, who was a personal friend of Captain Hull. The *Guerriere* had challenged any vessel of the American fleet to battle, and was cruising on the Atlantic, waiting for an answer. The *Constitution* went out to accept the challenge.

Years before this, Dacres and Hull had been talking about a possible battle between their frigates. "If we ever meet in combat, I wager a fine hat I will make you surrender," said Dacres to Hull.

"Agreed," was the laughing reply of Captain Hull. "I expect to win that hat some day."

In August, about seven hundred miles from Boston, the two vessels met. The *Constitution* and the *Guerriere* were the finest frigates in the world, their Commanders equally brave, their men equally matched. It was a question of ship management and gun power.

The British frigate flung out a flag of defiance from each topmast. Her guns began to roar, but the balls fell short of the *Constitution*.

"Don't fire until I give the word. Let the two vessels draw near together before we open. Keep steady and ready, and never mind their guns," said Hull to his men.

The two ships drifted nearer and nearer. The enemy's broadsides tore through the rigging of the *Constitution*. One of the enemy's balls struck the side of the vessel, and fell into the sea. A sailor, looking overboard, said,

"See the balls falling away from her. She's an old ironside, sir, an old ironside."

From that time on, the *Constitution* was called "Old Ironsides."

The two vessels came fairly abreast, near enough for the men to see each other, and for good pistol shot.

"Ready, men, do your full duty and fire," shouted Hull.

Broadside after broadside was poured into the *Guerriere*. First her mizzen mast fell, then her foremast was cut down, then her rigging and flag; she was soon a helpless hulk in the water.

Dacres surrendered, and came on board the *Constitution* to deliver his sword to his old friend. But Hull smilingly said,

"No, Dacres, you can keep the sword, for you are too brave a man to be without one. I want that hat you and I wagered some years ago."

When "Old Ironsides" sailed into Boston on the last day of August, you may well believe the people shouted themselves hoarse, and waved flags, and hung out bunting, and gave grand dinners in honor of this great naval victory.

Chapter 57

Tecumseh

Tecumseh was probably one of the greatest Native American that race has ever produced. He was the most eloquent orator ever known among the native tribes. When he spoke, his voice was deep and full, like an organ, his face shone with emotion, and his words were remarkable for their poetic beauty.

His father was a Shawnee warrior, and was killed in battle with English settlers, when Tecumseh was a mere child. This impressed him with a great resolve to keep the Englishmen out of the native lands, and to fight them whenever he could.

He possessed a sensitive dignity, as is shown by the following incident. Upon one occasion, when he came with his warriors to hold a conference with General Harrison, he looked around, after he had finished his address, to find a seat. Seeing that none had been reserved for him, he appeared offended.

A soldier, seated near General Harrison, arose and offered him his seat, saying, "Your father wishes you to sit by his side."

"The sun is my father, and the earth is my mother. I shall sit in his light and rest on her bosom," said Tecumseh. Whereupon, he sat down

Tecumseh

on the ground, in the full light of the sun.

Tecumseh was a noble soldier, and never allowed any prisoners to be tortured. He promised General Harrison that, in case of war between the natives and the Americans, he would not permit his warriors to massacre women and children. He faithfully kept his word. But at the siege of Fort Meigs, the natives began killing their prisoners. Tecumseh ran in, and bade them stop at once. Turning to General Procter, who stood looking on, he cried out,

"Why do you permit this outrage? Why did you not stop those men, and save those wretched prisoners?"

Procter replied that the natives could not be restrained, and that he could not prevent the massacre.

Tecumseh was furious at this, and said, "Begone, you coward. You are not fit to command men."

Procter was not a brave soldier, and, at one time, burned his stores and abandoned his fort, even though he had a thousand men and three thousand native allies. Tecumseh was so disgusted with his cowardice, that he compared him to a fat dog, who barked and held his tail high, when there was no danger, but who howled, and dropped his tail between his legs and ran, whenever any one attacked him.

When Tecumseh went to Alabama to stir up the Creek tribe against the settlers of that section, he found them unwilling to rise against their neighbors and friends. All his eloquence failed to move them, and, to all his appeals and threats, they merely shook their heads. Finally, in a burst of anger, he cried out,

"Your blood no longer runs red like the rising sun. You do not fight because you are cowards and are afraid to fight. You do not believe the Great Spirit has sent me, but you shall believe it. I am going back to Detroit. It will take me many days, but when I reach there, I shall tell the Great Spirit, and I shall stamp my foot on the ground, and shake every house in your village."

So saying, he left, and journeyed northward. The natives counted the days until he should reach home. Strangely enough, about the time he was due there, an earthquake shook the village. They rushed wildly for their dwellings, crying out,

"Tecumseh has arrived in Detroit; he has told the Great Spirit; we feel the stamping of his foot!"

The last battle in which this warrior was engaged was that of the Thames. The Americans had been pursuing the British and their native allies for some time, until Tecumseh was tired of the disgraceful state of affairs, and told the British officer, Procter, that he would retreat no longer. "We will stand here and give battle," said he. "I and my warriors were not made for running away from our enemies."

The result was the battle of the Thames. At the opening of the conflict, Tecumseh turned to his friends, and said,

"Brother warriors, I shall never come out of this battle alive. I go there to die, but I go. My body will remain on the field, I know it will be so."

He unbuckled his sword, and handed it to one of his Chiefs, and said, "When my son becomes a great warrior, give him this sword, and tell him his father died like a brave Chief and a hero. Tell my people I died for their rights." With that, he also took off the British uniform, which he had been wearing, and put on his own native dress.

The battle raged for a while with fury. Procter at last fled through the swamps and wilderness, escaping with a few followers. Tecumseh, however, brandishing his club, rushed upon his pursuers, and fell, pierced with many wounds.

Chapter 58

The Star-Spangled Banner

During the War of 1812, the British fleet blockaded our ports and sailed up our rivers to attack our cities and forts. Thus, they entered the Chesapeake Bay, and landed troops outside Washington City.

A battle was fought near there, but the British were not stopped from pursuing their way to the capital. The city was in great danger and the people hastened to gather their possessions and made their escape. There were only eight thousand inhabitants in Washington at that time. It was a small town, as compared with its great size and splendor, today.

A messenger rode in haste to bid the people flee. He came to the White House, where Dolly Madison, the wife of President James Madison, was waiting for her husband. He called out to her, "Mr. Madison says go, or the house will be burned over your head. The British are on the way to the capital. There is no time to lose. Escape as quickly as you can."

Dolly Madison did not go at once, but set about gathering the Cabinet papers, and the Declaration of Independence, which she made a servant pack in a trunk. Then she ordered a large portrait of Washington to be cut out of its frame, and rolled up so she could take that too. Having done these things, she escaped with her treasures, just as the British were entering the city.

The soldiers marched into the deserted town, and burned the Treasury Building, the Public Library, and the White House. A notorious officer, named Cockburn, followed by a mob of soldiers, entered the new Capitol, climbed into the Speaker's chair, and called out: "Shall this harbor of Yankee Democracy be burned?"

The mob of soldiers called out, "Aye," and proceeded to apply the torch to the building.

Dolly Madison found refuge with her friends in the country. When she and the President returned to Washington, they had to live in a rented house.

About three weeks after the burning of the city, the British began to attack Fort McHenry, which was built to protect the harbor of Baltimore. One evening, the British sent two bomb vessels, and a number of barges, filled with soldiers, to pass the fort and assail it in the rear.

But the noise of their oars was heard in the darkness, and an order was given to open fire on them. A deadly discharge was poured out from Fort McHenry upon the creeping craft, with the result that nearly all of them were sent to the bottom.

The English suffered so much from this repulse that they abandoned the attack and sailed away.

During the bombardment, Francis Scott Key, a young lawyer, was sent, under a flag of truce, to convey a message to the British fleet. His purpose was to secure the release of several prisoners.

Francis Scott Key

After delivering his message, Key and his party were on the point of departure, when an officer said,

"Mr. Key, I have orders to detain you and your party until the bombardment is over. You will, therefore, remain here."

Key did not like to be held, but there was no help for it. So he and his associates were kept in a little vessel moored to the side of an English ship, under guard of a body of soldiers. Here, on the deck, they witnessed the bombardment of the fort.

All night long the shells were fired. Key watched each one as it fell upon the fort, and listened for each explosion. Suddenly, before the morning dawned, the firing ceased.

"Has the fort surrendered, or have the British abandoned the attack?" was the anxious thought in the minds of the weary watchers.

There was no way to find out until day came. "If the flag is still flying, then the fort has not surrendered," said Key to his companions. Anxiously they paced the deck.

As day dawned, they turned their glasses toward the fort, and, to their great joy, they saw the flag was still there. Key was overcome with emotion. Drawing a letter from his pocket, he wrote on the back of it the opening lines of our national song, "The Star-Spangled Banner."

Later in the day, a small boat took him back to Baltimore. On his way he completed the poem. That very night, he corrected it, and wrote it out as we now have it. The next day, he showed the poem to a friend of his, who was so pleased that he had it printed in a Baltimore paper.

When the words appeared, they were eagerly memorized by an

actor, named Charles Durang, who stood on a chair and, for the first time, sang them to a crowd. Then, everybody joined in.

Soon the piece was being sung all over the country. It is our great national song, and whenever it is played or sung, we rise reverently and uncover our heads, proud of our great flag and of the deeds of valor it has encouraged.

To their great joy, they saw the flag was still there.

Chapter 59

Traveling by the Canal

Long before the days of railroads and automobiles, the people of the country had to travel from one place to another by means of stagecoaches and wagons, over rough roads, and with a great deal of discomfort. The pioneers made use of the rivers when they could, for traveling by water was much easier than jolting, or sticking in the mud every few miles.

The people began to think of a system of waterways, or canals, to connect the rivers with one another, and to open up communication with the Great Lakes and the Atlantic Ocean. The greatest of all these channels is the Erie Canal, extending from Albany, on the Hudson River, to Buffalo, on Lake Erie. By it, an all-water way was secured from New York to the Great Lakes, opening up traffic between the East and the rapidly growing West.

The Canal was a great enterprise. It took eight years to build, was three hundred and sixty-three miles long, forty feet wide, and, at first, only four feet deep. Later on it was made seven feet deep. It cost something over seven million dollars to construct, an expense which was borne by the State of New York. Governor DeWitt Clinton was the genius of the Canal, and devoted his energies to making it a success. People laughed at him, and called the Canal "Clinton's Ditch." But he went on, year by year, with an army of workmen, cutting down trees, leveling land, blasting through rock, building stone aqueducts across streams, and constructing locks from one level to another.

At last, the Canal was completed, in 1824. Governor Clinton went through it on the first boat. It was named the Seneca-Chief, and was drawn by four gray horses. It started from Buffalo, on its way to Albany. The boat carried a bear, two native boys, two eagles, and other things representing the Great West; also a keg of water from Lake Erie to empty into the Atlantic Ocean, so as to show that the waters of the two great bodies were united at last. Camion, stationed one every five miles from Buffalo to New York, announced the progress of the boat. It took eighty-one minutes to let the people in New York know that the boat had started from Buffalo. All along the way, she was greeted with the ringing of bells, the booming of cannon, the waving of flags, and the shouting of enthusiastic people. When the boat arrived in New York, a great celebration was held in honor of the event.

The canal-boat was a curious affair, about eighty feet long and twelve feet wide and three feet draught. On its deck was a cabin, in which were cramped sleeping-quarters. In the daytime, the bunks were folded out of sight, to make room for the tables at which the passengers ate. It was drawn by horses or mules, hitched to a long towline, and its speed was about two miles an hour. It was against the rules to go faster than four miles, for fear the wash of the water, caused by the motion of the boat, would damage the banks.

Stops were frequent, and passage through the locks caused much loss of time. Now and again, the passengers got off the boat to look around, and often they were left behind. Then they had to run along the banks, overtake the boat, and scramble aboard the best way they could. In fine weather, they sat in chairs on the deck outside the cabin, and enjoyed the scenery as they glided slowly along. Small villages were passed, then farms and forests. The canal wound among the hills, and went straight across a level area.

Sometimes, when the weather was good, the passengers were allowed to walk on the tow-path by the side of the canal. It was a slow but pleasant journey: fortunately, in those days, nobody was in a hurry.

One of the inconveniences was the frequency of the low bridges, under which the boat had to pass. If a passenger was not constantly on the lookout, he would be swept off the deck by a bridge, and find himself in the water. It was the helmsman's duty to cry out, "Low bridge!" and then all the passengers would either have

to duck their heads or go below. It was accounted great fun to leap from the deck on to the bridge, as the boat approached it, and then, having crossed, to leap back on the boat again.

Thus, the boat went along, full of freight in the hold, and passengers in the cabin and on the deck. It took six or seven days to cover the entire distance. We can cross the continent, or the Atlantic Ocean, in that time now, and go the same distance in less than a day.

On wet and cold days, travel by the Canal was not pleasant, for the passengers had to stay in the cabin, and suffer the discomfort of close quarters, with nothing to see and nothing to do.

After the coming of railroads, the Erie Canal ceased to be popular as a means of passenger travel. It was too slow and uncomfortable. But for freight it is still used.

Chapter 60

Lafayette's Return to America

In 1824, Lafayette, now an old man, longed to visit once more the people of America, and to see again the scenes of his youthful glory. Congress at once invited him to be the nation's guest.

More than forty years had passed since he had come to America's aid. The thirteen colonies were now twenty-four states. The nation was prosperous, peaceful, and a powerful Republic of twelve million people. Towns and villages had sprung up, and even the West was being opened to adventurous explorers and settlers.

Death had claimed many of the intimate friends of Lafayette. Washington had been dead for twenty-five years. Greene, Wayne, Marion and Morgan were all gone. Lafayette was the last surviving Major-General of the Revolution. But there were many veteran soldiers yet alive, and there was an entire nation of grateful people to welcome him to the shores of America.

Lafayette himself had had a busy and turbulent career since his part in the American War for Independence. He had fought the battles of liberty in his own country and had for five years been a prisoner in an Austrian dungeon. But in spite of this exciting life, he was still a strong and vigorous man.

In appearance, he was very tall and rather stout. He had a round face, with regular features and a high forehead. His complexion was clear, and his cheeks were red. He had lost his hair in the Austrian prison, and wore a curly, reddish-brown wig to conceal his entirely bald head.

Accompanied by his son, George Washington Lafayette, and his private secretary, Lafayette reached New York in August, 1824. Six thousand citizens aboard gaily-dressed vessels went out to meet his approaching ship. With cannon booming from the forts, and with flags flying from every masthead and building, the boat, bearing the distinguished foreigner, came to shore while many thousands of people lined the docks, and shouted, "Welcome, Lafayette! All honor to the nation's guest!"

In a few days, Lafayette went to Washington D.C., and President Monroe formally received him at the White House as the guest of the American people. From that time on, for more than a year, he was engaged in a long series of receptions in every state of the Union.

Having promised to attend the graduating exercises of Harvard College, Lafayette started for Boston. There were no railroads in those days and traveling was done by carriages. His party, therefore, traveled for five days from early morning until late at night.

Every village had its triumphal arch, and its procession of citizens and soldiers. Over the streets were mottoes of greeting to the great friend of Washington. Music and banquets and speeches of welcome greeted the party along the entire way.

People gathered from many miles around, and camped along the road to see his carriage pass. A large procession of horsemen followed him, as escort, from place to place. Cannon were fired, bells were rung, and bonfires were built by the eager and grateful crowds.

In this fashion the party came to Boston; and it was thus the people of the United States greeted their guest wherever he went.

A few weeks after his arrival, Lafayette went to Yorktown to attend the celebration of the anniversary of the surrender of Cornwallis, which had occurred forty-three years before. He was entertained in the house which had been Cornwallis's headquarters. Lafayette was provided with a bed; but many distinguished persons had to sleep in tents or on straw upon the floors of the houses, so great was the crowd.

A laurel wreath was offered to Lafayette at Yorktown; after wearing it on his head for a short while, he gave it to his friend, Colonel Nicholas Fish, who had helped him take a fort at Yorktown. "You must wear this also," he said. "It belongs to you more than it does to me."

As these two old comrades later on sailed up the Hudson River, Lafayette turned to Colonel Fish, and said, "Nicholas, do you remember when we were young, how we used to slide down those hills in an ox-sled with the girls from Newburgh?"

Then they fell to talking about the old times during the Revolution; often they would laugh over some remembered incident, and then again their eyes would fill with tears.

In Nashville, Tennessee, the hero was given a rousing welcome. In New Orleans, a band of Choctaw natives, who had been camped there for a month, awaiting his arrival, marched before his carriage to see "the great warrior, brother

Marquis de Lafayette in 1823

of our good father, Washington."

Lafayette visited Mt. Vernon, the home of Washington. He went through the rooms, the halls, and over the grounds, with which he had been so familiar. He went to the tomb of his good chief, and stood with bowed head before the stone coffin. Reverently, he knelt and kissed the last resting-place of the great man he had served so well and loved so truly. Tears were in his eyes as he rejoined his waiting companions.

Many other places did Lafayette visit in America. He was present at the laying of the corner-stone of the Bunker Hill monument; he visited the aged Jefferson in Virginia; he went to Philadelphia.

In September, 1825, he was given a farewell dinner at the White House by the new President, John Quincy Adams, and, shortly afterwards, sailed for France, amid the blessings and prayers of a grateful nation.

Chapter 61

Osceola, the Seminole Chief

When Florida was purchased by the United States from Spain, there remained on that territory the Seminole tribe, who had to be dealt with. But the Americans wished the natives to be removed at once.

They said to the natives, "We have bought all this land from Spain. You have no right to occupy it, and we propose to take it away from you. We will pay you for it, but you must give it up and go West, where we will give you other land."

The Seminole Chief replied, "This is the land of my forefathers. We owned it before the Spaniards ever heard of it. They never bought it from us, and they cannot sell it to you. We do not recognize your right, and we shall not move."

One of the Chiefs of the Seminoles was Osceola. His wife was the daughter of an escaped slave. She was born in the Everglades, and, when she grew to be a young woman, the Chief married her with all the ceremony of his tribe.

Once, when Osceola and his young wife were visiting one of the United States forts, she was seized and claimed as a slave by her mother's former owner. The law at that time was that the children of slaves belonged to the owners of their parents. The woman was, therefore, torn from the side of her husband and carried off.

Osceola stormed in his great wrath. He strove with those around him, and cried out in agony when he saw his wife thus being taken away. He was bound in irons, and kept a close prisoner, until she was safely gone. Then he was given his freedom, and told to be off!

When he reached the Everglades, he assembled his tribe, and described to them all his wrongs. Thereupon, he swore an undying vengeance against the United States government.

The Seminoles met in council with the agents of the United States to discuss a treaty which provided for their removal elsewhere. Osceola was present, and listened in silence to the talk of both parties. When called upon to give his answer, he drew his knife, and struck it deep into the table before him. "With that knife, and with that alone, will I fight for the lands of my forefathers," he said, and walked from the room.

Thus, began a long war between the Seminoles and the white men of Florida. Many a bloody battle was fought. The Seminoles had their homes along the edges of the swamp, and deep in the Everglades of Florida. These pathless and almost impenetrable regions furnished hiding-places for the natives, and it was almost impossible to track them to their retreats.

Word was sent by Osceola to all members of the tribe that any chief who signed a treaty with the whites, or who promised to go West should be put to death. He heard that one of his Chiefs was more peaceably inclined than the others. "Let him be slain for his treachery," ordered Osceola, and it was done the same night.

The settlers of Florida now felt the full fury of the Seminoles. Bands of natives and their followers roved over the state attacking mail carriers, stage-coaches, and small settlements. Troops were sent against them, but what could they do against such a foe, that fought from ambush, and, whenever pursued, disappeared in the swamps?

A body of soldiers, about one hundred and forty in number, was met by the natives in ambuscade. All were shot down but two.

The very same day, Osceola and a few followers surprised General Wiley Thomson, sent by the Government to urge the removal of the Seminoles. He and his friends were at dinner.

Bursting in upon them, with a loud yell, and brandishing his knife, Osceola seized General Thomson and killed him. The rest of the party escaped.

Thus did Osceola spread terror in Florida. The settlers became so alarmed, that whole towns in the interior were forsaken, the people hastening to the forts, or to the coast for protection. Hundreds of United States' soldiers were perishing from the fevers

Osceola, the Seminole Chief

of the swamps and the bites of venomous reptiles.

After the war had been going on for two years, Osceola came to General Jesup, Commander of troops in Florida, under a flag of truce. But no sooner did he enter the conference, with the rest of his followers, than General Jesup gave orders that he be arrested. He claimed that this was the only way in which he could stop the lawlessness of this Chief, who never felt himself bound by any obligation to the government.

Osceola was sent to Charleston, and there confined in Fort Moultrie. For two years he lingered a prisoner, broken-hearted and ruined in health. At length, in 1839, he died of a fever, and was buried just outside the fort.

The war went on for about seven years, and did not end until all the natives were found and sent to the West.

Chapter 62

An Early Journey by Railroad

Those of us who travel on the railroad trains of today, over smooth rails and in comfortable seats, taking our meals in the dining-cars, going to sleep in berths by night, and waking up for breakfast at our destination several hundred miles away, present a strange contrast to those who had the discomfort of early travel.

One of the first railroads of any size and importance, ran between Charleston and Hamburg, South Carolina, opened in January, 1831. It was a curious-looking affair. The locomotive was small, and, fed with fat pine, sent out clouds of smoke and red hot cinders.

The coaches for the passengers were like huge barrels, mounted on trucks. The conductor walked on a little platform outside, and collected fares through small windows. The rails were flat, and the wheels ran in deep grooves. Not being securely fastened to the ties, the rails would sometimes curve like snake heads, and run up through the bottom of the coach, much to the peril and alarm of the passengers.

When the road was opened, the stockholders made of the event a day of great rejoicing, though it was cold and cloudy and the journey any tiling but comfortable. Great crowds of people along the way met the train, and begged for a ride.

A sad accident befell the locomotive on one of its journeys. The fireman, tired of listening to the escaping steam, and thinking to save power, fastened down the steam valve, and then sat on it to make sure that it was closed. The steam mounted to exploding point, and the fireman was blown into a nearby cotton patch.

Another early railroad trip was across the Mohawk Valley. On this occasion, the engineer wore a dress-coat, out of compliment to some very distinguished guests who were aboard. The carriages were the bodies of old stage-coaches placed upon trucks. After collecting the fares, the conductor mounted a seat on the tender of the locomotive, and blew some notes on a tin horn, to signify that all was ready.

Amid the cheers of the crowd the locomotive started. The coaches were joined together by chains, and, as the slack was taken up, the passengers were jolted backward or forward, some of them being thrown from their seats. No one dared stand up, but held on to the seats for dear life.

The fuel consisted of dry pitch, and, when the train was well under way, a cloud of hot cinders, smoke, and sparks came from the funnel of the engine and poured into the coaches. After much coughing and rubbing of eyes, the passengers raised their umbrellas to shelter themselves.

This, however, was no protection, for the umbrellas soon caught fire and had to be thrown overboard. The passengers, in a state of frantic fear, spent their time beating each other with handkerchiefs, hats, and canes, in order to put out the fire that momentarily threatened to catch the clothes and endanger the lives of every one.

But that was in 1831. Today, one can travel across the continent, from ocean to ocean, with as much comfort as he can have by staying in a hotel or at home.

Chapter 63

Old Hickory

Andrew Jackson was born of Scotch-Irish parents on the border between North and South Carolina. His father died about the time he was born, and his mother had to support her three boys by spinning flax.

Jackson grew up to be a tall, slender lad, with red hair and a freckled face. He was very wild, quick-tempered, and mischievous. He had many quarrels with his companions, and many fights, but, at home, he was devoted to his mother, and showed kindness to the horses and other animals on the farm. He was a fearless rider, and all his life owned fine horses.

When Jackson was fourteen years of age, the Revolution was still in progress. The British army had swept through the neighborhood of his home, and the boy had seen his relatives and neighbors suffering and dying.

The local church was used as a hospital, and Jackson's mother often went there to nurse the sick and wounded. Andrew and his brother Robert ran errands for her, and were in and out of the church so often that they soon became familiar with the horrors of war.

At one time, Andrew and his brother were taken prisoners by the British, and were confined in the house of their own cousin. The English officers had everything they wished, and one of them ordered Jackson to clean his muddy boots.

Andrew replied, "I am a prisoner of war and not a servant. You may clean them yourself."

This enraged the British officer to such an extent that he struck at the boy with his sword, wounding him on his head and hand. Jackson carried the scars with him all his life. Robert also received rough treatment from the brutal officers.

The boys were carried forty miles away, to a prison camp, and not allowed any food or water. There, smallpox broke out, and both boys were quite sick with it. Their mother secured their release, but Robert, suffering from wounds and fever, died two days after he reached home, and Andrew was ill for many weeks. Before he was quite well his mother also died.

At seventeen years of age, he began to study law. When he was twenty-one, he moved to Tennessee, and became a prominent lawyer in that new and wild country. In his efforts to preserve law and order among the frontiersmen and adventurers of that section, he had many personal difficulties. He was hot-tempered and a good shot, and frontier life was rough.

During the War of 1812, a band of the Creek tribe attacked Fort Mimms in southern Alabama and killed four or five hundred people. Tennessee raised a body of troops to go after the Creeks and punish them. Jackson was chosen Commander.

He was in bed at the time, suffering from wounds he had received in a quarrel two weeks before. His physician ordered him to stay where he was, but Jackson arose, put his arm in a sling, and, though almost fainting from weakness and loss of blood, he mounted his horse and started on the campaign. He was gone eight months, and the Creeks were severely punished.

Once, during the campaign, some soldiers grew mutinous because food was scarce and they threatened to leave. Jackson, with his arm in a sling, rode up to them, and, taking his pistol in his free hand, said, "I will shoot the first man that moves." The soldiers knew he would do it, and there was no further trouble.

His endurance during this campaign earned for him the name of "Old Hickory" because he was so tough; and because, though he would often bend, he would not break. In appearance, he was tall, erect, and spare, with dark blue eyes and heavy eyebrows. All through life his temper was fiery, and easily aroused when he was opposed.

Andrew Jackson

His greatest fame as a general rests upon his victory over the British at the battle of New Orleans. Here, with a force of ill-prepared and untrained men, he gave a crushing defeat to a larger body of splendidly trained English soldiers. More than seven hundred of the enemy were killed, fourteen hundred were wounded, and five hundred were taken prisoners. Jackson had only eight men killed and fourteen wounded.

He became President of the United States when he was past sixty years of age. He was always a plain man of the people, who hated his enemies and wanted them punished; and who loved his friends and wanted them rewarded. He was a strong-minded President, who had his own way without asking advice.

Chapter 64

Daniel Webster

Daniel Webster was born on a farm in New Hampshire. He was the youngest of a family of ten children, and, as a child, was frail and delicate. For this reason, he was much petted by his parents and brothers and sisters, and was allowed to run free in the forests and fields near his home, in the hope that this freedom and exercise would bring him strength of body.

His mother and sisters taught him to read. In after years, he said he could not remember the time when he could not read the Bible. He had a very retentive memory.

His voice was musical, and when he read aloud, he gave great pleasure to those who heard him. Often, the men who came to his father's mill would get him to read to them while they waited for their meal to be ground. Sometimes the farmers, passing the house where he lived, stopped for an hour or two to rest their horses, and then they always sent for the boy, and generally they would say, "Daniel, read us something from the Bible."

Daniel had a brother, named Ezekiel, two years older than himself, of whom he was very fond. This brother always watched over the delicate boy, and kept him from too much exertion. The father told Ezekiel to let Daniel help him, especially in the light work of the farm. Once, the boys' father returned home from a trip, and asked Ezekiel what he had been doing.

"Nothing, sir," replied the boy.

The father then asked Daniel what he had been doing.

"I have been helping Zeke, sir," said Daniel, with a smile.

One day, when Daniel was at the village store, he saw a handkerchief for sale, on which was printed a copy of the Constitution of the United States. He resolved to be the owner of that handkerchief, and saved enough pennies to buy it. When at last he bought it, he did not rest until he had learned the whole great document by heart. In after years, he became its most able exponent and defender.

Webster's father was poor, and with but little learning himself. He was wise enough, however, to know the value of education. He told his son he intended to send him to college. Webster was so anxious to go that, for a moment, he could not speak for emotion. He afterwards said, "A warm glow ran all over me, and I laid my head on my father's shoulder and wept."

He became one of the greatest orators this country has produced, but, at first, he was much frightened when he stood before an audience. At school the boys made fun of him and of his clothes. Such ridicule caused him to be sensitive.

He said of this time, "Many a piece did I commit to memory, and rehearse it in my room over and over again. But when the day came, and all my companions were on hand, gazing at me, and I was required to stand before them, I was so frightened that I could not utter a word."

After leaving college, Webster began his law career in his native state. He moved to Boston later on, where he built up a large practice. He was soon called into political life, and spent thirty years in the service of his state. He was a close student of the Constitution, an orator of tremendous force, and a profound thinker on all political questions of his day.

Webster overcame the weakness of his boyhood days, and grew into a vigorous man. His appearance was noble, sturdy, and dignified. His eyes were dark, and his brow was massive. People said, "When Webster walks the streets of Boston, he makes the buildings look small." Once he visited Europe, and some one, passing him in the street, remarked, "Surely, there goes a king."

He is best known for his wonderful oration in defense of the powers of the Constitution to maintain an unbroken union of the states. A great debate was held in the Senate of the United States on the subject, and against Webster was Robert Hayne, of South Carolina, who spoke on the right of a state to declare null and void within its borders any act passed by Congress.

Hayne made a great argument, and Webster replied to him the next day. He had but one night for preparation, but he remarked to a friend, "That is enough. All my life I have been making ready for this occasion." On the morning of his reply, he said, "The people shall learn this day, before the sun goes down, what I understand the Constitution to be."

When he spoke, the galleries were crowded, the senators were all in their places, and every one realized a crisis was at hand. Webster took four hours, delivering one of the greatest speeches of his life.

At the laying of the corner-stone of Bunker Hill monument, he delivered another great oration. Thousands of persons were present, and the crowd pressed forward so

Daniel Webster

eagerly that they came near carrying away the platform on which the speakers were sitting.

Webster appealed to them to stand back. "We cannot, Mr. Webster," they cried; "it is impossible." "Impossible!" thundered the great orator, "I tell you that nothing is impossible on Bunker Hill."

The people, moved by his eloquent words, rolled back like waves from the shore.

Chapter 65

Henry Clay

This is the story of a poor boy, who, through his own energy and ability, rose to a position of power and usefulness. There are many such stories to be told in the history of our country.

Henry Clay was born in Virginia. His father died when he was a child, leaving a large family and a small farm. The brave mother had to struggle hard to provide for her children, and could give them but a limited education. All the schooling Henry had, he gained in a little log cabin in the country.

He had to work on the farm, and to help around the house. This meant getting up at daybreak, and going to bed early. As soon as he was big enough to guide a plow, he was entrusted with the plowing and cultivating. All this gave him vigor of body and independence of mind.

One of his duties was to ride an old horse to the mill, with a bag of corn or wheat for a saddle, and to bring back the meal or flour for the use of the family. In after years, he was called "the millboy of the Slashes," because the Slashes was the name of the district in which he lived.

When Clay was about fifteen, he moved to Richmond, and became a copying clerk in one of the Courts. It was his duty to keep a copy of the records. When he first entered the office, he was tall and awkward, and was dressed in a badly fitting suit of homespun clothes which his mother had made for him. But Clay had a genial, sunny nature, which did not mind what others said of him, and he soon made many friends.

Moreover, he was a careful clerk who wrote a good hand. Whenever the Judge wished a record particularly well done, he selected Clay for the job. When the day's work was over, Clay would go home to read, while the other clerks went out for amusement.

He now began to study law, and was soon admitted to the bar. He felt that he could become a great orator, and made special effort to train his voice and memory. He would read some good book, such as a history, and then attempt to recite the words or repeat the sense of what he had just read. In this way he learned history, and cultivated an excellent command of language.

It was also his custom to go into the woods, sometimes in his barn, and try out his speeches. He would select some subject, think carefully over all he wished to say upon it, and then rehearse by himself, or with only the cattle as audience. Thus he acquired the power of continuous speech.

He organized a debating club among the young men of Richmond, and they met regularly to discuss the burning questions which were then disturbing the public mind. In all these ways by study, practice, and persistence, he laid the foundation for his great career as a lawyer and statesman.

When Clay was twenty-one, he moved to Kentucky and began to practice law. He was successful from the start, and had many clients. It was said that no murderer, who was defended by Clay, ever suffered the extreme penalty of the law. His nature was sympathetic, especially toward the poor, and he was always glad to take their cases, and see that they secured justice.

Throughout his life, he was most polite and attentive in his manners. At one time, he was riding with his young son, when they met a slave man who lifted his hat most respectfully. Clay replied to the greeting, but the son did not notice the old man. Clay turned to his son and said, "My boy, courtesy towards others is always the mark of a true gentleman."

So pleasing was Clay in his manners that, upon one occasion, a political enemy refused to be introduced to him, saying, "I am afraid to meet Mr. Clay for fear his fine manners will change my opposition to him into admiration and support."

He held many public offices, and served the country most notably during a long life. He was greatly beloved by the people of Kentucky. But he could not please all the time, and often had to explain to his people the reasons for his actions.

Upon one occasion an old hunter became dissatisfied with the way Clay had voted upon certain measures, and declared he would not support him again. Clay met him a few days before the election, and said to him,

"You have a fine rifle that has not often failed you. Sometimes, however, it flashes in the pan, and it does not go off. Do you throw it away, or do you try it again?"

The hunter looked at Clay, and replied,

"Well, I pick the flint, and wipe out the barrel, and try it again. Any rifle will flash sometimes."

"Well," responded Clay, "I am a pretty good rifle, and if I have flashed in the pan once or twice, why throw me away?"

The man agreed that this suggestion was just, and voted for Clay the rest of his life.

Henry Clay always used his powers of persuasion to keep peace and harmony among the quarreling sections of the country. He tried to avert strife and war, and to be a peace-maker. For this reason he is called "The Great Pacificator."

He was a statesman of rare courage, as well as of remarkable power. He never went against his conscience for the sake of retaining office or of winning high positions. Once, when told that certain measures of his on compromising the disputes about slavery would ruin his chances to become President, he replied,

"I would rather be right than be President."

He never was President, though he was a candidate for that high office. But it is to his greater fame that he would not sacrifice any principle to win popular favor, or high position, or private gain. He was really a great man, for his policy was to do without rather than do what he thought was wrong.

Chapter 66

John C. Calhoun

Webster, Clay, and Calhoun are known as the great trio. They were all poor boys, they all worked on farms, and became great by force of keen intellect, hard study, and high resolve. They lived about the same time and were concerned with the same great national questions.

Calhoun was born and reared in South Carolina. When he was a boy, he worked in the fields with his father, and listened to stories of the Revolution, as the two sat by the fire on winter nights. From the first he loved to listen to the deeds of great men.

He grew up to be a quiet, thoughtful, studious boy, fond of rambling through the woods, and equally as fond of reading history. The schools at that time were poor, and Calhoun did not have much chance to get an education. Besides, he had to work on the farm.

He spent his spare time reading such books as he could borrow from his friends or buy from his small stock of money. When his father died, he took charge of the farm. He soon determined that he would be a farmer for life.

His brother, however, would not hear of this; he wanted John to be a professional man. Arrangements, therefore, were made to send him to school for two years, and then to Yale College for the study of law.

He was about twenty years of age when he entered Yale, and he became the leader of his class. He sometimes would get into discussions with the President of the College over political matters and expressed himself so openly and so ably that the President became filled with admiration.

Upon one occasion, Calhoun was asked his views on a certain point in politics. He arose and stated them so clearly and powerfully that the President of Yale was thunderstruck! He afterwards said, "That young man, Calhoun, is able, very able. He will become a great man, possibly the President of the United States."

But, like Webster and Clay, Calhoun was destined never to reach that high office. His very greatness made him unsuited to the demands of political campaigns. Such men as Calhoun need no office to fix their places in history.

After studying law for several years, he began to practice in South Carolina, but he confessed he did not enjoy it. He called reading law "a dry and solitary journey." He preferred history and loved to study and discuss the political issues of the day.

He soon entered public life and was sent to Congress just about the time the War of 1812 began. His associates were charmed with his powers of oratory. His great blue eyes glowed like coals of fire, his hair fell in masses about his broad forehead, and his full voice poured forth a rich volume of ringing words.

When Andrew Jackson was President, Calhoun had become one of the great leaders of the nation. It was the time of heated agitation over the question of the tariff. The Northern States wanted a heavy tariff to protect the home manufacture of goods, thus keeping out foreign competition. The Southern States wanted a low tariff, or none at all, so that they could buy goods anywhere at the cheapest prices.

It was a bitter controversy between the two sections, and Calhoun was ever the leader of the Southern States in their demand for a low tariff. At last, when the protective tariff bill of 1832 was passed, Calhoun wrote a letter to the people of South Carolina, advising them not to submit to it.

"It is unjust to the people of the South. It makes them pay high prices for everything they buy. It takes money out of their pockets and puts money into the purses of the Northern manufacturer," he argued.

The Northern manufacturers replied, "Without the tariff, we shall have to close our mills; we cannot go on with low prices for we cannot make the goods at such a rate. Our workmen will be dismissed, and our mills will be idle."

Thus, the two sections stood on the subject of the tariff. Calhoun advised the Legislature of South Carolina to nullify the

Clay proposed a compromise.

tariff law, so far as that state was concerned. South Carolina followed his advice and passed an ordinance to that effect. Thus, Calhoun led his state into open opposition to the laws of Congress.

President Jackson was resolved to carry out the laws, and he would have forced a conflict with South Carolina had not wiser measures prevailed to prevent a rupture.

Clay proposed a compromise, which both sections could agree to, and argued this remedy with so much force that South Carolina withdrew her ordinance, and the tariff was modified. Thus, the crisis passed.

Calhoun was in public office for nearly forty years. He was the great leader of the Southern people, the advocate of States' Rights and a firm believer in the institution of slavery. He was truly a great man, in whom there was no low or selfish motive.

Chapter 67

The Heroes of the Alamo

The Alamo is a fort in the town of San Antonio, Texas. It was built by the early Spaniards for a Mission; though the walls were strong and thick, they were only eight feet high, and ill-adapted for defense. Unsuitable as it was for warlike purposes, the Alamo was destined to be the center of one of the most heroic conflicts in American history.

Soon after Texas had declared her independence from Mexico, and had became a Republic, the Texans drove the Mexicans out of San Antonio, and took possession of the town. Santa Anna, the President of Mexico, swore vengeance against the rebels, and sent an army to punish them. It would have been well if the Texans had retreated, for they were few in strength, and poorly provided with food and ammunition, while the Mexican army numbered thousands.

But the Texans were heroes, and had no thought of retreating. When Santa Anna appeared near the town, the little force of two hundred Texans, under command of Colonel Travis, withdrew into the Alamo, and prepared for defense. The Colonel wrote a letter to his friends, in which he said, "I am determined to sustain myself as long as possible, and die like a soldier who never forgets what is due to his own honor or that of his country."

Among the defenders of the fort was David Crockett, the famous hunter of West Tennessee. He possessed wonderful skill with his rifle, which he called "Old Betty," and rarely missed a shot. Besides that, he was always in good humor, with lots of fine stories of his own adventures to tell. No wonder he was greatly beloved by all who knew him. Another defender of the Alamo was Colonel James Bowie, the inventor of the Bowie knife, a terrible weapon in the hands of a strong and resolute man.

Santa Anna planted his cannon around the Alamo, and began a steady bombardment. He waved a blood-red flag before the town to show the Texans what they might expect if they were overcome. Knowing their fate, the band of two hundred began their stout resistance.

At the close of the third day, Santa Anna's forces had increased to four thousand men, and the Texans were already worn out by excessive toil and watching. The end was not far off. The brave defenders knew that an assault would carry the fort; they were doomed. Travis called his soldiers, and assigned them their places.

Jim Bowie   William Travis   Davy Crockett

"Men, you are worn out by three days of fighting, with little rest, and scant food. Outside are thousands of Mexicans thirsting for your blood and mine. They are getting ready to make an assault upon this fort. All I ask of you is to fight to the very last, and die like men."

They went to their posts, grimly determined to slay as many

Mexican soldiers as they could before they, themselves, were slain. All night long the watch was kept up.

At daybreak the Mexican army advanced with scaling-ladders, which they placed against the walls. Up these ladders, the Mexican soldiers clambered, only to be hurled back by the defenders at the top. Again and again the Mexican soldiers rushed up, and again and again were they met with bullet, knife, and club. Hundreds fell, but there were still hundreds to take their places.

After several hours, the defenders were exhausted; the assailants by hundreds climbed over the walls, and attacked them from all sides.

James Bowie, too ill to stay in the fight, had crept to his room

Battle of the Alamo

and his bed. Here some Mexican soldiers found him and cruelly stabbed him to death.

Davy Crockett stood in one room, surrounded by dozens of his enemy, his rifle in hand. He had long since fired his last bullet, and had brought down dozens of his foes. Now, using his gun as a club, he laid about him, right and left, felling Mexican soldiers at every blow. At length, the brave hunter fell, pierced with many bullets. Not far away Colonel Travis, with a dozen Mexican soldiers surrounding him, fell also.

It was soon over. All the defenders, to a man, were slain, not one being left alive. But of the Mexicans, more than five hundred died on that bloody day. A thrill of horror went through Texas and the whole country, when news of this tragedy became known. In the subsequent battles between Texas and Mexico, the battle-cry of the Texans was, "Remember the Alamo! Remember the Alamo!"

Chapter 68

Sam Houston Wins Freedom for Texas

You have been told the story of the Alamo. The patriots of Texas had still other grievances against Santa Anna and the Mexican army. The defenders of Fort Goliad, led by Colonel Fannin, with more than four hundred men, had surrendered, and had been given solemn assurance of protection. They were immediately divided into small companies, marched in different directions out of town, and shot in cold blood, not a man being left alive. This was a merciless massacre, and infuriated the Texans still more.

Santa Anna now thought he was a conqueror. He had dealt with Travis, at the Alamo, and with Colonel Fannin, at Fort Goliad, but he still had Sam Houston to deal with. We shall now see how Santa Anna met his fate.

General Sam Houston was the leader of the Texans in their revolt against Mexico. His army was small, not more than seven or eight hundred men, and he had to watch very carefully for an opportunity to fight his stronger antagonist. At last, Houston took a stand at the San Jacinto River, and resolved, then and there, to pay the score for the Mexican outrages.

Sam Houston

It was not long before the enemy came in sight., eighteen hundred strong. They were very showy in appearance, but Houston knew they were not much, as soldiers and fighters. He grimly watched them.

Turning to his men, he addressed them thus,

"Men, there come the Mexicans, and with them is Santa Anna. They are many times our number, but we are Texans. If you wish to fight, here is your chance and now is the time. Remember, it is for liberty or it is for death. Men, remember the Alamo!"

His soldiers shouted, "We are ready, and we remember everything."

As they stood behind their breast works, awaiting the attack, a soldier rode up to General Houston and saluted. He said, "General, I have cut down the bridge, according to your orders." Houston smiled, and nodded his head, for he knew now that Santa Anna could not escape across the river, should he be defeated.

The day wore on, and the Mexican army halted, about noon, to rest and prepare for the attack. The soldiers began to cook their food, the officers lay down, and Santa Anna went to sleep. Houston said to his men, "Why wait for them to attack? Let us take them unawares."

The word was passed along the line, and, in a few moments, the whole Texan army was in double-quick, headed for the Mexican camp. As they ran, they shouted, "Remember the Alamo! Remember Goliad!"

The Mexicans sprang to their arms, the officers leaped from their couches, and Santa Anna woke up. It was too late, however, for the Texans were upon them. The Mexican soldiers fired on the approaching troops with little effect. A ball struck General Houston in the ankle, inflicting a painful wound, but the old hero kept his saddle until the action was over.

The Mexicans began to give way before the well-ordered advance and constant fire of the Texans. In fifteen minutes, they were in a panic of flight, the Texans in mad pursuit, filling the air with their cries, "Remember the Alamo! Remember Goliad!" The Mexicans dropped everything and fled. Behind them they left their cannon loaded, and their cooked food untouched. Some awoke just in time to flee, not waiting to dress. Others, playing games, threw down their cards, and hurried away as the Texans entered their tents.

The pursuit was kept up till night, by which time most of the Mexican soldiers were prisoners of war. More than six hundred were killed and seven hundred captured. Everything was taken, and Santa Anna escaped.

The next day, a body of Texan cavalry, scouring the country for prisoners, and especially watchful for Santa Anna himself, saw a Mexican soldier, whom they called upon to surrender. The Mexican threw himself upon the grass and covered his head with a blanket. They had to drag him to his feet, before he would answer them at all.

He then kissed the hand of the leader of the party, and said he was but a private soldier. He was much frightened, and begged them not to kill him. Noticing his fine clothes and jewelry, the soldiers took him back to camp. As they passed some Mexican prisoners, they heard one of them cry, "The President! The President! Santa Anna! Santa Anna!"

It was the infamous leader, the President of Mexico, who was now a trembling captive before General Houston, who spared his life. His capture put an end to Mexico's invasion of Texas, and made Houston the hero of the people of that young Republic.

It was the infamous leader, the President of Mexico, who was now a trembling captive before General Houston, who spared his life.

Chapter 69

The Invention of the Electric Telegraph

A packet-ship, named the *Sully*, was slowly making its way across the ocean from Havre to New York. Among the passengers was a New York artist named Samuel F. B. Morse who had been studying painting in Europe and was on his way home. He had once been a student at Yale College where he had become much interested in chemistry and other sciences.

In the cabin one day, the passengers began talking about improvements in electricity. One of them mentioned that Franklin had sent a current through several miles of wire, with no loss of time between the touch at one end and the spark at the other; also that recent experiments in Paris had proved conclusively that a current went almost instantaneously through a great length of wire run in circles around the walls of a large apartment. Morse listened attentively to the conversation.

"If it is true that a current passes so swiftly through a great length of wire, why could not messages be sent over the wire at any distance?" he inquired. The others agreed that it would be a splendid thing if it could be proven possible. Then the subject was dropped. But Morse was not a man to forget, and he kept the idea constantly in his mind.

Day after day, the ship made its way homeward, while Morse worked in his cabin on plans for sending messages by electricity. Before the voyage was ended, he had made drawings of an electric telegraph, and had devised the Morse alphabet of dots and dashes, the system used today the world over in telegraphy. His plans included laying the wires underground, afterwards abandoned in favor of stringing them in the air from pole to pole.

Before he left the ship, he said to some of his fellow-passengers, "I believe it will be possible to send a message around the world some day." Then he turned to the Captain: "If you ever hear of the telegraph as one of the wonders of the world, remember that it was invented on the *Sully*." The Captain was more skeptical than the hopeful inventor.

When Morse reached home, he began to work upon his great invention, but progress was slow. For he had to make a living; he was poor, and had no one to provide money for his experiments. At the end of three years, he had a circuit of seventeen hundred feet of wire, and a wooden clock, by means of which he succeeded in sending sounds from end to end of the wire. But it was not very satisfactory and those who witnessed its workings were not at all inclined to invest money in the enterprise.

Morse worked hard and neglected his business as an artist. He fell into abject want, and became poorer and poorer. He often went a whole day without food. Still, he kept to his invention, and did not once lose faith. It is of such courage and endurance that success always is made.

Unable to secure private help, Morse went to Washington and exhibited his apparatus to some Congressman. Then he petitioned Congress for an appropriation to build a line from Baltimore to Washington, a distance of forty miles. But Congress was slow to act and offered Morse little hope. Day after day passed and nothing was done.

Finally, the last day and indeed the last hour of the session of

Congress arrived. Morse, in despair, had left the capitol building and had gone to his house, the last hope of securing any appropriation having fled. He felt discouraged and disappointed, and was almost ready to give up the fight.

At the breakfast table the next morning, a young lady, Miss Annie Ellsworth, met him with a smile. "I have come to congratulate you, Mr. Morse, on the passage of your bill. Congress granted you the money at the very last hour."

Morse was delighted over the news. Congress had given him thirty thousand dollars. He could hardly believe his good fortune. It had been eleven years since he first conceived the idea and he had surrendered the best part of his life to working out his plans. He now saw success before him and entered with renewed hope upon his great labor.

The work was hastened. Morse found out that underground wires would be expensive and uncertain; hence he used poles. The telegraph was started from the Washington end, and a year passed before thirty miles of poles were set. The wires were tested as they were placed, and Morse was in constant communication with both ends of the line.

The first public test of the telegraph was made on May 11, 1844. The Whig National Convention, in Baltimore, had, on that day, nominated Henry Clay for the Presidency. The telegraph line was still ten miles from Baltimore. A train full of passengers started from Baltimore to

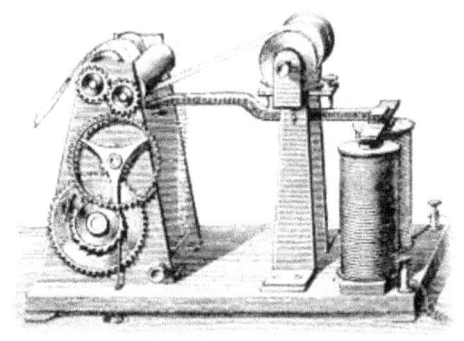

Morse Telegraph

carry the news of the nomination of Clay to Washington. When they reached the telegraph wire, Morse quietly asked for the news, and sent it on ahead.

The train arrived in Washington an hour or two later, and the passengers were surprised to find that the news they brought was already old news, for everybody in Washington had learned of it over the telegraph! This was a convincing proof that the telegraph could be used to convey intelligence; there was no longer a doubt of its value.

By May 24, the line was completed to Baltimore, and all the tests made. Everything was ready for the public exhibition of what the telegraph could do; the way was open for sending and receiving messages. Miss Ellsworth, who, more than a year before, had delighted the inventor by bringing him good news of the action of Congress, was given the privilege of sending the first message. She chose this line from the Bible: "What hath God wrought."

With these words the telegraph was born, and its use was spread to all lands. By its means, one can communicate in a few hours with family or friend in the most distant parts of the earth. The happenings of each day, the world over, are gathered in the daily papers by its means; business transactions are made in a few minutes across continents, and over seas. The telegraph has brought the people of the world into closer communication, has annihilated space and time, and expedited the world's business a thousand fold. And all because one man conceived a great idea, and would not give up until success had crowned his efforts.

Chapter 70

The Discovery of Gold in California

It had been the dream of the early explorers of America to find gold. Thousands had come to these shores in search of the precious metal. Many of them had died in their efforts, all of them endured great suffering, and, in the end, each one of them was disappointed. For over three hundred years the earth kept secret its hiding-place for gold in the New World.

After the Mexican War, California became a territory of the United States. Already a number of settlers were there, attracted by the fertile soil and fine climate. Among them was Captain John Sutter, who had moved to California from St. Louis about ten years before the Mexican War.

Captain Sutter had built a fort on the site of the present city of Sacramento. About fifty miles above it, in 1848, he was having built a sawmill on the American River. The mill was finished and started, when the tail-race was found to be too small to carry off the water. To deepen the race, the whole head of water was turned on to wash it out to the required depth.

One of the men, named Marshall, who had charge of the mill, watched the work of the water, and saw many shining particles lodged in the crevices of the rocks, or in the dirt the water had carried down. Thinking these particles might be gold, he gathered a small bag of them, without saying anything to anybody about his suspicions.

As soon as he could leave, without attracting notice, he

mounted his horse, and rode to the fort, fifty miles away, in order to show what he had found. He asked to see Sutter alone.

Sutter was surprised at the earnest manner of his foreman, and led the way into his private room; here he locked the door. "What is the matter, Marshall? Is anything wrong at the mill?" asked he.

"Nothing is wrong at the mill, sir," replied Marshall, "but I have something here to show you that may surprise you."

He then handed his employer the bag, which, being opened, was found to contain a handful of yellow metal, in small flakes and little lumps, which he said he had taken from the mill-race, and which he thought might be gold.

The two men by the light of a candle bent eagerly over the little heap of shining particles. Sutter could not believe it was gold. Marshall declared it was nothing else. Acid was applied, the metal was weighed, and other tests were used, until there was no doubt of the fact.

"You have found gold," said Sutter at last. "But let no one know of it until I can set my house in order; for this knowledge will change everything here."

His was an idle request. The next day the secret leaked out at the fort, and the news went at once to the mill. In a week, it was known for miles around, and everybody was saying to everybody else, "Gold has been found at Butter's Mill."

Sutter's men deserted him in a body, and the saw-mill was left without hands to run it. Every person in the neighborhood began searching the streams, the gullies, the mountain sides, and the bed of the river for gold particles. The miners then began to straggle down to San Francisco with their pouches of gold-dust, and to show them to the people there.

This was enough to start a panic rush for the gold fields. In three months most of the houses in San Francisco, and in Monterey, were shut up, and their occupants turned in mad haste for the hills. Sailors left their ships in the harbor, carpenters abandoned their benches, lawyers closed their offices, physicians deserted their patients, even the newspapers suspended indefinitely.

Everybody who could get a shovel and a pan, and a week's supply of provisions, was off for the mines. The people were as wild for gold-hunting as ever were the Spaniards of former days.

The result was that mills were left idle, fields of wheat were turned over to the horses and cattle, houses became vacant, and farms went to waste. People had no thought for food or anything else.

Tents were built near the mines, and along the river-beds where the gold was found. There were fabulous stories of men who made fifty dollars a day. One miner, with a common tin pan, washed out gold to the value of eighty-two dollars in a single day. A man who made less than ten dollars a day was not considered a good miner.

Prices went bounding higher and higher. Flour was worth fifty dollars a barrel, a common spade sold for ten dollars, rooms were rented for a hundred dollars a month each, and a simple two-story house at Slitter's fort brought five hundred dollars a month as a hotel.

In the meanwhile, gold was

Panning for gold

found in other areas. Every day new stories were heard of some rich "find" somewhere, followed by a mad rush to the place. In a few months, four thousand people were washing for gold, as , if it were the only business in life.

Vessels, returning from San Francisco, carried the wonderful news to all parts of the world. Everywhere was blazoned the story that gold was found in the streams, on the mountain sides, and in the gullies of California. There was a mad race for the gold-fields! Adventures from the islands of the Pacific, from South America, even from China, began to pour in by every arriving ship.

The news reached the Atlantic ports, and society was stirred to its very depths. First there was wonder and distrust, but the stories kept on coming, until the East went wild with the fever for gold. How to get to California was the one great question!

It was three thousand miles across the plains, and a still longer journey by the Isthmus of Darien, or by water around Cape Horn. This did not deter or dismay the eager people. Ships were fitted out in every port, caravans were made ready for the overland journey, and thousands of gold hunters started for the land of wealth.

In one year, a hundred thousand people moved into California, coming from all sections of the country, and from nearly all parts of the world.

Chapter 71

Crossing the Continent

The great rush to the gold fields of California took place in 1849. The "gold fever," as it was called in sport, broke out in many parts of our country, and, indeed in many parts of the world, and thousands of people started for the West. Those who went to California at that time were called "Forty-niners."

The demand for ships was great. Any kind of seaworthy craft was fitted out for the voyage. Even old whale-boats were used, crowded to their limit with passengers. The streets of the seaport towns presented an odd appearance, with men dressed in red woolen shirts, slouch hats, and cowhide boots, carrying rifles on their shoulders, and wearing pistols and knives in their belts.

Ship after ship sailed on its way around Cape Horn, or bore the passengers to the Isthmus of Darien. Men of all classes were aboard, lawyers, doctors, scholars, clerks, farmers, business men, for all kinds and conditions of men had caught the fever. Love for gold is a magnet that levels all distinctions of society.

The sailing of ships was followed by the march of thousands across the plains. Like colonies of ants, the long trains of wagons crept along the roads, crossing the dreary deserts, climbing the mountains, dragging their weary but hopeful freight of human souls on the long quest. It was a dreadful journey, but there were many at that time who undertook it.

Generally, the gold-hunters started out in a caravan of a dozen or more big canvass-covered wagons, drawn by teams of horses, loaded with provisions for the journey, and with tools for digging. The women and children rode in the wagons, while the men were astride their own horses, carrying guns and pistols for protection.

The caravan usually started from St. Louis early in the spring, so as to get good weather and grass for the teams. Months would pass, however, and winter would be on them before they arrived at their destination. Slowly they wended their way along, the women talking, the children sleeping or playing, and the men riding ahead. It was a long and tiresome trip.

Crossing the Continent

At night, the caravan would stop at some place where there was water. The teams would be unhitched; the horses fed and watered and bedded for the night. Campfires were then built, and supper was cooked and eaten. As soon as it was dark, everybody went to sleep in the wagons, except those who kept guard.

By daylight, the caravan was astir, and, after breakfast was over, and the sun began to show its first rays, the journey was taken up again. Another twenty or thirty miles were added to the number already traveled.

Sometimes, there were the blinding sand storms to be encountered, when the trails would be covered, and the travelers would lose their way. In this manner, many perished of hunger and thirst.

Then, there was the danger from wild beasts that often stampeded the horses or killed them outright. Sometimes water was hard to find, or the grass gave out, or the provisions spoiled, or the teams died. Long after the gold fever had subsided, there might be seen along the plains abandoned wagons or the skeletons of dead animals.

But there were thousands of caravans that made the journey safely. After many weary months, Salt Lake City was reached a new and small town just founded by the Mormons. Here, the weary emigrants tarried a while to rest and to recruit fresh horses for the remainder of the journey.

Then to the road again, struggling through the parched valleys, where horses almost died of thirst, and the women and children cried out in their distress! Up the granite sides of the Sierra Mountains they went, almost dropping from exhaustion, till they came to Sacramento Valley, and Mount Shasta burst upon their view!

At last they were in the land of their dreams, the land of untold wealth for some, and of bitter disappointment for others! They found San Francisco a city of tents and shanties, scattered about a few wind-swept sand-hills. Everything was rude and disorderly, and everybody lived in great confusion. Rooms cost seven to ten dollars a day. Food was scarce and high.

In this confusion, every man was his own protector, and he placed his trust in his own right arm and quick fire. So long as he was peaceable he was safe, but justice was swift to those who broke the law of the camp.

Thus, the emigrant crossed the land, or sailed the waters, to find the gold fields of the New World.

Chapter 72

The Pony Express

When gold was discovered in California, thousands of persons moved to the Pacific Coast. The lack of mail facilities for these emigrants was keenly felt. At first, it took months for a man in the East to exchange letters with any one in California.

In 1854, it was proposed in Congress to establish a weekly mail between St. Louis and San Francisco. The time required would be ten days, and each trip would cost the Government five thousand dollars. Congress thought this was a wild scheme, and so nothing was done about it.

California had to content itself with getting mail by way of Panama. If the ships were not delayed, a letter would be delivered in about three weeks. It took so long to cross the continent that, when Utah Territory was created, in 1850, three months passed before the news reached Salt Lake City.

Eight years later, the stage-coaches of the Southern Overland Mail covered the distance of twenty-seven hundred and fifty-nine miles, between St. Louis and San Francisco, in three weeks. The fare was one hundred dollars. The outfit consisted of one hundred stage-coaches, one thousand horses, five hundred mules, and seven hundred and fifty men, of whom one hundred and fifty were drivers. Letters were carried for ten cents a half-ounce.

It was a long, tiresome, and sometimes exciting journey. The mail was put in big bags, securely strapped on top, or in the back of the stage. The passengers were inside, while the intrepid driver forced his plucky horses from station to station, along the rough roads. Often the traveler had to hold on for dear life, while the coach went over ditches or down the steep incline of the mountains, rocking from side to side, and threatening to pitch over or slide down a precipice at any moment.

Sometimes it rained; it was very cold in winter and hot and dusty in summer; and there was always the possibility of an attack on the coach. Then again, the bold appearance of a band of highwaymen resulted in a hold-up, while the mail-bags were robbed, and the passengers were searched for their money and jewelry. An attack on the mail-coach was by no means an unusual occurrence.

Horses were changed at regular stations. The passengers alighted, ate their meals, visited awhile, or stretched their cramped limbs while the new teams were being hitched. Then up and in place, the crack of the whip, a whoop from the driver, and the coach disappeared down the road! Three weeks of this was anything but a pleasant journey. In 1860, a system of carrying mails and small parcels by the use of ponies was established. It was called the "Pony Express." The schedule was fourteen days in all, by rail from New York to St. Joseph, and thence by running ponies to Sacramento. The little animals made wonderful distance, and were very accurate in their schedule, always arriving on time.

The ponies employed were selected with care for their speed and endurance. They were housed, and fed, and rubbed down with every possible attention. Ten miles, at the full limit of his speed, was demanded of each little animal, if the road was bad, and more, if the road was good.

Across the prairies, where the land was level, and the traveling good, pony and rider flew like the wind, scarcely noticing the sweet grass or the wild flowers by the way. Up the mountain sides, across streams, through the forests, around sharp turns, went the Pony Express at top speed. In summer heat and winter cold, in rain and snow and dust and drought, the rider and his pony made schedule time. At the end of the run, flecked with foam, panting with exertion, and covered with dust or mud, but still full of fire and strength, the pony would be rewarded by a rub down.

The rider dismounted, stretched his legs a little; then he remounted another waiting pony, received his precious bundles, and was off like a flash down the trail on another lap of the journey. Thus, one rider made several changes, and the pony he left behind, after its rest, was prepared for another rider taking him back to his first station.

Nearly two thousand miles had to be covered in eight days. There was no idling for either pony or rider. Once under the saddle, the little animal leaped to his course like a fire horse to his harness. The rider was trained to the saddle, and could ride better than he could walk.

The packet of letters made a bundle not much larger than an ordinary writing-tablet, but every letter had been paid for, five dollars in advance. There were hundreds of them, written on the thinnest paper that could be found.

Twenty pounds was the limit of the weight of the mail-bag. In all, six hundred and fifty thousand miles were covered by the riders of the company, and only one small package was lost. Each rider was provided with pistols to protect himself from attack, and had to be a courageous, skillful and trustworthy man.

But the Pony Express never paid expenses. It was operated for sixteen months, and lost money all the while. At the end of that time, it was abandoned. When the telegraph was completed across the plains, the rate of postage fell to one dollar a letter, and the pony and his rider went out of business.

However, the Pony Express opened the way for the cross-continent telegraph and railway, and was evidence of how enterprising the early emigrants were while they were settling and developing the wonderful country beyond the Rocky Mountains.

Chapter 73

The Boy Who Saved a Village

In western pioneer days, out on the Pacific Coast, the adventurous life of the settlers was beset with many dangers. About the time the "gold fever" struck the people of the United States, a family named Goodman, started from one of the eastern states to find a home in the Northwest, somewhere along the coast. The region was inhabited only by a few natives and hunters, engaged in trapping wild animals for their fur.

After weary months of travel overland, in slow carts drawn by oxen, suffering from hunger, thirst and sickness, and harassed by the native people there, the family at last reached a place on Puget Sound and built themselves a home. There were two children, a little girl, and a boy who, even though only nine years old, was quite useful in helping his father build the log cabin and plant the garden.

As the boy grew larger, he went with his father hunting wild game, and fishing. So that by the time he was twelve years of age, he could use his rifle with deadly aim and could paddle a boat as well as any native person along the coast.

After a while, other settlers came and, for protection, moved in the neighborhood; thus, after a time, quite a colony grew up. The native people there looked on with distrust and alarm. The settlers were coming in such numbers that the natives feared they would be driven away and lose their hunting and fishing grounds. The natives held a big meeting of all the tribes before they agreed to make war on the little town and kill all the people in it.

The settlers heard nothing of the intention of the natives and went on with their planting and building and fishing, not knowing of the deadly danger that hung over them. They had been kind to the natives, had furnished them with guns and powder, and had given them presents; they had every reason to believe that the tribes were friendly.

One day, however, word came that a group of natives had appeared at a remote farmhouse, and, after burning everything, had slain all the inhabitants. The next day, news arrived that other settlers had been killed in the woods, and that the natives had put on their war-paint. This so alarmed the settlers that they prepared for defense.

A friendly native woman brought word to Mr. Goodman that the natives were on the way to destroy his house. It was a few miles from the village itself, so he hastily sent his wife and the girls to the hamlet, while he and his son stayed behind to discover the purpose of the natives. That very night the barking of the dogs gave warning that the natives were near. Looking out, the father saw dusky, painted forms, and was greeted with a shower of arrows.

Closing the door, he and his son escaped through the back, leaped into a canoe, and were soon beyond the reach of their foes, though arrows fell thick about them as they paddled away. It was not long before they came to the sleeping hamlet a few miles up the coast.

"The natives are coming. Awake and arm yourselves!" they cried, as they landed.

Then commenced a great hurrying of men and women. All night long they built a big clay fort, brought water and food, loaded guns, and made ready for the attack which they knew was not far off.

About noon the next day, a fleet of war canoes was seen approaching. They came within gunshot of the village fort, and opened fire. The settlers replied with deadly aim. The natives were in open boats, and the settlers behind clay walls, so that many a native fell into the water with a bullet wound, while only a few of the settlers were hurt. Late in the afternoon, the natives decided they had had enough for one day and withdrew for the night.

They intended to renew the attack the next day, so they drew off about a half-mile, to a neck of land, beached their canoes, and built fires for cooking and dancing. They had a great feast of meat and corn, and then began to beat their drums and dance their war-dances.

Now, let us return to the hero of our story, young Goodman. All day long he had been firing his gun with unerring aim, causing many a native to fall from his canoe. When night came, and the natives retired, the boy cautiously left the fort, and crept through the bushes to see what they were doing. No one missed him, for he told no one where he was going. Slowly and carefully, he crept nearer and nearer, until he was quite close to the dancing crowd. Then, he formed a bold plan of stealing all the canoes of the natives, so that they could not go back to the village. Besides which, the canoes held the guns and powder and much of the provisions owned by the natives.

He waited till nearly midnight, then undressed, and, tying his clothes around his neck, he waded into the water and swam until he rounded a point which brought him near the canoes and close to the native camp.

He was very quick and swam as silently as a fish. Slowly, he crawled up to one of the canoes, and cut the thongs that held it to its moorings. He was glad to see it swing loose and drift away from shore. Then he began to cut them all loose, one after the other, and push them from shore. He worked silently; for, if the natives heard him, it would mean certain death.

After he had cut away about a dozen canoes, a native came toward the shore, but the night was dark, and the native was tired and sleepy; so Goodman hid himself behind one of the boats and waited. The native took some food out of the canoe nearest him and went back to his companions.

In about three hours, all the boats were cut loose and adrift. Some were far out, and all were being carried away by the tide. Goodman jumped into the last canoe, seized the paddles, and rowed away, uttering a loud yell of triumph, for now he was out of danger.

The natives rushed to the shore, but it was too late. Day was breaking, and they could see their canoes adrift, and they realized that they were helpless. They yelled in anger and fired off their guns and some of them even started to swim for their canoes. But Goodman was too sure a shot to miss a single swimmer; he lay flat in his canoe and fired at them one by one.

They gave up the pursuit, and, by sunrise, were on their way home overland. When Goodman reached his own fort, the old men patted him on the back, while the women, with tears in their eyes, hugged and kissed him. To this day, they tell the story of how Goodman saved the village.

Chapter 74

The Rescue of Jerry McHenry

Sometimes slaves in the South escaped and ran away to places in the North where slavery was not allowed. But there was a law known as the Fugitive Slave Act that allowed Southern slave owners to capture runaway slaves in the Northern states, and returned to them to the South.

Jerry McHenry was one such runaway, who had lived as a free man for a number of years in Syracuse, New York, working quietly and expertly as a cooper. No one inquired where he came from, or how he had reached the town, or who he was. The people were content to let McHenry alone, and not ask too many questions. If he was an escaped slave, it was the duty of the officers of the law to return him to his previous owner. And no one wanted to do that.

One day, an agent came to Syracuse, and obtained a warrant for the arrest of McHenry, declaring he was a former slave, owned by a Mr. Reynolds of Missouri; and that, under the Fugitive Slave Law, he must be arrested and sent back to the slave-owner.

Going to his place of business, the agent, accompanied by an officer, said, "Jerry McHenry, you are an escaped slave, and belong to Mr. Reynolds. You must come with us and stand trial."

McHenry was struck with astonishment and dismay. He said little, but, with despair in his heart, he laid aside his tools, and went with the agent to appear before the Judge.

The testimony was one-sided. The agent thus stated the case: "This man, Jerry McHenry, is by birth a slave. He belongs to Mr.

Reynolds of Missouri. He escaped and has been hiding in the North. The law requires him to be returned to his owner."

McHenry said nothing in his defense, and was not asked any questions. He sat looking on, and not very closely guarded, though his hands were in hand-cuffs. The Judge and the agent were arranging some papers, and were talking about the case. A young man, standing near the prisoner, leaned over, and whispered, "Now, Jerry, here is a good chance for you to slip out of the court room."

In a moment McHenry had risen from his seat, slipped through the bystanders, run down the steps, and was in the street below. The crowd cheered him, and made way for him. There was no vehicle for him to escape in, but McHenry was a swift runner, and disappeared up the street.

The police officers raised a great cry, and started in hot pursuit. McHenry had turned a corner, and was fleeing as fast as his manacled condition would let him. He had run about a mile, and was quite out of breath before his pursuers came near to him.

"Stop, and surrender, or it will be the worse for you," they cried.

"Never!" he answered, and made one last despairing effort before they closed in on him.

McHenry fought like a tiger, against overwhelming odds. He was surrounded by the police and their followers, and struck from before and behind. He was thrown down, and bruised, his clothes being sadly torn.

In this condition, he was put in a wagon, four policemen guarding him. He was brought back to the city, and confined in the back room of the station, under a heavy guard. The crowd of citizens outside watched the proceedings with ill-concealed anger.

They proposed to rush in, and rescue the poor man. But one of their number advised them in this fashion:

"Wait a little while, and it will be quite dark. Proper arrangements can then be made for the poor fellow to be hidden after we rescue him. Stay nearby until all is made ready."

In the meantime, McHenry was in a perfect rage of passion. He beat his iron-bound hands on the table before him, and cried out in his fury, "Take these irons off my hands, and give me a chance. I will fight my way through all the guard, and escape; if I do not, you can send me where you will."

One of his friends came in to quiet him, and told him, in a low voice, that a crowd was getting ready to rescue him when it was dark. He then sat down, with his head on the table, and said nothing else.

About thirty men met outside, and planned how to effect the escape of the prisoner. They did not sympathize with the Fugitive Slave Law, and were anxious to give McHenry a chance to get away. All arrangements were carefully made. At a given signal, the doors and windows were smashed in, and the rescuers rushed into the room. The officers were seized and held. There was little opposition, for the crowd was so determined that any show of force would have been useless.

Several men seized McHenry in their arms, and bore him outside to a waiting buggy, to which a swift horse was hitched and where a willing driver sat ready.

"Now, go for your life," was the order, and the horse started at a rapid pace. The driver managed to escape all followers, and, after about an hour's journey, he delivered McHenry into the hands of a kind woman, who gave him shelter for the night. His pursuers were off the track, and McHenry was safe for a while.

After a day or two, a covered wagon, with a pair of fleet horses, was seen standing in front of the house where McHenry had found lodging. An old and infirm man was noticed coming out of the house and getting into the vehicle, which started off at a rapid rate.

Several persons saw the unusual sight, and told the police that they were suspicious of the old man, and thought he might be McHenry. The police at once started in chase. The pursuit lasted for a short while, but they were not very eager to capture their former prisoner, and did not go very far. After ten miles, they gave up and returned to town.

The supposed old man was in reality McHenry, who was making his way into Canada. There, no person could be held as a slave, and, once there, all fugitive slaves were safe. In fact, there were many provisions made for helping escaped slaves get over the border into Canada.

After several days, McHenry and his rescuers came to one of the Great Lakes, where a friendly Captain took him on board a boat. At dark, the boat sailed across the Lake, and Jerry McHenry landed in Canada, where he soon established himself again in business as a cooper.

Chapter 75

Abraham Lincoln

Lincoln was born in a cabin, in a dreary region of the state of Kentucky. It was a one-room house, about fourteen feet square, built of logs. In this one room the family cooked, ate, and slept. Very few children have started life in so poor and barren a home as did Abraham Lincoln.

When he was seven years old, his parents moved to Indiana, into a wild and wooded region, and there built a rude place to live in. It was still a cabin, with the roughest of furniture. A log, smoothed on one side, was used as a table. The bedsteads were made of poles, fastened to the walls. The chairs were blocks of wood. All the cooking was done in the fireplace.

Here, Lincoln spent his childhood in toil and hardship. The family was poor, and every member had to do hard work on the farm. After laboring all day, the young boy would often lie down before the fireplace, and read by the light of the burning fire. Then, when too tired to read any more, he would climb a ladder, made of pegs driven into the wall, and go to sleep in the loft on a pallet of straw, covered with skins.

He had but little chance to get an education. He did not go to school more than a year, all told, and had very poor teachers. But he learned to read such books as *Aesop's Fables, The Pilgrim's Progress*, and the Bible.

He borrowed the *Life of Washington* from a neighbor, and sat up far into the night reading it. He kept it in a crevice in the wall, near his bed, for safety. One night it rained, and he found the book soaked through and through. The owner made him work three days to pay for it, and then let him have it. It was the first book the boy owned.

He was accustomed to hear every preacher and stump orator that came into his neighborhood. Once, he walked fourteen miles to hear a trial in Court. When one of the lawyers finished his speech, Lincoln walked across the room in his bare feet, with his trousers rolled up, and said quite audibly, "I want to shake your hand. That is the best speech I ever heard." Years after, when Lincoln was President, the lawyer, grown old and feeble, came to the White House and reminded him of the incident.

When Lincoln was about twenty-one years of age, his father and two of his neighbors moved to Illinois. Through mud and water, and over rough roads, Lincoln walked all the way, driving an ox-team. They settled about ten miles from Decatur, and started life afresh.

Lincoln aided in clearing the land, and he fenced it with rails. He helped build the cabins and plant the spring crops. Though he was of age, and could have done as he pleased, he stayed with the family until they had started in their new surroundings.

He needed some clothes, for he still wore the buckskins of the frontier. He bargained with a neighbor to make him a pair of trousers out of brown jeans, dyed with white walnut bark, agreeing to split rails in payment. He had to split fourteen hundred rails before the trousers were paid for.

Lincoln was now a grown man, six feet and four inches tall, spare of frame, but muscular, and in perfect health. He was much beloved by the community in which he lived, and was popular with his companions. He could out-run, out-jump, and out-wrestle anybody in the neighborhood. And, as a rail-splitter, nobody could approach him in the number he could split a day.

For he had precision and power with a sharp ax. Every blow fell in the right place, and with great force. To see him cut down a large tree, and split it into rails, was to witness an exhibition of rare skill.

He was also a good story-teller. All his life he had an inexhaustible supply of funny stories to fit any occasion. He gained a reputation for honesty and square dealing in all his business transactions. That is why he was called "Honest Abe."

One day, a woman came into the store where Lincoln was engaged as clerk. After she had gone, he noticed that she had given him six cents too much. That night, after his job was finished, he walked five miles to the woman's house to return her the money.

By dint of hard study and hard work, Lincoln began to be a leader in the town of New Salem, where he was employed. He studied law, was admitted to the bar, and was elected to the Legislature. He was sent to Congress, and was a candidate for the United States Senate.

As a lawyer, he was very shrewd and successful. Upon one occasion he defended the son of a poor woman, who

Abraham Lincoln with his son, Todd Lincoln

was accused of murdering a man at night. Lincoln was satisfied in his own mind that the boy was innocent. The trial began, and the witnesses were called.

The chief witness said, "I saw him strike the man and kill him."

Lincoln inquired, "What time was it when you saw him?"

"It was about eleven o'clock," the witness replied.

"How could you see so well at night?" asked the lawyer.

The man replied, "The moon was shining, and I could easily see by its light."

Lincoln sent for an almanac, and showed the jury that there was no moon shining on that night, whereupon the witness retired in confusion, and the man was acquitted of the crime.

In after years, Lincoln was President of the United States, during the trying period of the Civil War. His was a deep responsibility, and he felt the burden of saving the Union very keenly.

He was a man of strong convictions and of great firmness. He was cast by nature in a heroic mold, yet he was always sympathetic and tender in his dealings with men. His disposition was melancholy, in spite of his humor, and he brooded deeply over the welfare of the country. His great hope was to save the Union at any cost, and it grieved him profoundly to see the Southern States secede.

Chapter 76

Robert E. Lee

Robert E. Lee was the son of General Henry Lee, a hero of the Revolution, known as "Light Horse Harry." He was born in Virginia. He was no more than a mere boy, when his father died, leaving him to the training of a devoted mother. When Robert was not at school, he spent his time with her, helping her to keep house, taking her out to ride in the old family coach, and reading aloud the books she liked to hear.

Some days, however, he spent in hunting, of which he was very fond. Then he would ride all day with his hounds, or tramp for hours through the woods looking for game. In this way, he developed the splendid strength that never failed him in his after life.

When he was eighteen years old, he went to West Point to be trained as a soldier. He was there for four years, and never received a demerit. He was a model cadet. His clothes were always clean and well cared for. His gun, belt, and sword were as bright as they could be polished. His lessons were studiously prepared. So good a record did he make that he graduated second in his class.

Lee served as a Captain of Engineers during the War with Mexico. It was his duty to make roads and bridges, to plant big guns, to draw maps, and to direct the marches of the fighting men. He was with General Scott in all the big battles, and was of such assistance that that General said, "Lee is the greatest soldier I have ever known."

In after years, General Scott said, "If I knew that a battle was to be fought for my country, and the president were to say to me, 'Scott, who shall be my commander?' I would say 'Robert E. Lee! Nobody but Robert E. Lee.'"

In Mexico, while the battle of Cerro Gordo was raging, Captain Lee heard the cries of a little girl, and, following the sound, found a Mexican drummer-boy badly wounded, and lying on the ground with a big Mexican soldier, who had been shot, fallen on top of him. Lee stopped, had the Mexican soldier thrown off the boy's body, and the little fellow taken to a place of safety.

His small sister stood by, her eyes full of tears, her hands crossed over her chest. Her feet and arms were bare, and her hair hung down in a long plait to her waist. She looked up into the kind face of Captain Lee, and said, in her own language, "I am very grateful, kind sir. May God bless you for saving my brother."

Once, on a long march, a part of Scott's army had lost its way. General Scott sent seven engineers to guide the men into the right road. They had to cross a huge bed of lava and rocks. Six of the engineers came back, and said they could not get across. Captain Lee, however, on foot, and alone, pressed on through darkness and danger, and brought the men out in safety. General Scott said, "It was the greatest feat done by any one man during the war."

When the Civil War came on, Lee resigned from the United States Army to fight for Virginia and the South. He was offered the chief command of the Union forces, if he would remain in the service of the United States. He said to Mr. Blair, who came to offer him this command,

"If I owned the four millions of slaves in the South, I would give them all up to save the Union, but how can I draw my sword upon Virginia, my native State?"

After the war had been going on for nearly a year, Lee became the commanding General of all the Confederate Army. His soldiers were devotedly attached to him, and had supreme confidence in his ability.

On one occasion, General Lee placed himself at the head of a body of Texas troops, and, waving his sword, ordered them to follow him into battle. The situation was critical, and Lee wanted to save the day.

But the soldiers would not move. They cried out, "Lee to the rear! Lee to the rear." One of his Generals rode up and, taking his horse by the bridle, said, "General Lee, there are Georgians and Texans here willing to charge, but unwilling to see you in danger. If you will go back, we will go forward."

To this Lee replied, "You are brave men, and do not need me"; and, turning his horse's head, he rode back of the charging lines.

An old soldier relates that one day he was in the trenches, when a big gun was ready to be fired. Lee came in, and walked about, asking after the men and speaking words of cheer. Approaching the big gun, he asked an officer to fire it that he might see the result. The officer hesitated, and said,

"If I fire this gun, the enemy will return the fire at once in great force. Some of us will be killed, but that does not matter so long as you are not here. You might get hurt. If you will retire out of danger, I shall fire it as long as you order, but I beg you not to have it fired while you are here."

Lee was greatly touched by this devotion, and did not insist upon the big gun going into action while he was present.

General Lee ever felt kindly toward Union soldiers. He never called them "the enemy," but always spoke of them as "those people." Once, he remarked about the Northern troops, "Now, I wish all those people would go home and leave us to do the same."

A lady, who had lost her husband in the war, spoke in sharp terms of the North, one day, to General Lee. He said gently, "Madam, do not train up your children as foes of the Government of the United States. We are one country now. Bring them up to be Americans."

Throughout his life, he had but one purpose, and that was to do his duty. He often said, "Duty is the sublimest word in the English language," and, in accordance with this belief, he regulated his great life upon what seemed to him to be the only course he ought to pursue at the time.

Chapter 77

Stonewall Jackson

His real name was Thomas Jonathan Jackson, and he was born in what is now West Virginia, of poor parents who had to work hard for a living. His father died when he was three years old, leaving his mother to support three little children. They all lived in one room, where the mother taught a little school, and did sewing for her friends and neighbors.

Thomas grew up rosy-cheeked and blue-eyed, with waving brown hair, very determined to have his way, and full of confidence in himself. Fortunately, his way was a good one, and, from the start, he was a very dependable boy.

He was fond of arithmetic, and easily learned all the hard rules and could work any of the problems given him. His other studies were not so easy, but he never stopped anything he had once started, until he had mastered it, or it had mastered him. One of the maxims of his life was, "You may be whatever you resolve to be."

He gained a reputation for telling the exact truth. At one time, he walked a mile in the rain to correct a statement he had made.

"Why do you go to so much trouble for such a mere trifle as that?" someone asked him on his return.

He answered, "Simply because I found out that what I said was not true, and I never carry anything to bed with me that will rob me of sleep."

He was a leader in sports, particularly in climbing and jumping.

He was generally selected as Captain of one side, and this was the side that nearly always won, for he was a master of strategy in games.

At eighteen, he resolved to be a soldier. Dressed in a plain homespun suit and carrying his clothes in a saddlebag, he rode into Washington, and asked to be made a cadet at West Point, the military academy of the nation. He received the appointment.

His appearance caused much sport among the students there, for he was awkward and ill at ease, but always good-natured. It was not long before his ability to master his studies, however, made him sought after by others, and he soon won admiration and respect.

From early life, he was very religious. He taught in the Sunday-school, and even gathered the slaves of his town together every Sunday afternoon, and made them familiar with the truths of the Bible. Later on when he had become a great soldier, it was his habit to go off to a quiet place and pray before a battle.

When the Civil War began, Jackson threw his lot in with Virginia, and enlisted in the Confederate Army. He was commissioned a General. The first great battle of this war was known as Bull Run, or the Battle of Manassas. The Confederate troops were driven back but were rallied on a half-plateau by General Jackson.

Here they stood immovable, for Jackson refused to retreat a step. An officer rushed up and said, "General, they are beating us back, and we are without ammunition."

"Then, sir," replied Jackson, "we will give them the bayonet."

A few minutes later, seeing the troops around Jackson, standing their ground so firmly, General Bee, a Confederate officer, cried out to his own men:

"Look at Jackson's brigade! It stands like a stone wall."

After this incident, the great soldier was known in history as "Stonewall" Jackson.

Like many other soldiers Jackson never used coffee, tobacco, or whisky. Nor could he bear to hear any one utter profane language. He never reframed from expressing his disapproval of swearing.

Often, in winter, he would go without an overcoat, saying, "I do not wish to give in to the cold." Once, when told by his surgeon that he needed a little brandy, he replied, "I like it too well; that is the reason I never take it. I am more afraid of it than of Federal bullets."

Jackson always shared the hardships of his men. On one occasion, when his brigade was worn out with marching, he said, "Let the poor fellows sleep. I will guard the camp myself." Accordingly, he acted as sentinel during the night, while his tired men took their rest.

Jackson became the ablest Lieutenant of General Lee, who relied upon him implicitly. He was often sent upon most important and most dangerous missions, but his skill was so great that he always returned victorious. So rapid were the movements of his troops, that they became known as "Jackson's foot cavalry."

At the battle of Chancellorsville, Lee sent Jackson around to the rear of Hooker's army. Jackson fell so suddenly upon the flank of the Federals that they were thrown into confusion. The result of the attack was to defeat Hooker's plan, and to check his advance.

The victory was dearly bought. Jackson had ridden out in the gathering darkness to reconnoiter the positions of the enemy and was returning to camp. He ran into a body of his own troops, who, mistaking his party for Federal cavalry, fired upon them. Jackson fell from his horse mortally wounded.

He was borne on a stretcher to a farmhouse nearby where he died after a few days. His final thoughts were of the battle, and he muttered orders to his men as his life ebbed away.

His last words were, "Let us cross over the river, and rest under the shade of the trees."

His death was a great loss to the Confederate cause. Lee wept when he heard the sad news, and said, "I have indeed lost my right arm."

Chapter 78

Stealing a Locomotive

One day, in April, 1862, a passenger train was on its way from Marietta, Georgia, bound North. At Marietta, about twenty men, in civilian clothes, had boarded the train, nobody paying any special attention to them. Yet these men were bent upon a desperate adventure.

Eight miles beyond Marietta the train stopped ten minutes for breakfast at the station, called Big Shanty. Everybody was hungry, and soon the passengers, the conductor, the engineer, and the fireman were in the breakfast room. The men who had boarded the train at Marietta quietly stole toward the locomotive, instead of following the others. No one paid any heed to their movements, in spite of the fact that a sentinel was walking his beat hardly a dozen steps away.

One of the men climbed into the cab of the locomotive, another slipped in between two cars and pulled out the coupling pin, while the others climbed into an empty box-car. Finally, the man in the cab laid his hand upon the throttle. The engine moved off with three box cars, leaving the passenger coaches standing on the tracks.

The sentinel, in alarm, fired off his gun, and the passengers ran out just in time to see the locomotive and cars disappearing in the distance. The engine had been stolen, and the men were on their way to the Federal lines. The conductor was so frightened by this disaster that he started on a run up the track, in frantic but useless haste to overtake the fugitives. The amazed passengers stood helplessly on the platform, quite powerless to do anything.

The men who had stolen the locomotive were a party of Northern scouts, who had made their way in disguise into the Southern lines, with the intention of stealing a train, burning the bridges behind them, and make useless the only railroad by which troops could be sent to Chattanooga to oppose the Union forces. Their enterprise had succeeded thus far, and they were rapidly making their way North.

Their only peril seemed to be the telegraph wires, by which information could be sent on ahead, and their flight arrested. Therefore, they stopped a few miles out of town while one of the men climbed a pole and cut the wires. Then they started again on their way. Occasionally, they had to stop for wood or water. The leader of the party, named Andrews, answered all questions by saying, "We are taking a trainload of powder to General Beauregard," and pointed to the boxcars as evidence of his statement.

At Kingston, thirty miles from Big Shanty, the party drew into a siding to let a local train go by. Andrews expected to move away after this, but, to his dismay, the train carried a red flag, showing that another train was just behind.

"How does it happen that this road is blocked when I have orders to hasten with this powder to General Beauregard?" he asked sharply of the conductor.

The conductor replied, "We have orders to move everything out of Chattanooga, and there are a number of trains on this track. You will have to wait, or run into a collision if you go on." This was bad news for the Union soldiers, for they had to wait an hour while tram after train passed, carrying the red flag. At last, one went by without that signal, and Andrews and his men gladly leaped on board their own train and started wildly up the track, hoping to escape before they were suspected or pursued.

"The race was on."

Yet they must guard against pursuit. Stopping their train, they sprang out to tear up the rails of the track in order to check any such danger. Hardly had they gotten out their tools before they heard, far down the track, the ominous whistle of a locomotive, evidently coming under full speed. Abandoning their intention, they sprang aboard in alarm and haste, and started ahead under full steam.

The race was on, for the conductor and engineer of the stolen train had secured another locomotive and cab, and, filling it with Confederate soldiers, had started in hot pursuit of the daring scouts. Andrews and his men well knew their fate if they were caught. They were not only robbers, but they were also spies, and capture meant death.

On went the Union soldiers at full speed; on came their pursuers hardly a mile behind! The locomotives were well matched, and thundered over the rails at a perilous rate. If the scouts could only stop long enough to tear up a rail, or even to pile up an obstruction of ties, all might be safe, but the pursuit was too hot, and there was no safety except in flight!

Andrews now uncoupled the rear boxcar, hoping thus to wreck his pursuers by a collision. The Confederates saw the danger in time to slow down, pick up the car, and push it on ahead of their engine. Andrews tried the same trick a second time, but again the Confederates caught the boxcar, and went on pushing two cars. On reaching a siding, at Resaca, the Confederate engineer pushed the two cars into a switch and left them there, while he started again in pursuit.

Not far beyond was a bridge, which Andrews hoped to destroy. Setting fire to the third boxcar by means of oil, he stopped it midway on the bridge, and left it there in full blaze. The bridge was covered, but fortunately the roof was wet because of recent rains. Dense smoke poured from each end of the blazing car, but the Confederate engineer was not dismayed. Right into the smoke he ran, caught the boxcar and pushed it off the bridge. In a few minutes, the flames were extinguished, and all danger was over.

The Union soldiers were now in a sad plight. Their wood and water were exhausted, and their steam was getting low. Their engine was slowing down, and escape was impossible. The men sprang from the engine, and rushed into the woods, scattering in every direction.

Soon, the Confederate engine arrived, and a hot pursuit of the fugitives began. The alarm spread rapidly, and the whole country was aroused. In a few hours several of the men were captured. The rest hid in the woods and swamps, and lived the best they could on roots and berries. But by the end of the week, all had been found, and put into prison. The leaders were executed "as spies and robbers."

Chapter 79

Sam Davis

In times of war it is necessary to have scouts, whose duty it is to go into the enemy's lines, and far into the enemy's country, in order to get valuable information, and bring it back to their commanders.

These scouts are called "spies" by the enemy, and if they are caught, they are put to death by the rules of warfare. They frequently disguise themselves by wearing the enemy's uniform, or the clothes of a civilian. Sometimes they dress and act as if they were quite different persons from what they really are. A young scout may play the part of an innocent old farmer, even of a woman; or take any character that will suit his purpose.

It is a life full of danger and adventure. A scout must be very brave and quick-witted. He has no one to depend upon but himself, and his wits are often called upon to do their best to get him out of trouble. He is sometimes absent for days and even weeks, and no one hears a word from him, until he returns with the information wanted.

He brings word of the size of the enemy's army, of their equipment, and of the strength of their positions. He often learns the plans of their pro- posed battles, and the next movement of their troops. In this way, his commander will know exactly when to attack his enemy, and how best to defend himself.

Sam Davis was a young Confederate soldier, detailed as a scout. He was only seventeen years old, but he was a fine rider, and knew all the country into which he was expected to go. General Bragg, of the Confederate Army, desired to know the strength of the Federal forts in middle Tennessee, and he selected Sam Davis to bring him the information.

When Davis came before him. General Bragg said, "Davis, I wish you to get this information for me. It is a dangerous task, my boy, but you know the country and you are the best one to go. Be very careful, for if you are caught, you will be shot as a spy. You need not go if you do not wish to."

Davis stood erect, saluted the General, and said, "I am not afraid. I know the country and am ready to go. I also know the dangers, and what will happen to me if I am caught. What are your instructions, sir?"

He rode off early one morning dressed in a disguise. What he did or where he received the information or from whom he obtained it, will never be known, for it was never told by anyone.

After several weeks' absence, Davis had procured all the data he needed, and was on his way back to his own lines. In his possession were very important papers and drawings. As he was riding along, thinking that in a few hours he would be beyond danger of capture, he saw a body of Federal soldiers in the road. Hoping to pass them without disturbance, he rode boldly on as if he were going to work somewhere.

One of the soldiers said, "We had better stop that boy. He might be a spy." So they called upon Davis to halt, and to get down from his horse. In spite of his protests of innocence, he was searched, and the papers were found in his clothes.

Hurriedly, the boy was taken before the Union General, and the papers found upon him were shown. He was court-martialed, and, according to the rules of war, was ordered to be shot the next day at sunrise. Davis heard the sentence without uttering a word, or even changing color.

The Union General was much affected by the brave conduct of the young scout. Sending for him to come to his tent, he said to him,

"My boy, you are very young, and you are very brave. I hate to take a life like yours. If you will tell me who gave you those papers, I will let you go free. Think of your mother and father, and of the life before you, and save yourself."

Davis shook his head, and said, "General, I received those papers from a friend, and I shall not tell his name."

The General then said, "Davis, if you do not tell me the name of your friend, I shall be compelled, by the rules of war, to order you shot tomorrow morning. I hate to do this, for I should like to save your life. But I cannot help you if you refuse."

Davis answered, "Do you suppose I would save my own life by betraying a friend? I have never betrayed anything in all my life, and I shall not do so now. I would rather die a thousand times than betray any secret committed to my care."

There were tears in the eyes of the General. He thought of his own boys, and of his own scouts who had done similar service for him and had gotten off safe. Turning to the guard, he said simply, "Take the lad away. It nearly breaks my heart to sign this order."

The next morning, Davis was led before a file of soldiers. At the very last, he was firm in his refusal to give any information as to where he received the papers. Those around him begged him to change his mind, but he answered quietly,

"No, I shall not betray my friend. I have given my word. I am ready to die as a soldier and a man."

The bandage was placed over his eyes, and, in a few moments, the reports of the rifle told of the end of Sam Davis's life. On the grounds of the capitol in Nashville there is a beautiful monument erected to his memory by the State of Tennessee.

Chapter 80

An Escape from Prison

Libby Prison was in Richmond, Virginia. Before the Civil War, it was a tobacco warehouse, close by the Lynchburg Canal, and not far from the James River. It was three stories high in front, and four in the rear, built of brick and stone, with thick partition walls which divided it into three sections, with a cellar under each.

The first floor contained three apartments, one for the prison authorities, one as a hospital, and the third for cooking and dining purposes. The upper stories had sleeping quarters for the prisoners. In this prison, one thousand Union soldiers were confined.

There was little chance of escape from it. A strong guard surrounded the prison, and every precaution was taken. The only attempt at escape that even partially succeeded was made by a number of Union prisoners through an underground tunnel.

The enterprise was undertaken by a few of the most daring of the Union soldiers, and was carefully kept secret from the others. One of the cellars, reserved for the storage of old boxes and barrels, was used as a starting place. Fortunately, it was never visited by the prison authorities, and, once at work, the prisoners could proceed without much fear of detection or interruption.

How to reach the cellar and begin excavating the tunnel was the first question to be solved. It was decided to remove the stones and brick in the fireplace of the cooking room, and to make a sloping entrance into the cellar. All this work was done at night, with as little noise as possible, by several prisoners who were stonemasons by trade. By day, the bricks and stones were carefully replaced, and all evidence of their labors was covered up. In a few days the cellar was reached, and all was ready to begin digging the tunnel.

This proposed tunnel was to be just large enough to admit one man, crawling on hands and knees. It was to cross a narrow street, and enter a lot used as a stable yard, which was concealed from the street by a high board fence. Once in this yard, and behind the fence, the prisoners would be safe from detection from the street, and could make good their escape through the other side of the stable yard.

The work on the tunnel began. It was eight or nine feet underground, and only one man could dig at a time. The only tools they had were pocket knives, small hatchets, a broken fire-shovel, and pieces of firewood. But the earth was soft, and the prospect of liberty was alluring.

Night after night the work went on, one man digging forward and another one passing the dirt back to others who scattered it on the floor of the cellar and covered it with straw. The air in the tunnel was very close; the positions of the men were cramped; and there was constant danger of the earth caving in. But these daring men worked on, for they were struggling to gain their freedom.

In about three weeks, the tunnel was considered to be long enough, and so the forward workman began to dig upwards. In a short while, he had made an opening, and cautiously stuck his head out. To his dismay he found he was on the wrong side of the fence, and still in the street, with a sentry only a few yards away. Fortunately, the sentry did not see him. Quickly concealing the opening with grass, and packing it from underneath so it would look like a hole in the ground, the workman succeeded in avoiding detection, and work on the tunnel was renewed.

Ten feet further on brought them well inside the stable yard, and behind the protecting fence. The opening was now made, and, to the joy of the prisoners, the way of escape seemed plain. The evening of February 9, 1864, was appointed as the time to make their dash for liberty. The hour set was nine o'clock. One can well imagine the intense eagerness and excitement with which the men awaited the moment for their adventure.

About one hundred men, who were in on the secret, assembled and, in single file, one by one, they crawled through the opening in the fireplace, across the cellar, and into the tunnel. There was no crowding and no rushing. The men proceeded silently on their knees, one behind the other, and climbed out into the stable yard.

As soon as two emerged, they made off together, and, crossing the yard, came into a nearby street. They strolled away, conversing in ordinary tones, as though they were citizens bent on their own affairs. They wore no prison clothes, so their appearance excited no suspicion. In about three hours, one hundred and nine men had escaped, and had scattered through the town. Not one of them had been challenged by the guard, who was pacing his rounds on the other side of the fence.

The fugitives found themselves in well lit streets, filled with people, and with shops open.

But they gave no sign of haste. Talking and laughing, they proceeded to the outskirts of the town, and disappeared into the open country.

The absence of so many at roll-call the next morning excited the suspicion of the prison authorities. A search was immediately begun, and, as soon as the facts were established, an alarm was sent out to scour the country for the escaped prisoners. Of those who had gone, fifty-five reached the Union lines in safety, but fifty-four were recaptured.

Chapter 81

Running the Blockade

During the Civil War, the harbors of the Southern ports were closely blockaded, so as to cut off supplies from foreign countries. In spite of the watchful gunboats patrolling the coasts, there were many adventurous blockade-runners, that slipped past the patrol, carrying supplies to the Confederacy, and bringing out cotton and other products for foreign trade. The life of a blockade-runner was full of perils and thrilling experiences.

This is the story of how a blockade-runner made its way into Wilmington, North Carolina, which lies about sixteen miles up Cape Fear River. At the mouth of the river was Fort Fisher, whose guns kept the blockading fleet some distance away, thus giving a blockade-runner a chance to slip in, once under protection of the fort.

The mouth of the river was heavily patrolled by Federal vessels. There were three sections of them, one cordon as near shore as was safe, and two others lying outside, so that a blockade-runner must needs be very alert to get by their vigilance.

The Banshee was a blockade-runner operating from Nassau. On her first run into Wilmington, she left the shores of the Bahamas, and crept noiselessly along, invisible in the darkness, and keeping well out of sight of vessels in the daytime.

During the day, a man was stationed in the cross-trees, and the moment a sail was seen on the horizon, *The Banshee* would turn in the opposite direction, until the sail was lost beyond the horizon. Every time the look-out man saw a sail, he was given a dollar. If the sail was discovered first from the deck, the look-out man was fined five dollars.

Thus, two days passed, and *The Banshee* neared her destination. The night was dark, but calm and clear. No lights were allowed, not even a cigar. The steersman had to see as much of the compass as he could through a shield that came almost to his eyes. Absolute silence prevailed, as the blockade-runner moved into the danger zone.

At length, they were opposite the mouth of Cape Fear River.

"Better cast a lead, Captain, to find the bottom," whispered the Pilot.

A muttered order down the engine-room tube and *The Banshee* slowed down and then stopped. The lead was cast, and the report was "Sixteen fathoms – sandy bottom with black specks."

"Not far enough in, and too far southward," said the Pilot. "We must get away from that bottom before we head in shore."

At the end of an hour, the lead was cast again, and the Pilot whispered to the steersman, "All right, we are opposite the mouth of the river. Starboard, and go easy."

The ship crept along slowly in the darkness. Not a sound was heard except the beat of the paddle floats. Suddenly, the pilot grasped the Captain's arm.

"There's one of them, on the starboard bow," he whispered.

A moment afterward, a long, low, black ship was seen, not a hundred yards away, lying still on the water. *The Banshee* drifted by as noiselessly as possible. Not a movement was seen on the patrol boat, and, in a half-hour, it was lost in the darkness.

Not long afterwards came the whispered alarm, "Steamer on the port bow." Another cruiser was close by.

"Hard-a-port!" said the Captain to the steersman, and *The Banshee* swung around, barely missing the cruiser.

Hardly had this second ship been passed, before a third one loomed up, dead ahead, steaming slowly across the bow of *The Banshee.*

"Stop her," was the quick order down the engine-room tube, and *The Banshee* lay dead on the water.

"Instead of going around those blockaders, we are going through them," said the Pilot to the Captain. "Our only hope is that they will not recognize us and will take us for one of them."

Day was not far off, and *The Banshee* must make haste to get inside the cordons of the blockade. She was headed straight for the white line of surf on the shore. As much speed as possible was made, and all eyes were strained for any familiar landmarks.

Daylight now streaked the East. Fort Fisher was some distance off and the gunboats were still on the watch for blockade-runners. In a half hour, *The Banshee* would be safe or else captured.

Six or seven gunboats appeared out of the mist, and headed for the blockade-runner, to discover her identity.

"Full steam ahead, and a race for the fort!" cried the Captain.

Displaying her flag, she ran full steam toward the protecting guns of the fort. It was now a question of speed and distance, for *The Banshee* was discovered, and her purpose was known! Boom! came the roar of guns across the waters. Splash! Splash! fell the shells uncomfortably near the runner, which was carrying a cargo of ammunition.

But Fort Fisher was now awake, and the guns began to roar. Every minute brought *The Banshee* nearer to safety, and the gunboats into greater danger. The guns from the fort rained shells over *The Banshee* and into the sides of her pursuers.

With a sullen roar, and a parting shot, the gunboats drew off, and the blockade-runner glided under the walls of the fort.

In and out, ran *The Banshee*, trip after trip, bringing in guns, ammunition, and medicines, and carrying out cotton and tobacco. Her daring crew had many narrow escapes before the war came to an end.

Chapter 82

Through the Heart of the South

The Civil War was drawing to a close. The exhausted Confederacy was bleeding to death. There was a shortage of men and supplies, but the South was hanging on desperately to a cause that already was doomed. Grant and Lee were fighting it out in Virginia, while Sherman, the Northern General, having captured Atlanta, was making ready for his march to the sea.

His army of sixty thousand men was unopposed. The fair, open country was before them, with the harvests of the fall already gathered in the barns. It was to be a march of destruction, but without violence to the people themselves.

"The people must feel the hard hand of war. It is better to lose property than to lose lives. This is the best means to end the war," were the reflections of General Sherman, as his men started out on their six-week long march to the sea.

The distance was three hundred miles, and the soldiers were told to live on the country, as they advanced. There was no need of wagon trains, when the land was provided with food which was being gathered for the Confederate soldiers in Virginia.

The Federal army spread out to cover a front of forty miles. The men had orders to march about fifteen miles a day, and to forage as they went along. These foragers brought in poultry, vegetables, cattle, and food supplies of all kinds. They had orders not to destroy property needlessly, but these orders were not strictly observed, and, in many instances, farm houses, gin houses, and cotton crops were burned, while fields were laid waste. Often, the horses were taken from the farms, and the cows and hogs were driven away or else slaughtered for the immediate use of the soldiers.

In spite of regulations, a large number of "bummers" and thieves followed the army, who were not responsible to any orders. Before these bandits the Southern people were helpless. They not only robbed houses of their provisions, but took away silverware, clothing and valuable articles of furniture.

In order to do as much damage to the Confederacy as possible, the Union soldiers tore up the railroad tracks, burned the ties, and, heating the rails, bent many of them around the telegraph poles. In this way, a path of desolation was cut through the heart of the South, that did much to hasten the inevitable end of the conflict.

The Union army was followed by crowds of slaves, many of them neither knowing where they were headed, nor what the march meant. They were just moving along with the soldiers, careless and happy, singing songs by night, and helping the marching men by day.

"Bless the Lord, we are free, and we're going along with these soldiers," said one old woman with a child in her arms.

"But where are you going, and what will you do when you get there?" asked one of the officers.

"That makes no difference now. That's a month off. I never look that far ahead," was the woman's philosophical reply.

The soldiers traveled along leisurely. The weather was good, the supplies were sufficient, the march was unopposed. All the telegraph lines were cut, and no news of their whereabouts was sent to the North.

Finally, General Sherman reached Savannah. On Christmas Eve he sent a message to President Lincoln:

"I beg to present to you, as a Christmas gift, the city of Savannah, with one hundred and fifty guns, and plenty of ammunition; also about twenty-five thousand bales of cotton."

President Lincoln replied, "Many, many thanks for your Christmas gift – the capture of Savannah. When you were leaving Atlanta for the Atlantic coast, I was anxious, if not fearful; but feeling that you were the better judge, and remembering that 'nothing risked, nothing gained' I did not interfere. Now, the undertaking being a success, the honor is all yours . . . Not only does it afford the obvious and immediate military advantage; but . . . it brings those who sat in darkness, to see a great light. But what next? I suppose it will be safer if I leave Gen. Grant and yourself to decide. Please make my grateful acknowledgements to your whole army, officers and men."

Thus it was that Sherman's army marched through Georgia, doing no violence to the people, but doing a property damage that was estimated at one hundred million dollars. Such is the sad havoc of war.

Chapter 83

The Surrender of General Lee

At a house, in the little town of Appomattox, Virginia, on April 9, 1865, a memorable event took place. General Robert E. Lee here met General Ulysses S. Grant, and surrendered the Confederate Army under his command.

For four years, the terrible war between the North and South had been going on, until the Southern Army was reduced to a bare handful of ill-fed and badly clothed men. The South had been drained of her men and supplies, and Lee saw it was useless to continue the unequal struggle any longer.

The two great Generals met by agreement in this village to arrange terms for the cessation of hostilities.

The contrast between the two men was striking.

Grant was forty-three years of age, five feet, eight inches tall, with brown hair and full brown beard. He wore a single-breasted blouse, of dark blue flannel, an ordinary pair of top-boots, with his trousers inside; he was without spurs, and he had no sword. A pair of shoulder-straps was all to show his rank. Around him sat or stood a dozen of his staff officers.

Lee, on the other hand, was six feet tall, and faultlessly attired. His hair and beard were silver gray, and quite thick for one of his age. He was sixteen years older than Grant. He wore a new Confederate uniform, and, by his side, was a sword of exquisite workmanship, the hilt studded with jewels. It was the sword presented to him by the State of Virginia. His boots were new and clean, and he wore a pair of handsome spurs. He was attended by a single officer, his military secretary.

Lee was the first to arrive, and, when Grant entered, he arose and bowed profoundly. Grant and his officers returned the greeting. Grant then sat at a marble-top table, in the center of the room, while Lee sat at a small oval table, near a window.

General Grant began the conversation by saying, "I met you once before, General Lee, while we were serving in Mexico. I have always remembered your appearance, and I think I should have recognized you anywhere."

"Yes," replied Lee, "I know I met you in Mexico, and I have often thought of it. Those were wonderful experiences for us, when we were young soldiers."

After a few more remarks about Mexico, Lee said, "I suppose, General Grant, that the object of our meeting is understood. I asked to see you to find out upon what terms you would receive the surrender of my army."

Grant replied, "The terms are that all officers and men surrendered are to be paroled, and are not to take up arms again; and all guns, ammunition, and supplies are to be handed over as captured property."

Lee suggested that the terms be written out for his acceptance. This was done, Grant adding that the side-arms, horses, and baggage of the officers were not to be included in the terms of surrender. There was no demand made for the surrender of Lee's sword, nor was there any offer of it on Lee's part. In fact, nothing was said about it.

When the document was written, Lee took out his glasses, and slowly put them on. Reading the terms of surrender, he remarked,

"I would like to mention that the cavalry and artillery own their horses. I would like to know whether those men will be permitted to retain their own stock."

Grant immediately replied, "I take it that most of the men in the ranks are small farmers, and, as the country has been so raided by the armies, it is doubtful if they will be able to put in a crop to carry them through next winter without the aid of the horses they now have. I will instruct the officers to let the men, who claim to own horses or mules, take the animals home with them to work their farms."

Lee appreciated this concession, and said, "This will have the very best possible effect upon the men. It will do much toward conciliating our people." He then wrote out his acceptance of the terms of the surrender.

When this was done, General Grant introduced the members of his staff to General Lee. Some of them Lee had known before, and the conversation became general and cordial. Lee at length said,

Lee surrenders to Grant

"General Grant, I have a thousand or more of your men as prisoners, a number of them officers. I shall be glad to send them into your lines as soon as possible, for I have no provisions for them. I have indeed nothing for my own men. They have been living for the last few days on parched corn, and we are badly in need of both rations and forage."

General Grant immediately offered to receive the prisoners back into his own lines, and said, "I will take steps to have your army supplied with rations at once." Turning to an officer, he gave the command for the issuing of the rations to the hungry Confederate Army.

The two Generals then shook hands, and, bowing gravely to the others, Lee prepared to depart. Reaching the porch, he signaled for the orderly to bring up his horse. When it was ready, he mounted and rode away, to break the sad news to the brave fellows he had so long commanded.

The news of the surrender reached the Union lines, and firing of salutes began at several places. Grant sent orders to stop this, saying,

"The war is over, and it is ill-becoming to rejoice in the downfall of a gallant foe."

Chapter 84

Laying the Atlantic Cable

A number of years before the Civil War, a wealthy, retired merchant of New York City, named Cyrus W. Field, sat in the library of his home, studying a large globe of the world. He was thinking about the electric telegraph that Morse had invented, and was wondering how far it would carry a message.

He was also thinking about what a friend had said to him a short while before that the ocean bottom was a table-land along a certain direction, and could easily hold an electric cable, if it were laid properly.

"What an advantage it would be to civilization if the electric telegraph could be used between countries on opposite sides of the ocean," he said to himself. "Tomorrow I will speak to my friend Peter Cooper about it."

The next morning, he not only talked the matter over with Peter Cooper, but wrote a letter to Samuel Morse.

Peter Cooper afterwards said, "I am glad that Field chose me among the first to discuss this great enterprise, but I felt sure at the time that most people would think us crazy."

Cooper, however, agreed to the enterprise, because he saw that a great deal of good could come of it, and he wanted to help his friend, Cyrus Field. Together, they went to their wealthy friends, and raised a large sum of money to form the Atlantic Telegraph Company.

The first undertaking was to lay a line on the ocean bed, from the mainland to the island of Newfoundland. This was readily done, and was a success, showing that cable lines could transmit messages under the water.

Field and Morse then went to England, and appeared before the British Government. "We have come to propose to your lordships that you join us in uniting, by an electric cable, the two great countries of Great Britain and America. It will take a great deal of money, but, in the end it will bring much benefit to both peoples. We are ready to do our part."

"But suppose you make the attempt and fail, and your cable is lost at the bottom of the sea. Then, what will you do?" asked an Englishman.

"Why, if the cable is lost, I shall lay another, and another, until one does reach and hold. Every cable I lose I shall charge to profit and loss, and then I shall start over again," was the reply of the American.

This so pleased the British that they at once offered to furnish money and a vessel to help lay the cable. Congress also appropriated money, and thus the two Governments were pledged to the great enterprise.

The British ship, *Agamemnon*, and the American ship, *Niagara*, were set apart for the work. Each vessel carried a load of cable, and they sailed from the coast of Ireland. On board the American ship were Field and Morse.

The Niagara began the work. The cable was securely anchored to the shore, and unwound along the bottom of the ocean, as the vessel steamed slowly along. Mile after mile was paid out in this way, the big cylinder slowly revolving, and the long, dark cable falling into the ocean bed. Day and night the work went on, the other vessel standing by to take up the work when the Niagara had exhausted her supply of cable.

At the end of three hundred miles there was a wrench and a tug, and the cable snapped in two. There was a great cry; "The cable has parted; the cable has parted."

Naturally, this caused bitter disappointment and much discouragement. "You will never succeed. It is too great an undertaking. You had better give it up," was all that Field heard on every side.

"I shall not give it up," said he, "but will start in mid-ocean, and let the vessels go in opposite directions, one toward Ireland and the other toward Newfoundland."

And so he did. With a new supply of cable, he started, in mid-ocean, having spliced the ends of the cable together. Each vessel sailed towards its own country, slowly paying out the cable on the ocean bed from the great coil in the stern.

In a few weeks, there came the news, "The cable is laid." The people were now as excited over the success of the cable as they had been gloomy and doubtful beforehand. Bells were rung, guns were fired, and great placards were hung about the streets of New York. And there were many speeches of congratulations!

On the 16th of August, 1858, Queen Victoria sent a cable message to President Buchanan, and the President sent a courteous reply. They were messages of friendship and good-will between the two countries, now united by a cable nearly three thousand miles long, over which a message could travel in the fraction of a second.

But amidst all the rejoicing came word that for some reason the cable would not work. No more messages could be transmitted, and nobody could find out the reason why. More than a million dollars had been spent, and nothing profitable had come of it!

Then the Civil War began, and for four years the American people thought of little else than the great struggle. Cyrus Field was forgotten, but he did not forget, nor did he lose hope.

"When the war is over, and the mind of the world is settled, I shall try again, but not until then," he said to some friends.

At last, the time came, and Field renewed his efforts. He now had but one vessel, *The Great Eastern*. It was a monster ship, remodeled for the purpose of carrying the cable and laying it on the ocean bed. Another failure was added to the list of early attempts, for the cable parted in midocean, and sank to the bottom.

Again an effort was made, and *The Great Eastern* set sail with its coil of cable. This last trip was crowned with success, and the cable was laid.

Then *The Great Eastern* returned to mid-ocean, and began grappling for the cable she had lost on her first voyage. The broken ends were found, welded together properly, and, before the end of 1866, two cables were working between Ireland and America.

Field had labored for thirteen years, and had spent a great deal of money, but at last he had succeeded. More than a dozen cables crossed the Atlantic, and many stretched over the vast bed of the Pacific; all shores are were in touch with each other, and messages could be sent around the world in a few hours.

This is due to the energy and perseverance of the man who did not know how to fail, and who would not give up trying!

But the inventor kept on working, and, the year after the

Centennial, the telephone was put into practical use by the public. People at first thought it was a luxury, and they were slow to adopt it. But then it became a household convenience and a business necessity. It is no longer regarded as a toy, but it has been added to the long list of American inventions that facilitate business and make life more comfortable.

Chapter 85

The Story of the Telephone

There was a great Exposition held in Philadelphia in 1876. It was called the Centennial, because it celebrated the one-hundredth anniversary of the Declaration of Independence. Nearly every country in the world contributed to the exhibits, and people from every nation came to see the wonderful display of art and industry.

Among the visitors was Dom Pedro, the Emperor of Brazil. He was a man of great knowledge, and was much interested in invention. The officials of the Exposition showed him special attention. Among other things, he was asked to a room where the judges were passing on the objects offered for exhibition. A young man was speaking to the Committee.

"I have here a new invention," he said, "the purpose of which is to convey the human voice over a wire by electricity, so that it can be heard a long distance off. I call it a telephone."

The judges were tired, and the hour was late. They were about to dismiss the young man without even trying to see whether his invention would work. They did not put the receiver to their ears, nor did they speak in the mouth-piece when the inventor asked them to do so.

Dom Pedro stood in the doorway, and listened to what was going on. He saw the eagerness in the face of the young man, and noticed the indifference of the judges. He felt indignant that so much enthusiasm should meet with so great a rebuff.

Stepping into the room, he was surprised to recognize the young man as Alexander Graham Bell, whom he had met in Boston, and to whom he had already taken a great fancy.

"Let me examine your instrument, if you please," he said politely, and put the receiver to his ear.

Bell went into another room, where the other end of the wire was, and recited into the transmitter some lines from a great poem, which Dom Pedro heard distinctly.

"This is very wonderful," he said. "I think, gentlemen, you will make a mistake not to allow Mr. Bell to exhibit his telephone, for it is a very interesting device, and may some day be a serviceable one."

The judges were anxious to please their distinguished visitor, and so allowed the telephone to have space.

"It is merely a toy, and it might amuse the public, at any rate," said one.

Alexander Graham Bell demonstrates the telephone.

But this toy proved to be one of the great attractions at the Exposition. Crowds came every day to hear the voices of their friends over the wire. The question asked by many was, "Have you tried the telephone yet?"

Alexander Graham Bell also taught lip-reading to the deaf. They were taught to know what others were saying by watching the motion of their lips. The system had been worked out by Bell's father, but young Bell had greatly improved upon it. He had succeeded in teaching persons, born deaf, and those who had become deaf in infancy, not only to understand the motion of lips, but also to speak.

One of his pupils was a young girl who had lost her hearing when a baby, and, in consequence, her speech also. She was a lovable, bright girl. Bell taught her to speak and to understand what others were saying. She afterwards became his wife, and helped him with his telephone.

Work on the telephone was done by the inventor at odd hours, after he had finished his day's teaching. He was very poor, and could not afford to buy material or tools. The first telephone was made out of an old cigar-box, two hundred feet of wire, and two magnets taken from a toy fish pond.

Chapter 86

Thomas Edison, The Great Inventor

The story of our great inventors would not be complete without telling about Edison, the greatest of them all. When he was a boy, he sold papers for a while on a train. On one occasion, while he was standing at a station, he saw a little child playing on the track. Just at that moment, a train came thundering along. Edison jumped on the track, in front of the moving engine, and rescued the child. The father was the telegraph operator at the station. To show his gratitude, he offered to teach telegraphy to the young newsboy.

In a few years, Edison became a swift and competent operator. He was offered employment in a Boston office. When he appeared, dressed in shabby clothes, for he was very poor, the other operators in the room made fun of him. But Edison did not care, and took his place at his desk. In a short time, an operator from New York, noted for his swiftness, called up the Boston office.

"Let the new man take the message," said the chief. He desired to try out Edison, of whose ability he knew nothing.

Edison sat down, and for four hours and a half wrote the message, as it came over the wire. Not once did he ask the operator to go more slowly, but kept up with him easily. Faster and faster ticked the instrument, while Edison's fingers flew over the pages, taking down every word as it came.

The other operators gathered around in amazement to see this exhibition of speed. Edison paid no attention to them.

At the end of a long period, the operator sending the message

inquired over the wire,

"Who are you taking this message?" Edison replied, "I am Thomas A. Edison, the new operator."

"You are the first man in the country," was the reply, "who could ever take me at my fastest, and the only one who could sit at the other end of my wire for more than two hours and a half. I am proud to know you."

All the time that Edison was an operator, his mind was busy on inventions and improvements. When he was seventeen, he invented the duplex telegraph, by which several messages could be sent on the same wire at the same time, even in opposite directions, without causing any confusion. This was a great saving of time.

Shortly afterwards, he went to New York, where he soon became known as an electrical expert. The first invention that brought him any considerable money was the ticker for stockbrokers' offices. This ticker was an electrical machine for recording quotations in the stock market. He was paid forty thousand dollars for this invention.

He next persuaded some men in New York to furnish the money for him to experiment in making a lamp for the electric light. They agreed to pay all his expenses, and, if it was a success, they were to share in the profits. Edison moved to Menlo Park, New Jersey, and opened a little shop and laboratory.

After awhile, he announced that he

Some of Edison's first light bulbs

had made an electric lamp that would burn, and soon had eighty electric lights in Menlo Park. This was very promising, and everybody was greatly interested in the results. Suddenly, the lamps went out, and Edison was much discouraged, but he was not the man to give up.

For five days and nights he remained at his laboratory, sleeping only a few hours at a time. The world declared the electric lamps a failure. One prominent man said they could not be made,

"I will make a statue of that man, and light it with electric lights, and put a sign on it, saying 'Here is the man that said the Edison lamp will not burn,'" was the inventor's reply.

After much hard labor, Edison discovered that the reason why his lamp would not burn was because the air had not been sufficiently exhausted from the glass bulbs. So he set about remedying the defect, after which the lamps burned brightly and lasted a long time. Soon all the world used electric light.

Edison invented the first electric railway, and because of him the electric cars are used on the streets of nearly every city, large and small. He invented the phonograph for recording and reproducing sound. He also invented the kinetoscope, which was the beginning of moving pictures.

Many other inventions have been made by him; so many, indeed, that he accumulated a large fortune, and was known as "The Wizard of Menlo Park."

It is quite certain that no other inventor has produced so many things that have added to the comfort and pleasure of the world as Thomas A. Edison.

Chapter 87

Clara Barton and the Red Cross

At the outbreak of the Civil War, a young woman who was a clerk in the Patent Office in Washington, gave up her position, and volunteered to nurse soldiers without pay. She knew that the sick, wounded, and dying men would need comfort. Her name was Clara Barton. She did not go to hospitals, where it was safe for her to be, but she went on the battlefields, where the awful carnage of death was around her.

Inspired by her example, other women undertook the same work, some going to the hospitals, and others following the armies, but all nursing the sick, comforting the dying, and keeping their last messages for the loved ones at home.

Years before, on one hot day in the summer of 1859, there was fought the great battle of Solferino in Italy, at the end of which more than thirty-five thousand men lay dead and wounded on the field of battle. There was no aid for them. For hours and even days they lay where they had fallen. A Swiss, by the name of Henri Dunant, visited the battlefield, and was so overcome by its horrors that he wrote circular letters, and delivered lectures, calling upon all nations to form some sort of a society to relieve the distress of the wounded.

"If nations will go to war, then there should be some means to help those who suffer by it. I call upon all nations to send representatives to Geneva, Switzerland, in order to establish a society for this purpose," said he.

The conference met, and formed an organization, which had for its purpose the care of the sick and wounded on the battlefield and in hospitals. The society adopted a badge, or flag, which was a red cross on a white ground. This was done in compliment to the Swiss Republic, whose flag was a white cross on a red ground. The organization soon became known as The Red Cross Society. Many nations signed an agreement to respect the principals of this Society.

When Clara Barton, who was in Switzerland in 1869 to recover her health, heard of this society, she was filled with joy and hope. It was the kind of work she most loved, and she resolved to give her whole life to the Red Cross.

At the beginning of the Franco-Prussian War in 1870, Clara Barton saw her opportunity for service. After the siege of Strasburg, there were twenty thousand people without homes and employment, and starvation threatened them all. Clara Barton secured materials for thirty thousand garments, and gave them out to the poor women of the city to be made up. She paid good wages for the work. Everywhere she went, the soldiers and people lent a helping hand.

After the war, the city of Paris was in the hands of lawless men of the lowest character. The Army of the Republic besieged the city, and the most dreadful scenes of conflict occurred. There was fighting on the streets, and many innocent persons were killed. In the midst of these horrors, Clara Barton entered the city on foot, and began her work of helping the sick and wounded.

One day, a great crowd surged through the streets of Paris, crying for bread. The soldiers were powerless before such a mob. Clara Barton raised her head as if to speak to them. The crowd stopped, and she spoke in calm and hopeful words. In the end, they cried out, "It is an angel that speaks to us," and quietly went back to their homes.

When the war was over, there were removed from Paris ten thousand wounded men, who otherwise would have suffered and perhaps died through lack of care. All this was done by the Red Cross Society, working under the direction of Clara Barton.

She now returned to America, to found a similar society in this country. It was not until 1882 that the United States signed the treaty of Geneva, and joined the family of nations in this great work. The American plan, however, went further in its purpose than relief in times of war. It included relief for the distressed at any time, and to meet any calamity, such as earthquake, flood, fire, and pestilence. Clara Barton was the first President of the American Red Cross.

Clara Barton

A great fire swept through the forests of Michigan. For many days, it raged in unchecked fury. Homes, farms, woods, were swept away, and thousands of people were left homeless and penniless. The Red Cross Society was there promptly with its offers of relief. The call for aid went forth, and supplies poured in from every direction, until eighty thousand dollars in money, food, and clothing were available for the suffering people of Michigan.

Then came floods along the Ohio and Mississippi rivers, fearful cyclones in the West, an earthquake in South Carolina, and a long and terrible drought in Texas. To them all the Red Cross went, with

Clara Barton as its inspiration.

In 1889, the city of Johnstown, Pennsylvania, was swept away by a flood, caused by the breaking of a dam. Nearly five thousand lives were lost, and twelve million dollars worth of property was destroyed. It was a most dreadful calamity. Hardly had the news reached the country, before Clara Barton and the Red Cross were in Johnstown, organizing relief for the severely stricken people. For five months she stayed amid those scenes of desolation and woe.

"The first to come and the last to go," said one of the newspapers, "she has indeed been an elder sister to us; nursing, tending, caring for the stricken ones through a season of distress such as no other people may ever know."

When the war with Spain occurred, Clara Barton was seventy years old, but she went to Cuba, and did heroic work there. At the time of the Galveston flood, she was eighty years old, but she went to that stricken community, and for many days labored to relieve the sufferings of the people.

The American Red Cross has grown into a very large and useful society, and has many thousands of members. It has contributed a great deal of money to a suffering world. Wherever humanity has a need, wherever it raises a cry for help, the Red Cross holds out its hand in relief and comfort.

In World War I, the American Red Cross sent its workers into the home camps, and overseas, to be with the soldiers in time of need. Whatever the men desired in the way of comfort and help, which the government could not supply, the Red Cross was ready and willing to give. Its doctors, nurses, and directors numbered many thousands. What they did for the wounded and the dying will be the subject of many an inspiring story for years to come.

Chapter 88

Hobson and the *Merrimac*

The Spanish-American War in 1898 was undertaken for the purpose of delivering Cuba from the oppressive rule of Spain. It was therefore natural that the main object of the United States Government should be to drive the Spaniards from that island.

When the war began, there was some uncertainty as to the size and strength of the Spanish navy. We knew that Spain had fine battleships, but we did not know how they were equipped and manned, or what training their gunners possessed. It was feared that the Spanish fleet might appear off the Atlantic Coast, and bombard New York or Boston.

The Spanish navy was under command of Admiral Cervera. Our own fleet hunted for weeks, before it was discovered that the Spanish fleet had taken refuge in the harbor of Santiago. Immediately, the American fleet blockaded the harbor so that the Spanish boats could not get out. The Spanish admiral knew the weakness of his vessels. He had five ships, but his crews were not trained, and his gunners had but little practice; they were by no means the equal of the American marksmen.

Days and weeks passed in idleness. Cervera refused to come out, and the American Commanders guarded the mouth of the harbor day and night. It was feared that the Spanish ships would slip out under cover of darkness, and be free to inflict damage along the United States coast before they could be destroyed. But they did not attempt to offer battle to the American fleet.

To prevent their escape, a daring exploit was planned by Lieutenant Richard P. Hobson. He proposed to sink the collier, *Merrimac*, in the channel of the harbor so as, effectually, to prevent any ships from passing in or out. Lieutenant Hobson, with seven companions, started out on the collier, in the dead of night, and slowly steamed away.

When the Spaniards discovered the approach of the collier, they opened fire upon her from the shore batteries on both sides. It seemed that the shells must certainly pierce her through and through. Escape for the men aboard appeared impossible.

But they were cool-headed and kept on until they reached the desired position. Just before they were ready to sink the collier, and take to their boats, the rudder of the *Merrimac* was shot away. Hence, she sank diagonally instead of across the channel. The position of the wreck did not entirely block the entrance; it left a passage open for the unfortunate dash for liberty which was made later by the Spanish fleet.

When the *Merrimac* was sunk in the channel, Hobson and his men took to a raft, and there they clung till morning. It was impossible to escape the searching fire of the enemy, afloat as they were in the open harbor. But, when day came, and the Spaniards saw their helpless plight, they sent a boat out and took them prisoners. Admiral Cervera, himself, helped lift Hobson out of the water, and was so filled with admiration for his daring that he sent a flag of truce to the American fleet with the news that all the men were safe in his hands.

The prisoners were treated with great respect, and, later, were exchanged for a number of Spanish prisoners, held by our forces.

Chapter 89

Dewey at Manila Bay

The beautiful islands, known as the Philippines, were the possession of Spain. When war between that country and the United States seemed inevitable, Commodore George Dewey was ordered to collect a fleet at Hong-Kong, and hold it in readiness for instant action.

Nothing suited Dewey better. He purchased a large supply of coal and provisions, called for a few more ships, collected stores of ammunition, and put his men under strict orders. By April, of 1898, he found himself in command of a fleet of nine ships, ready for battle, and quietly awaiting orders.

He had not long to wait. He received a cablegram from the Secretary of the Navy, "War has commenced between the United States and Spain. Proceed at once to the Philippine Islands. Capture vessels or destroy them. Use utmost endeavors."

Dewey smiled with deep satisfaction. The chance of a lifetime had come, and he was ready. He issued orders to sail at once, and the very next day the fleet began its long voyage of six hundred miles to the Philippines. For three days and three nights they struggled through a boisterous sea, before they reached the mouth of Manila Bay.

This bay is a very beautiful harbor. Two small islands stand like sentries at its mouth, with their cliffs rising five hundred feet above the water. On those cliffs, as well as on other points of the mainland, were forts bristling with guns. Twenty-five miles up the bay, lay Manila, the capital of the Philippines, with its quarter of a million inhabitants. Its low-lying ground, intersected with many water-ways, made it known as the Venice of the East. It was Dewey's purpose to enter the Bay of Manila and to find the Spanish fleet there.

Night had fallen on April 30, 1898. As silent as ghosts, with all lights out, and in close order, the American battleships crept through the channel under the frowning forts. The moon, rising over the eastern waters, gave the ships the appearance of gray specters gliding in a smooth sea. "I believe they will not see us," remarked an officer quietly, to the watchful Commander. "Evidently they are not expecting us so soon."

The ships were now half-way in the channel, and opposite the forts. Suddenly, a shot from a shore battery broke the stillness of the night. Then another and another were fired in quick succession. The fleet answered at once, and put on full steam ahead, for there was no longer any need of concealment. In a short while, the danger-point was passed, no damage was done, and the fleet was on its way up the bay to Manila, and to the Spanish men-of-war.

All night long the fleet steamed forward, silently and slowly. The rising moon made a silver path over the waters. The tropical breeze fanned slowly over the decks, and the hills loomed dark against the sky line. There was nothing on this beautiful night to indicate the approach of one of the decisive battles of modern history.

The next morning, the ever-memorable first day of May, the vigilant American Commander saw what he was looking for – the Spanish fleet, lying close under the guns of Cavite, a small town a few miles from Manila.

"The hour has come," said Dewey. "Nothing can prevent a battle. They cannot escape us, for we command the outlet of the harbor. It is their day or ours." Whereupon he gave orders for immediate action.

With Dewey there were nine vessels, only six of which were to be engaged in battle, the other 3 being supply ships and a revenue cutter. The best vessel of the American fleet was *The Olympia*, the flagship. The Spanish fleet numbered ten, the largest of which was the *Reina Cristina*. None of the Spanish ships could be compared in size and strength with Dewey's *The Olympia*.

The two fleets were well matched, both being equipped with modern guns, about equal in number, as well as having about the same number of men. The advantage was slightly with the Americans, but, on the other hand, the Spanish fleet was backed up by the shore batteries at Cavite.

"Order the supply-ship out of range, place the fleet in line of battle, and prepare for immediate action," directed the Commander. It was then about six o'clock in the morning.

Promptly the American fleet swung into line, and moved toward the enemy. The Spanish guns opened on them as they approached, but they gave no reply. Silently and steadily they came nearer and nearer, until within a range of five thousand yards.

Dewey turned to the Captain of *The Olympia*, and said, "If you are ready, Gridley, you may fire."

The American ships now formed in a half circle, swinging before the massed enemy. An eight-inch shell from *The Olympia* sped across the water toward the Spanish flagship. A little later on, the order to open with all the guns brought every ship into action, as the fleet moved forward in a graceful curve. A terrific fire from the Spanish fleet and forts was the answer, and the battle of Manila Bay had begun.

Again and again the great American battleships swept around, pouring a deadly fire into the Spanish vessels, coming each time nearer and nearer, and doing more and more damage. In the midst of the action, the Spanish flagship, *Reina Cristina*, moved out to give battle to *The Olympia*. Dewey concentrated all the fire of his whole fleet upon her. Amidst an awful raking of shells, the Spanish vessel halted, broken and torn, and turned to flee. She was hardly able to struggle back to her companions; two hundred and fifty of her crew lay dead or wounded upon her shattered decks.

Five times did the American fleet swing past the enemy, each time doing more deadly work than before. Then Dewey drew his fleet off to the opposite shore, to prepare for the final engagement. The Spaniards thought he had withdrawn entirely, and cabled to Madrid that the battle was over, and that Dewey had retired to bury his dead. They were soon to find out otherwise.

The men ate breakfast, and then brought up fresh supplies of ammunition. The decks were cleaned, the guns examined, and at eleven o'clock came the order to continue the battle. Slowly, the American fleet swung around in its half circle and began its destructive work. One by one the Spanish ships went down, until the whole fleet was utterly destroyed. In a few hours the battle of Manila Bay was over.

Admiral Montojo, the Spanish Commander, escaped by land to Manila, while Dewey was destroying the shore batteries with the unerring marksmanship of his gunners.

The victory was complete. The Spaniards lost every ship of their fleet. The American ships were not seriously damaged, not a man had been killed, and only eight had been wounded. The Spanish rule of three and a half centuries in the Philippines was broken forever.

Chapter 90

Conquering the Yellow Fever

There was an enemy that for hundreds of years no one learned to conquer. Its presence spread terror wherever it appeared. It lurked in Southern cities, but, often, it stalked broadcast over the whole country, scattering death wherever it came. That enemy was the yellow fever.

Its ravages had been endured with hopeless despair, with no chance to escape but in flight; and, often, flight was denied to those who lived in the stricken districts. Quarantine was rigidly enforced. So terrified were those who lived in the uninfected regions, that refugees from yellow fever cities were turned back by loaded shotguns.

Household goods were destroyed, bedding and clothing and even houses were burned, to prevent the spread of the disease. Yet it was only held in check, and the people continued to live in terror of it. Just the announcement that yellow fever had appeared in a town was enough to make the bravest heart turn sick with the awful consequence of the horror it might mean.

Yellow fever had always been present in Cuba. Ships from that island brought it into Southern cities, and the contagion, once started, went on its ravages for months at a time. When Cuba was occupied by the United States, the problem of the yellow fever was in the hands of our Government.

Our soldiers were going into Cuba, and it was said that those who went would sooner or later have the fever. Many lives were thus imperiled. It was for our Government to find out what measures could be taken to save the men.

A Board of Medical Commissioners was appointed to go to Cuba and investigate the yellow fever. Of this Board, Major Walter Reed, an army surgeon, was appointed chairman. Major Reed had never had the fever, but he was too brave an officer and too devoted a surgeon to do otherwise than welcome this opportunity for service.

He had to deal with a treacherous enemy, that stalked up and down in the dark, attacking its unsuspecting victims. No one knew how it came, or by what means it spread. It was found wherever filth and darkness prevailed, and was supposed to be a filth disease.

Dr. Walter Reed

"The first thing we will do will be to clean up Havana, and not leave any place for fever germs to lurk," said Major Reed.

For a year and a half the most rigid sanitary measures were enforced. Deaths from other causes were reduced, but yellow fever went on its way unchecked. Plainly it was not a filth disease. Dr. Carlos Finlay, a physician in Cuba, offered the suggestion that the fever might be carried by the bite of a mosquito. The other members of the Commission scoffed at the idea.

"Everything else has failed in explaining why the disease spreads. I see no reason why we should scoff at this idea," remarked Dr. Reed. "It is certainly worth investigating."

There was but one way to find out, and that was for those who had not had the fever to be bitten by a mosquito that had come from the body of a yellow fever patient. The members of the Commission tried the experiment on themselves. Dr. Carroll was bitten by an infected mosquito, took the fever, and came near dying. Dr. Lazear allowed himself to be bitten by a mosquito, took the disease in its worst form, and died a martyr to the cause of science.

"It seems that we must try this experiment on a large scale, and build special houses for the purpose," said Dr. Reed to the Commission. "I am beginning to think the mosquito has much to do with it."

An experiment camp was therefore built, named "Camp Lazear" in honor of the dead doctor who had sacrificed his life in the cause of investigation. Two houses were erected. One was filled with infected clothing, soiled articles, bedding, and everything that could possibly spread the disease from one person to another. All mosquitoes were carefully excluded from this building. Nothing was left to carry the disease, but the clothing and bedding.

The other building was clean, airy, free from infected articles of any kind. But inside the screens were placed a number of mosquitoes that were known to be infected. Then came the call for volunteers. Dr. Reed addressed the soldiers:

"Men, I shall not detail anyone to enter these wards. I am asking for volunteers. Dr. Lazear has just died from the results of an experiment. It may mean death to some of you, but it may mean the saving of hundreds of thousands of others."

One by one the soldiers volunteered, until Dr. Reed had enough for his purpose. He explained to them their danger and their duties. He then offered to each one a sum of money. "We take no money for this," they replied. "It is a condition of our going that we receive no pay."

"Gentlemen, I salute you in the name of humanity and your own great government," said Dr. Reed.

For twenty days and nights, the men lived in their different quarters. In the clothes-infected house the men slept in the yellow fever beds, handled the clothing of patients, and breathed the air that had passed over infected articles. Not one of them took the fever.

In the other house, clean, sweet, airy, but full of mosquitoes, ten out of thirteen came down with the fever, but the cases were light and not one of them died.

The experiment proved conclusively that yellow fever was carried by the bite of a female mosquito, which had previously bitten a yellow fever patient. It was not carried by the clothing, and it did not infect the house. Its spread could be controlled by killing the mosquito, or by screening the sickroom.

Dr. Reed died shortly after he had announced the results of his investigations. In a letter to his wife, he wrote,

"The prayer that has been mine for twenty years, that I might be permitted in some way and at some time to do something to alleviate human suffering, has been granted."

Chapter 91

The Sinking of the *Lusitania*

During World War I, it was the declared policy of Germany to torpedo any vessel flying an enemy flag in the waters adjacent to the British Isles, regardless of its character, or who was on board.

One bright morning, the first day of May, 1915, the huge British liner, *Lusitania*, lay at her dock ready to sail from New York to Liverpool. Her decks were crowded with passengers. They had read, in the morning papers that "vessels flying the flag of Great Britain, or any of her Allies, are liable to destruction and that travelers sailing in the war zone on ships of Great Britain or her Allies, do so at their own risk."

In spite of this warning, the ship was crowded with a large and happy throng, who were not deterred by any threat of destruction. She steamed down the harbor amid the waving of hands from the shore, and the sound of music on her deck. There were many confident souls on board, but along with them were many who were wondering if destruction really lay in wait for the great vessel.

The voyage was full of pleasure. The decks were crowded with promenaders, and the smoking-room and cabins were centers of amusement and conversation. There was little thought of danger, and but few discussed the possibility of the ship being torpedoed. It was an event that no one wished to consider for a moment.

The morning of May 7 came with a heavy fog over the sea. The blowing of the siren awakened the passengers, and some of them commented on the fact, saying it might attract the submarines. Later on the fog lifted, leaving the sky without a cloud and the sea as smooth as glass. The shores of Ireland were in sight. Everybody was glad that the voyage was nearly over, and that, in a few hours, the ship and its passengers would be safe.

The morning passed, and the ship steamed steadily on. Luncheon hour came, and the passengers thronged below for their midday meal. Nearer and nearer came the friendly shores, and less and less grew the danger that threatened the vessel. The British flag was flying, as if in defiance to the threat of Germany.

Having finished luncheon, some of the passengers came on deck, some went to their rooms to rest, while others turned to the smoking rooms. The ship settled down to the usual afternoon routine.

At a few minutes after two o'clock, some of the passengers saw what looked like a whale or porpoise, rising about three-quarters of a mile to starboard. They knew that it was a submarine, but no one dared name it. All eyes now fastened in silence and dread on the menace that lay so quietly and sullenly in the distance.

Then a long white line, making a train of bubbles across the water, started from the black object. It came straight for the ship. No one spoke until it was about sixty yards away. Then some one cried out, "It is a torpedo!"

There was no chance for the great ship to get out of the way. Its movement was too ponderous for the swiftly coming torpedo. It was plain that it could not miss its mark. It was aimed ahead of the vessel, and timed to strike under the bridge. As the missile of death came nearer, it dived, and the passengers held their breath. Would it hit or would it miss?

Suddenly, there was a terrific explosion, and the fore part of the ship was torn into great holes. Pieces of the wreckage came through the upper deck, and fell among the frightened passengers. Germany had carried out her threat, and had dealt death to the great trans-Atlantic liner.

There was no second torpedo; there was no need of one. The boiler exploded immediately, and the ship listed heavily to starboard. The passengers rushed to the high side of the deck the port side. There was such a list to starboard that the lifeboats on the port side swung so far in that they could not be launched.

The vessel began to settle, and the lifeboats on the starboard side were launched. The first boat dropped clear of the ship, and floated away with no one in it. One man jumped from the deck, swam toward the boat, and got in alone.

Everyone was frightened, but there was no panic. The cry was raised, "Women and children first!" These were placed in the lifeboats that were launched. The ship settled down on the starboard side, and also by the head. Those who could not get into the lifeboats trusted to the life-preservers, and made ready for the plunge

The *Lusitania*

into the cold water. The officers of the ship acted with bravery and coolness, trying to launch the lifeboats and get the women and children into safety. The wireless telegraph apparatus was put out of commission shortly after the explosion, but not before a distress message, calling for help, was sent out and answered.

So quickly did the ship sink that it was impossible to get life-preservers from the lower deck cabins. Many had to leap into the sea without them. The shock of the cold water was so benumbing that those who jumped in were not able to swim, and many of them soon sank out of sight.

With one great plunge, the stricken vessel, that so often had crossed the Atlantic, and that, only an hour before, was so full of life and power, sank head foremost into the sea. A great wave, rushing over her decks, cast the remaining passengers into the water.

Then followed a scene of indescribable tragedy. Two boats, full of people, were overturned. Another was swamped as the vessel went down, and still another was dragged down by catching in the davits. The sea was piled with wreckage to which people were clinging. Some were struggling to swim, others were depending on life-preservers, all were battling with the waves in mad endeavor to save their lives.

Thus, eleven hundred and fifty-two were drowned. Of these, one hundred and fourteen were known to be American citizens. Of the two thousand and more passengers, nine hundred and fifty-two were saved in the life-boats and on the rafts picked up by friendly vessels that hastened to the scene of disaster.

Thus did the German submarine carry out the threat of the German government, and sink a noble ship with its precious freight of human lives.

Chapter 92

The Last Race of Private Treptow

The American soldier felt individual responsibility in the Great War. He was ready, by himself and alone, to do his part. Often he showed the spirit which meant, "It is for me to win this war, right here and now."

"Over there," it often happened that through a rain of fire the soldiers had to carry messages from the company to the battalion. There was no way to get these messages through except by runners, and the man who undertook the mission was racing with death as a companion.

It was like dodging fate every second. The bullets flew in every direction, the air was full of noise of men's cries and of smoke and dust.

These messages were usually taken by word of mouth, for there was no time to write; besides which, writing is dangerous if it should fall into the hands of the enemy.

Some of these runners got through safely, and delivered their message. Others never got through. And there were some who crawled on over the awful bat-

Private Martin Treptow

tlefield, and delivered their message with dying lips. But they all went!

On the day the Americans crossed the Ourcq river in France in 1918, a terrible machine-gun fire opened up, and it was necessary to send an important message to the battalion which was across the field. The noise was deafening, the danger great, the need imperative. The officer in charge dreaded to order any man to go. He knew what it meant to be sent into the open at that time. But it had to be done.

"Send for Private Treptow, of Iowa," he called, after much hesitation. Private Martin Treptow came, saluted, and waited attentively while the message was delivered to him.

"You understand that you are to go across the field, connect with the battalion, and deliver this message as I have given it to you?" said the officer.

"I do, sir," replied the intrepid private, bowing.

"You know the importance of the message, and the great risk you run, and are not afraid?" asked the officer,

"I shall not fail, sir," was the answer.

The private saluted, the officer returned the salute, and went to other duties, while Treptow made ready to depart.

As he looked over the field, and measured the distance, it did not seem so far to that battalion. It was a matter of a few minutes, if there were no snipers or machine-guns lying in wait for him.

"Here goes," he said to those around him. Putting his cap down over his eyes, and grasping his gun, he stepped out of cover, and faced his fate. There were others to follow him with the same message, in case he failed; for it had to be carried through at any cost.

He began his race against death. On he went, with the bullets tearing after him. Hiding as best he could behind whatever cover the field afforded, dropping into pits when there were any, running boldly across the open, he moved here and there, now up, now down a very fury of fire about him all the time.

He ran, a prayer on his lips for his loved ones at home, and for the safety of the men dependent on his message. A bullet tore through his clothes, and made a jagged wound in his side. But he ran on. Another wound, and he was faint from loss of blood and from the exertion of the race.

He was half-way over. He was running now with whatever spark of life there was left in him. Just as he was nearing his goal, a German sniper took careful aim, and a deadly bullet crashed through the body of the brave runner. Private Treptow fell and lay quite still. He thought for a moment of those across the seas, and then he did not think at all. He had run his last race.

The battle raged for awhile, and then passed elsewhere. Over the broken, scarred field came the ambulances to find the wounded, and with them were those to bury the dead. The searchers came to the place where the runner lay.

"This is Private Treptow," said one. "He was sent across this field yesterday with a message."

They lifted him up, and carried him back of the lines. They searched his clothes before they buried him to see if they could find anything to send to his family. In a pocket, there was a diary, on the first page of which he had written these words: "America shall win the war. Therefore, I will work, I will save, I will sacrifice, I will endure, I will fight cheerfully, and do my utmost, as though the whole issue of the struggle depended on me alone. My pledge." And to this he had signed his name.

When these words were read to the men of his company, many a one had a new vision of courage, and that night many a soldier rewrote the same pledge.

CHAPTER 93

FRANK LUKE, JR., AVIATOR

The life of an aviator is full of danger and adventure; the annals of the World War are filled with his exploits. It is the business of the aircraft, its pilot, and observer to note the enemies' positions and movements, to take photographs, to direct the fire of big guns, to bring down observation balloons, to drop bombs, and to destroy or drive off the enemy's machines. The aviators fly all the way from a hundred feet to three miles high, and often at a rate of a hundred miles an hour.

Frank Luke, Jr., came from Phoenix, Arizona. He was twenty years old when he entered the service. He had his training as an aviator, and found himself near Chateau-Thierry, France, late in July, 1918. He had an insatiable appetite for flying, and was deeply interested in machine-guns and incendiary bullets.

About the middle of August, the enemy planes were in large

Frank Luke Jr.

number over the sector where Lieutenant Luke's squadron was operating. He felt that if he could get across the lines unobserved, he could take the enemy's formation unaware, and swoop upon the rear man and shoot him down.

One day, he went off alone, rose to a great height, and crossed into the enemy's territory. Far below him he spied six machines getting ready to land on their own aerodrome. The odds were against him, six to one, but he was not an aviator to count the odds, and prepared for action.

He swooped down from fifteen thousand to three thousand feet in one long dive, speeding at a rate of two hundred miles an hour; he closed in on the rear man, and, from a distance of twenty yards, sent him crashing down.

The enemy formation was taken completely by surprise. Before they could realize what had happened, or engage Luke in combat, he had dropped to four hundred feet, had dodged all anti-aircraft fire- and machine-guns, and was off like a rocket to his own lines.

On September 12, 1918, began the St. Mihiel offensive. At daybreak, Luke rose in his plane, and observed a German balloon far to the right. He returned to his aerodrome, and learned that the balloon was doing great damage by directing an enfilading fire on our advancing troops. He volunteered to destroy the balloon, and flew away with his flying partner, Lieutenant Wehner.

In a short while, he was seen to drop out of the clouds, surprise the balloon, and, at the second dive, he shot it down in flames. This was Luke's first experience with a balloon-gun, a gun designed to shoot a heavy incendiary bullet.

Two days later, the enemy were keeping three observation balloons in the air. They were operating at a low altitude, so low, indeed, that an observer could not use his parachute to escape, the height not being sufficient for the parachute to open and land the observer safely. Luke volunteered to destroy these balloons, and was sent out with other pilots detailed for protection.

A few moments before Luke was ready to shoot down one of the balloons, his escort became engaged in a fight with an enemy formation, and it seemed hopeless to make the attack. Undaunted, however, Luke darted in underneath the fight raging above him in the air, and, descending repeatedly on the balloon, sent it down in flames, despite the shower of machine-gun bullets that rained around him.

When he reached his own lines, it was found that his machine was so riddled with holes that it was on the verge of a collapse. Under a little more strain, it would probably have fallen to pieces in the air. "A narrow escape, that," was all the daring aviator said, when he looked at his riddled plane.

The same afternoon, he set out to bring down one of the other balloons. Again, his escort was engaged with the enemy aircraft. Again, Luke dived under the fight to attack his prey; but he himself was attacked by a formation of eight enemy planes. Diving with great speed to the level of the balloon, he delivered a burst of machine-gun bullets, saw the envelope blaze into fire, and then escaped his pursuers by a zig-zag course, back to his own aerodrome.

Day after day, Luke went up for enemy planes, or in search of observation balloons. Escorting patrols engaged the enemy, while he darted in, and fired upon the balloons, bringing them down in flames, and escaping the terrible machine-gun fire from the ground.

In seventeen days, he brought down eighteen enemy machines

and balloons. His name became a terror to the Huns, and they lived in dread of his daring attacks upon their observation balloons. The observers in those balloons would frequently leap into their parachutes and descend before Luke had actually set fire to the balloons.

On September 29, he went out for the purpose of destroying three balloons. On his way, he flew over an American aerodrome and dropped a weighted message, asking that a sharp lookout be kept for three German planes which he had sighted. His machine was then seen to go over in that direction, and to rise to a very high altitude. When nearly over the three machines, he was attacked by ten enemy planes. He engaged all of them, single-handed, and sent two crashing to the ground.

He then dropped out of the fight, and descended to the level of the balloons, which he shot down, one after another all three of them. This made five victims in one engagement.

Now, the sad story of his death is to be related. His machine, surrounded by a flock of enemy planes, was forced to descend on to Germany territory. He was wounded in the shoulder, but was full of fight to the last. Drawing his pistol, he opened fire until he was killed by an overwhelming number of the enemy.

The Germans took his clothing, and rifled his pockets of their contents, and left his grave unmarked. Months afterwards, the inhabitants of the village told the Americans the story of his last brave fight, and showed them the grave in which the great American ace was buried.

About the Author

Rachel Lebowitz is the owner of A Charlotte Mason Plenary. She and her husband have always homeschooled their two children using the Charlotte Mason method of education. She has a Bachelor of Arts degree from the University of Houston where she studied Communications and Political Science. Before attending college, she travelled as a member of Up With People, a performing arts organization with a mission to transcend cultural barriers and create global understanding through music. After college, she spent many years as a Radio and Television Journalist. She currently resides in Texas with her husband, two children, two dogs, and one guinea pig.

Other Books by the Author

The Plenary Annotated Home Education Series

Home Education: Annotated Edition (Volume 1)
by Charlotte Mason, Rachel Lebowitz, and Ruk Martin

A Philosophy of Education: Annotated Edition (Volume 6)
by Charlotte Mason and Rachel Lebowitz

(Other Annotated Volumes by Charlotte Mason coming soon)

The Plenary Plutarch Series

Plutarch's Life of Publicola: Plenary Annotated Study Guide
by Plutarch and Rachel Lebowitz

Plutarch's Life of Pericles: Plenary Annotated Study Guide
by Plutarch and Rachel Lebowitz

(More Plutarch Guides coming soon)

For a complete listing of books and study guides,
or for more info about the Charlotte Mason method of education,
please see The Plenary website at:

WWW.CMPLENARY.COM

www.ingramcontent.com/pod-product-compliance
Lightning Source LLC
Chambersburg PA
CBHW052008070526
44584CB00016B/1668